Socrates in Silicon Valley

Other books by Tom Morris include:

NonFiction

Making Sense of It All
God and the Philosophers
True Success: A New Philosophy of Excellence
If Aristotle Ran General Motors
The Art of Achievement
Philosophy for Dummies
The Stoic Art of Living
Superheroes and Philosophy
If Harry Potter Ran General Electric

Fiction

The Oasis Within
The Golden Palace
The Stone of Giza
The Viper and the Storm
The King and Prince

Tom Morris

Author of the National Bestsellers
If Aristotle Ran General Motors
If Harry Potter Ran General Electric

Socrates In Silicon Valley

The Essential Jobs@Work

Steve Jobs and his Philosophical Operating System

Wisdom/Works
Published by Wisdom Works
TomVMorris.com

Published 2017

ISBN 978-0-9993524-1-0

Printed in the United States of America

Set in Adobe Garamond Pro
Designed by Abigail Chiaramonte
Cover Concept by Sara Morris

"I would trade all of my technology for an afternoon with Socrates."

Steve Jobs, 2001

Contents

Introduction: The Unlikely Success 1

Part One: The Fourteen Principles 15

1. Focus 16
2. Simplify 36
3. Take Responsibility End-to-End 52
4. When Behind, Leapfrog 78
5. Put Products Before Profit 93
6. Don't Be a Slave to Focus Groups 103
7. Bend Reality 122
8. Impute 137
9. Push For Perfection 146
10. Tolerate Only "A" Players 162
11. Engage Face-to-Face 173
12. Know Both the Big Picture and the Details 183
13. Combine the Humanities With the Sciences 189
14. Stay Hungry, Stay Foolish 202

Part Two: The Seven Conditions 211

15. The Deep Operating System for Success 212

Appendix One: A Self-Diagnostic Check-up on The 7 Cs 246
Appendix Two: A Short Formula 250
Appendix Three: The NeXT and Last Horizon 254
For Further Reading 256
Acknowledgments 258
About the Author 260

Introduction

The Unlikely Success

Steve Jobs: In some ways, he was like a Socrates in Silicon Valley. Throughout his life, he embodied a spirit of endless curiosity on a quest to expose limited assumptions and leave behind the flimsy opinions of those who had not dared to think deeply enough. He stripped away people's illusions through fierce challenges and tough questioning. He would not suffer fools gladly, and insisted on a higher standard, the ideal of the *insanely great*—in what was perhaps his favorite phrase. As a result, he blazed new paths whose influence will likely never disappear. He did something new, something that has changed the course of history. In his time, he had, of course, both loyal followers and rabid critics. And he still does, just like his ancient predecessor who revolutionized his own field of endeavor. Additionally, as also in the case of his intense philosophical forebear, Jobs seems somehow both to have succeeded beyond all reasonable measure due to his intense personal intransigence, or a sort of extreme willful stubbornness, and then he also died because of it. Neither man was focused on money. Both lived simply and gave all their energy to an ideal and a form of purity in their quests that set them apart from the norm.

The parallel isn't perfect, of course. But no useful and potentially revealing analogy is. Cupertino isn't Athens. And I don't think any toga or tunic, however sporty, would work that well with a black mock turtleneck and tennis shoes. The Californian and the Greek, however, both did start out with some pretty rough attire and more than questionable grooming habits. They were each known to go around barefoot, even into important meetings. A tumultuous personal life made it easy for both of them to spend more time at work than might be normal. But one focused on truth. And the other favored beauty. The old guy wanted to transform people inwardly. The modern man was more concerned about outward revolution. Both stubbornly overturned the assumptions and beliefs of their day. Each was in his own way the clichéd bull in a china shop. And each left a big legacy. The salient points of connection between the two are perhaps interesting enough for us to play with for a bit, and may even spark some new understanding. Their surface commonalities are at least sufficient to give us the possibility of a new angle into the extraordinary success of the man most iconic for a company that he named after the legendary fruit whose tempting nature reportedly launched the human adventure as-we-know-it. But his hope was that his bite of the apple, and then ours, would actually get us back to the Garden, through great technology and elegant design.

Both Socrates and Steve Jobs knew how to "Think Different." And both changed the world. In each case, it was because of their embodied philosophy. Steve was and remains the most unlikely, successful, and fascinating leader of the modern era. He built what became in time the world's most valuable company and, in the process, he basically invented the way we now live. It seems that nearly everyone knows of his many quirks, flaws, and foibles. He was quite a character. Even books that seek to defend him or soften his image have had to admit his wildly rough edges and "sharp elbows." As a result of all the stories about his life, we have many accounts of his behavior whose details can make his astonishing achievements almost utterly mystifying. But that's because almost no one has understood the full philosophy that powered his success—the deep personal operating system that produced amazing results in different ways throughout his working life. In this book, we're going to take our own very big philosophical bite out of the most valuable apple in history and chew on what we can learn about the ultimate essentials for extraordinary achievement that can be transferred into our own lives.

Many commentators have identified and distilled a few techniques or qualities that seemed to set Jobs apart. But no one has yet done a thorough analysis of what overall nexus of ideas and imperatives lay behind his epic accomplishments and how these insights might be used more commonly. Even the most exhaustive and well composed narratives about what he did, and when, and under what circumstances, and with whose collaboration or resistance only give us hints as to how he attained such things and managed to succeed at a unique level that as a result shaped our world. This book is about the full and integrated array of distinctive insights, prescriptions, and principles that led this one man to an incredible height of modern business success. It's my conviction that they can be viewed as a set of universal tools any of us can use in whatever we do. They will give us the essential jobs for any endeavor.

No one before now has unearthed and analyzed the full array of philosophical principles, ideals, and orientations that fueled the outrageous success of Steve Jobs. That's my skill set, and will here be my job. I'm a philosopher. My task is to take in enormous amounts of information and spot the deep patterns at work beneath it all. Many entrepreneurs in our time want to live the life of Steve Jobs, in at least certain salient respects. But, as the original Socrates once put it, "The unexamined life is not worth living." We need to examine our chief exemplars of success in the modern world, like Steve Jobs, and ask what he did that's worth trying in our own experience, and what's best to be avoided. The cautionary tales about Jobs are everywhere. What I want to focus on are the philosophical lessons that can help any of us to attain our own levels of the insanely great.

This is not another biography, and it's not an account of the things that happened at Apple, NeXT, and Pixar while Jobs was running the show. There are many fascinating histories of all that, already easily available. This will be a book of ideas. I want to dig down and isolate the conceptual underpinnings behind the successes. What can we learn from the legacy of Steve Jobs that might apply in our own circumstances, in our lives, and throughout our distinctive business and leadership challenges? That's my question. And it may be yours. I want to strip things down to the essential Jobs at work in his storied accomplishments that can be transferred to our own work right now. In a sense, my aim is the quintessential Socratic task. I've had to ask lots of questions and question lots of answers to get beneath all the appearances and uncover the underlying realities behind the biggest success story ever to come out of Silicon Valley, or anywhere else, in recent times.

As I begin this little book, American corporations are sitting on more cash then ever before and many are unusually hesitant to spend, playing it safe instead, guarding against unforeseeable economic turns and unpredictable global events. And yet, we often find in life that playing it safe is the riskiest path of all. We need to use our resources to innovate and grow. We should seek to be creative and bold. But, the question is: How?

We can learn a lot from past innovators who've used their resources well and, as a result, have had great forms of success. In this short account of one such instance, I'm excited to be focusing on one of the most remarkable business creators of our time, or of any time. People have called him the king of innovation, and even the man who invented the new century. But in many ways, Steve Jobs was probably the most unlikely leadership success story of the past one hundred years—perhaps even in the entire modern era. And, until now, a full grasp of how he achieved such results has yet to be attained.

The early story is well known. Adopted as a baby into a hard-working, middle class family, Steve was treated like a prince by his new parents. They wanted to indulge him and grant him any wishes they could. If we can trust the standard accepted accounts of his childhood and teen years, he grew up largely having his way and making his own rules. He eventually became the quintessential California Hippie—a long haired, barefoot, LSD tripping, Zenned Out maverick who truly believed that a strict vegan diet would exempt him from the onerous, bothersome, time-consuming duty of bathing. He was, unfortunately also opposed in theory and practice to the use of deodorant. In his initial adult years of life and work, the sweet smell of success did not surround him.

And this was not just a passing adolescent phase. In a delightfully long conversation one afternoon, the first man to whom he ever sold a computer described to me the young entrepreneur in unforgettable terms. Hippie Steve went into early business meetings shoeless, sloppy, smelly, and without any of the normal social skills. If you've read about him at all, you know that he was in many ways what we now call a hot mess, a complicated hair-trigger emotional disaster with a mercurial personality given to rants and tirades and personal insults as a motivational device. Acquaintances variously viewed him as obsessive-compulsive, maybe bipolar, and a malignant narcissist to the extreme who believed that normal rules didn't apply to him. He never put a license plate on his car. He'd rather go get a new Mercedes than deal with the hassle. He parked in handicap spaces as often as possible, because, as he explained to the perplexed, they were "always close" to where he was going—which, of course, may well have led some to speculate that there must be at least a few handicap spots right outside hell. He once got a speeding ticket for driving a hundred miles an hour and started blowing his horn at the policemen writing the citation, to urge him to hurry up, so he could get back on his way, once again, at a hundred miles an hour.

He practiced staring without blinking, in total silence, as a technique for getting people to back down in business negotiations. Sometimes, he would alternate between silent staring and intense bouts of fast, loud talking, for the sole purpose of intimidation. And when that didn't work, he could quickly burst into tears. No one had ever seen anything remotely like this in a business setting. To put it mildly, he did not fit in easily with those around him. He did his own thing. And often, he did it quite harshly. I recently decided to follow the example of a writer who years ago did something interesting while investigating the negative side of Steve's behavior. He Googled together the words, 'Steve Jobs' and 'asshole.' When I tried it, I got 509,000 results. Among those who knew him well, it must not have been a minority opinion.

Jobs had what his colleagues called a Reality Distortion Field that put both Don Quixote and Donald Trump to shame. He saw what he wanted to see, and he refused to acknowledge the reality of anything he didn't like. His longtime girlfriend had a baby and for years he refused to accept that he was responsible, even after a DNA test confirmed it decisively. And while rejecting his daughter, he oddly embraced a new computer model that he named after her—as if he could accept only a Lisa he could control, and not a real human creation that might impinge unpredictably on his prior, steely-minded plans for himself and his world. He did what he wanted to do, and didn't tolerate anything that he thought to be stupid and a waste of time. Unfortunately, there were a great many things in normal life that he thought to be both stupid and a waste of time. The thinly disguised novel that his sister Mona Simpson eventually wrote about him famously started with the simple sentence, "He was too busy to flush a toilet." The World According to Steve was a quite distinctive place.

In his relatively short time among us, he altered the face of many industries. He changed personal computing, desktop publishing, the music industry, the whole shape of telecommunications, and even animated film, during his days of helping to build Pixar into the powerhouse it eventually became. He oversaw the creation of the machine on which the world wide web was invented, the first server was launched, and so much else was initiated that's responsible for how we now live and work. He altered our basic expectations regarding brick and mortar retail with his designs for the Apple Stores of the world, and through their spectacular success. He gave us the iMac, the iPod, iTunes, the iPhone, the iPad, and so much more. In many ways, this Zen-ful counterculture creator invented the interconnected iLife that we all now experience, day-to-day.

Michael Malone, a technology writer and the author of *Infinite Loop*, has put it like this:

> "He wanted Apple to be like the Beatles and have this amazing run of landmark albums. Well, he did it. He hit one home run after another. Edison didn't do that. Ford didn't do that. Hewlett and Packard didn't do it. Noyce, Moore, and Grove at Intel didn't do it. I have never seen this happen where someone could introduce one product after another, and their success was a *fait accompli.*"

I was in a major airport recently and looked around the gate area as we all waited for the announcement to board our plane. Half the people sitting in chairs throughout the area were using tablet computers. It looked like about three quarters of those devices were iPads, and the others, close imitators. It also seemed that, among the few people not on iPads, most were using their iPhones, or close imitators. In a matter of just a few years, it's become hard to imagine what life would be now without the devices that Jobs pioneered, created or inspired.

So, how did this really challenged dude, actually handicapped in so many ways, go from a small business startup in his parents' garage to building what was to become in his own time the world's most valuable company? How did he actually succeed on such a grand scale that he fundamentally altered the way we live? His high school grade point average of 2.65 didn't exactly bode well for a future career of world changing creativity. Nor did the fact that he officially dropped out of college with no more than a semester under his belt. He wasn't a computer scientist or an electronics expert. He hadn't been trained in principles of design, or in manufacturing, or sales, or marketing. He had no academic degree or experience in business. He often seemed to have the personality of a part-time sociopath who would inevitably wind up in jail. What made the difference for this admittedly strange, abrasive guy, and led him to outrageous success after success in a field completely crowded with very smart and ambitious people?

Many have called him a visionary genius of the highest order. Others have said that he was an outrageous, unique, incredible iHole. His philosophy, as propagated to the world by his favorite advertising agency, was indeed: "THINK DIFFERENT," a slogan whose very grammar nicely exemplifies its own content. In this short look at the thought behind the achievement, we're going to dig into what that meant and how it worked. I believe Steve Jobs intuitively pieced together a deep philosophical operating system for success, and that the story of this system has yet to be told. That's my intended task.

When Walter Isaacson's big authorized biography of Jobs was published just nine days after Jobs died in 2011, it seemed like almost all early readers came away from it saying, "This guy was a massive jerk! How could anyone work for him or with him for more than a week? Why would anyone have ever done business with him?" Readers and early commentators were focusing on all the quirks, flaws, eccentricities, and utterly obnoxious personality traits the book had revealed. Friends of Jobs were sometimes horrified at what they saw as a one-sided portrayal that failed to capture the inner complexities of the man. Isaacson heard the reactions and worried that people were missing all the positive and powerful lessons of Jobs' career. So he wrote an article for the *Harvard Business Review* on "Fourteen Leadership Principles" that Jobs exemplified throughout his work life. Those principles are going to get us started and structure the first part of this look at his success and leadership secrets. I want to begin by using these principles primarily because they're so well known that they've attained an almost canonical status, perhaps even beyond the renown of Isaacson's massive biography itself. But I also want to dive deeper into each of them. Then, I want to plunge a bit deeper still, with aspects of an operating structure that Isaacson apparently didn't glimpse in all his conversations with Jobs, or at least in his own analyses of what he was hearing.

This topic came to me in an interesting way. I had spoken to the top leadership team of an international company at their annual gathering three different times, on three distinct subjects that I had extensively researched, written about, and already spoken on at dozens, or even hundreds, of previous occasions for other corporate groups and trade associations. When the CEO of this company emailed me about their next upcoming session, he told me that his direct reports had established a book group, and had been reading Isaacson's big biography on Jobs. And, like many readers, he had found various aspects of the book to be both fascinating and troubling. He had then discovered Isaacson's article presenting all the positive insights that could be gleaned from the extensive interviews and research he had done. This CEO then asked me if I could structure a talk for his global leaders around those fourteen principles. I had never used anyone else's contemporary framework of ideas for a talk of my own, but once I was able to look at the principles and give them an intense scrutiny, I agreed to the request, knowing that as a philosopher I could find my own way in, with a distinctive analysis and spin, and perhaps a novel, innovative sense of how we could implement the wisdom to be learned from Jobs, as filtered initially through these ideas. Then, in addition to Isaacson's book and his article, I read everything else about Jobs that I could get my hands on. I watched podcasts and videos, slogged through blogs, talked with people who had worked with Jobs directly, both on the phone and over coffee, and began to form a solid sense of my own as to what his fundamental philosophy, or personal operating system, might have been, and what we can learn from it that might be useful in our own work and lives.

The day of the meeting arrived. I gave my talk bringing together all this, and the executives in the room reacted strongly, in a very enthusiastic and appreciative way. I had the sense that I might be on to something. So I kept up the research. And I kept testing what I learned about Jobs against experiences in my own life, and in the lives of the many and diverse companies I've served as a philosopher. Each test then pushed me a little deeper, and on to something else well worth pondering and employing in whatever challenging business endeavors we might undertake. This little book is the result.

Isaacson's fourteen principles are quite insightful. But in my view, they don't capture everything that's important about the success and leadership secrets of Steve Jobs. If you've read much about him at all, you may look over these principles in the preliminary list I'll give you in just a second and find yourself asking things like "Where's the mention of his unique passion, of his intensity, of his charisma, of his drive?" Or you might note that there's no acknowledgement of his legendary perseverance, or stubborn persistence in the face of failure. And if you've read much about Silicon Valley in the years Jobs and Wozniak created Apple, you may wonder where any mention is of the overall cultural context in which he worked. No one attains greatness in a vacuum. Jobs was around lots of very talented people with similar interests who were always going about helping each other, providing new ideas, and showing each other how to do interesting new things. Our main character capitalized on all this like no one else. He was a collector of ideas and insights who knew better than anyone how to put them to good use. He wasn't born in coastal North Carolina, where I live, or in Iowa or Maine, but in just the right part of the right state at the right time where the future was waiting to be made in precisely the field in which he was most interested. And his success arose out of this matrix, as well as from his personal intellect and habits of thought and action. The fourteen principles alone don't capture everything that we need to understand about Jobs. But they can give us a useful place to start.

My job as a philosopher is the full Socratic quest. It's a task of relentless examination. I can start with what other people observe and report, but can never be content to stay there. I have to question everything. My challenge is to get below the surface and dig out anything of universal application that can be learned from a form of success or failure, but especially when it's on an unusual scale. Here, my focus is on what we can learn and use from the leadership and business success of one rebel who became a revolutionary. But there are, of course, plenty of cautionary tales in his story, too. We want to know how to replicate the good and avoid the bad that's to be seen just as amply in this man's life and career. And we'll find that there is indeed a philosophy to be unearthed from his extraordinary accomplishments, a toolkit of powerful ideas that can be applied in anything we do.

And we'll begin with the fourteen principles. In anticipation, a principle is an ideal, a rule, or a general guideline for thought or action. And guidelines, of course, can range from strict and inviolable laws or demands, on one end of a spectrum, to rough rules of thumb, or mere casual suggestions, on the other end. The guidelines we'll be examining were lived by Steve Jobs as more like absolutely firm requirements than mere suggestions. And, as such, they were meant to order both the thoughts and behaviors needed for success at Apple, or in any context. They can be read off his own conduct, throughout his life, and represent what he insisted on in the lives of his leadership team.

Like Socrates, we can identify the principles that underlie successful thought or action by questioning appearances, interrogating behaviors, listening well, and distilling down what we discover into the most fundamental, essential truths. You'll be able to appreciate right away the universal applicability of these truths that result, and the imperatives to which they give rise, across industries and types of business. They're the sorts of guidelines that can be used by leaders in any commercial enterprise. And they will facilitate excellence in any business endeavor.

Before we analyze them in appropriate detail, let's initially here have a sneak preview of the fourteen keys to the success of Steve Jobs from which we'll start, the basic rules first outlined by Isaacson, and stated here as they were originally, as directives or imperatives, and with only a few small tweaks:

1. Focus
2. Simplify
3. Take Responsibility End-to-End
4. When Behind, Leapfrog
5. Put Products Before Profit
6. Don't Be a Slave to Focus Groups
7. Bend Reality
8. Impute
9. Push for Perfection
10. Tolerate Only "A" Players
11. Engage Face to Face
12. Know Both the Big Picture and the Details
13. Combine the Humanities with the Sciences
14. Stay Hungry, Stay Foolish

Walter Isaacson is a very good journalist, an insightful historian, and an immensely engaging writer. As in the case with his previous biographies of Benjamin Franklin and Albert Einstein, his authorized book about Jobs was extensively researched and very well written. But even in all its heft and detail, it didn't go into all the depths of the philosophy behind the extraordinary success that Steve Jobs had. That, of course, wasn't its mandate, or Isaacson's intent. But it is mine. As a business and life philosopher seeking to understand success in our time, this is at the core of my concern. I'm not writing here a new short life of Jobs, or a new account of his business decisions. All of that is readily available in many other places. I'm not a journalist, historian, or biographer. And I'm not a tech guy. I'm glad others have those skills and have used them well to do such vital work. That makes it possible for me to do mine.

I wish I had known our man Steve. At this point, I almost feel like I did. I've watched untold hours of video where he was talking about this or that. And I've found him to have an intriguing mind and heart in many ways. We never met, but he's the only person who ever paid my full corporate speaking fee for me to stay home and not speak. Even in this, he was an innovator. I remember my surprise at getting the check, for an amount more than what had been my annual starting salary as a professor at Notre Dame. I said to my wife, "Wow. Maybe this is a new business model. If enough companies are willing to pay me not to speak, I'll just shut up altogether." And then a real flash of insight came to me. "If every company in the world would simply adopt this amazing and novel practice, I could just stay home and retire, and we might even end up with almost as much money as—Steve Jobs!"

But it was an unusual time. Apple was in big trouble. There was turmoil. Things were going downhill fast. I had been asked by their leadership to come and speak on the universal conditions for success in anything we do, based on the wisdom of the ages. Contracts had been signed. Anticipations were high. But, then, if memory serves me well here, something big happened and interrupted the plan. It was exactly the time when Steve came back from his long exile away from the company he had founded. He quickly needed to reinvent Apple. He wanted to use the meeting where I was supposed to speak to do his own talking to the leaders of the company, to all those he would most depend on to turn the enterprise around. It would be entirely The Steve Jobs Show, and could not now include The Tom Morris Hour. So my engagement was cancelled. Jobs didn't have to pay my full fee when the plug was pulled. The cancellation came far enough in advance of the date that this wasn't at all required or even expected. But it was a nice gesture, and one I fondly remember.

Despite his hard edges and ragged sides, there's a lot about him that those who did know him remember even more fondly, years later. It's my job here, as a beneficiary of this remarkable individual in many ways, to dig deep and discover the things that powered his success, things that we can also learn from, emulate, and put to work, in whatever we're doing. I've used his products since the day in 1984 I walked into my office at Notre Dame and the administration surprised me with a brand new Mac on my desk. The little machine with the small screen intrigued me. And it launched me into what would become a life of All Things Apple. Over the years, I've seen a lot of the Jobs philosophy reverberating through various Apple products. And so, I've also had a lot of personal experience as a customer to draw on as I've pondered what was going on behind the scenes, and in the brain of Apple's wild, Socratic CEO. Augmented by extensive research, I think I've found the most important elements of his leadership philosophy and the operating system behind his creative success.

We're going look at, and ruminate together on, the wisdom and deep structure to be found in the purpose, passion, people, processes, and products that lie behind the legend of Steve Jobs. It's been an eye-opening adventure for me. And I can't wait to share it with you.

So, let's begin.

Part One

The Fourteen Principles

I

Focus

Every sort of confusion is revealed within us.
Socrates

Focus. Focus. First of all, the operative word here, and the entirety of our first principle, is essentially a verb. Even the noun form is an action word. Focus is something you have precisely when it's something you do. Those who do it well have exactly what they need. Everyone who knew Steve Jobs will tell you that he was a man of intense focus. This, according to Walter Isaacson, was the first secret of his success.

To understand better what the vital element of focus involves, why it's important, and how it can work for each of us, I want to present three simple imperatives, or clear implementation guidelines, as keys to grasping what, in my view, this principle involves. I'll then do the same in the following chapters for each of the other principles that Isaacson has so helpfully identified. These imperatives are my own invention, or really, my way of understanding each of the fourteen principles. Exploring these imperatives, or requirements, will both help us to grasp the philosophy behind the principle, and also steer us into its proper use for anything we're doing. Along the way, I'll tell you some stories from my own life that may bring insight, as my first intellectual inspiration and philosophical hero—the original Socrates—has done for me through the recollections of his closest students, like the great thinker Plato, and the outstanding leader, Xenophon.

1. Ignore Distractions. Ask What Matters.

There's an old saying that the two most common elements in the universe are hydrogen and stupidity. That could be true. And if there's a third, it just may be distraction. We're almost always surrounded by distractions—news, gossip, emails, texts, phone messages, the ever alluring and never ending streams of social media, the various forms of old fashioned media, people stopping by to shoot the breeze or tell us about their problems, or their sister's problem, or their friend's disaster, or even their new idea for a great business, or the best place in town for lunch. Everyone wants our attention, or our help, or some advice. Or they're distracting us just to get us to return the favor. The buzz of diverting distraction is incessant. And it's all around us.

Socrates, even in his time, complained that we're unbelievably beset by distractions. He once said that, on account of this, the least important things we think about and talk about the most, and the most important things, we think about and talk about the least. We live life backwards, or upside down. We need to turn that around. A proper focus is necessary. And it's often hard to attain. According to Plato's depictions of him in the famous dialogues, Socrates himself was a person of unusually intense focus. He had learned to ignore distractions, and would strongly urge the same for us.

But, of course, we can take this advice to ignore distractions only if we can recognize one for what it is. What's relevant to our concerns, and what's off target, even if just slightly? What can advance us along our path, and what would merely detain us, or derail us and hold us back? We're able to draw this crucial distinction only if we have a clear purpose and clear goals, precise targets around which to structure our focus, along with helpful strategies and tactics for properly getting there. Those organizing aims, ideas, and principles then become the test for anything that enters our consciousness: Will this new thing or idea or opportunity or conversation help us properly to attain our goals, or not? Is it useful, or not? Will it keep us on the road, or detour us off course?

Focus is a skilled behavior, and is what the most careful students of human activity think of as a practice. The most interesting aspect to anything that's a skill is that we can, through deliberate and careful engagement, or intelligent practice, get better at it. We talk about the practice of medicine and the practice of law, in part, for exactly this reason. Both domains involve many skilled behaviors. There are spiritual practices that involve skilled behaviors that can be improved and enhanced over time. Some who are involved in a given practice are better at it than others. And in every case, the most skilled practitioners—the true masters—are those with the greatest ability to focus well and properly. The skill of focus is one of the very few skills that can contribute vitally to all the others. It is a practice that's a crucial ingredient in every other practice.

And that's a breadcrumb to pick up on the path of success. It's a key for our own achievements. The more we consciously and deliberately focus on the challenge of focus, the more proficient we can get at it. And, yes, you can tell we're doing philosophy any time we end up thinking about thinking and, as here, focusing on focus. It will help us to succeed at succeeding, which, ironically, is the same thing as to fail at failing. But, then, that's enough philosophical flourishes, already. Our point here is actually simple. Every time we fight to attain a clear focus and maintain it successfully, the better we get at the art of focus, however incrementally, and the less we'll have to struggle on subsequent occasions with the minor distractions that can disturb a less practiced and skilled mind.

The best way to identify and ignore distractions is to question, at least implicitly, everything that crosses our path. Ask what matters. Is this new thought, suggestion, piece of information, or potential activity germane to our path, or off the best track? Is it relevant? Is it likely to contribute to my progress? Do I need to spend time on this, or is it simply an energy-waster, however well disguised? Should I delegate it, or ignore it and avoid it altogether? Masters of achievement are masters of avoiding distraction. True wisdom consists, in part, in precisely this sort of careful discernment.

When Jobs returned to Apple after his sojourn at NeXT and Pixar, he confronted a company that had lost its focus, a chaotic business with around three hundred products. He quickly cut the product line down to ten. And that was the beginning of the revolution that eventually brought Apple to the exemplary and dominating position it went on to attain. Focus had its intended effect.

If we survey a cross-section of world philosophies and religious traditions, we'll find, amid all the manifold diversity, a relevantly interesting point of overlap and insight. The great thinkers and spiritual pioneers seem to agree on something that's very practical. We are defined by our focus. What we pay attention to ends up forming and delineating who we are. It also governs what we can become.

A strong focus on what we're doing leaves clearly irrelevant things behind and relegates all dubious candidates for our attention to our peripheral vision until they can be proved more relevant to our plans and needs. And that's in itself an important point to realize. A helpful and powerful focus isn't so narrow and intense as to be utterly blind to things outside the range of its chosen gaze. It does have peripheral vision. And there's a reason for this. When you focus on the right things, you tend to get the right results. When, however, you focus on the wrong things, your focus can still yield vital benefits. A wrong focus can take you so quickly to the wrong results, and sometimes no results at all, that you learn you need to adjust and shift what you're doing. And as you've moved forward, you're more likely to have had in your peripheral vision the things that you truly need to be focused on, instead. As Aristotle pointed out, we learn by doing. And we learn quickest when we focus best in that doing.

The metaphorical idea of a range of peripheral vision around our center of focus can lead us to another insight. The virtue of focus may allow for the sort of overall analysis that Aristotle, the philosophical grandson of Socrates, once gave for any of the virtues he identified as strengths for human living. His idea was that every virtue, or strength, is something like a midpoint between two vices or extremes. For any virtue like, for example, courage, which is a proper response to danger, there is an extreme of too little—in this case, timidity, or cowardice—and an extreme of too much: here, temerity, or a crazy and rash foolhardiness. Courage as a virtue is a midpoint between the deficiency and the excess, or between the too little and the too much.

With respect to the virtue of focus, not recognized by Aristotle as one of his canonical virtues but, in my view, one nonetheless, there is clearly an associated "too little" which we might label as either vagueness or distraction, as the case may be. Many people and companies are hamstrung by a surprising degree of vagueness in their plans and goals. They allow slogans to substitute for clear thought. Or they could be in a situation where either enthusiasm or desperation quickly summons a haze of possibility that merely masquerades as a new focus. Then, like at Apple during the years Jobs was in exile, a lack of real focus leads to a lack of success. There can also, in other cases, be a deficiency of focus because of constant distraction or diversion, a wavering fragility of concentration that can't stay put. But can there be, with respect to the consideration of focus, anything like a "too much"? I think the answer is yes. And it's something that Steve Jobs struggled with at various points in his life, when he was arguably so obsessed in his focus as to become monomaniacal and narrow in unhealthy ways—in a manner that excluded normal relationships and any sort of balance in his life, which is a situation hard to sustain. A proper focus is one thing, and an unhealthy obsession or addiction is something else altogether. So when we seek to emulate Jobs by fighting for greater focus, we mean to avoid both vagueness and distraction and, if we're wise, also the obsessive mania that can at times be even more destructive and self-defeating than the confusion that comes with no clarity. What's important in business and life is a powerful, healthy focus that can be sustained.

2. Select. Eliminate.

One of my neighbors in Wilmington, North Carolina once worked for Steve Jobs as a close associate for six years, during a crucial period at his startup business, NeXT, while he was away from Apple. Right before I met this interesting man, I had just read lots of descriptions of the outrageously unpleasant personality that Steve often displayed to people close to him at work, and to others whose paths he crossed, day-to-day. So, when Tom Looney introduced himself to me and told me of his extensive time with Jobs, my first thought was that you'd have to be at least a bit loony to work for that crazy man as long as he had. But Tom seemed utterly sane, as well as exceptionally bright and kind. And he had been around Jobs enough to learn a lot about what made him tick. He had seen the famous and intense focus he had, up close and personal for a long time.

According to my new friend, Jobs was above all things a man on a mission, and that mission was guided by a conception of what matters most in any challenging business environment. He had a clear and idealistic purpose. And he had great passion around that purpose. He also had a saying about focus as it relates to purpose, something he often repeated and that's extremely insightful. Looney recalled hearing it a lot. Steve would say, "Deciding what not to do is as important as deciding what to do." He would then usually add that, "Good things have to be set aside so that we can do really, really great things." Tom had illuminating insights to share with me about the unpleasant side of this highly focused man, and they are some revelations we'll consider shortly. But for now, I want to keep my focus on focus and Steve's firm commitment to carving away anything that didn't belong—in a company, a product line, a process, or a product.

To select is to eliminate. We all have limited time and energy. The power of choice allows us to cut through the tangled thicket of what's possible and carve out a path we can follow. The famously groundbreaking modern painter Piet Mondrian claimed that the most difficult brush stroke in any painting is the very first one. Prior to that, he explained, a blank canvas presents to an artist infinitely many possibilities. The first stroke begins a process of elimination. To choose is to exclude. When we do this, we can't also do that. To put it even more vividly, to choose for any one thing is to choose against innumerably many other things we could have done, instead. Many people don't seem fully to understand this, in at least a deep existential sense. Metaphorically, they seek to swim while keeping one foot on the side of the pool and their options open. Or they think that a masterful exercise of multi-tasking will allow them to select without really eliminating. And that's simply false, however common an illusion.

Without elimination, there is no selection. You may think you've made a new choice and set a new goal, but if that hasn't resulted in the exclusion of other contrary behaviors, you don't really have a new choice or a new goal, at all. "No" is just as important as "Yes," and must be much more frequent, as an attitude and an answer.

Every yes in fact presupposes a no, and requires many more, in addition. Now, clearly, some people take this to an extreme, and say no to things that it would be in their best interest to accept or do. The great leader and high achiever need not be an overly narrow, harsh, one-dimensional soul. We should be open to things outside our current focus that could be important. And we ought to embrace a diverse array of things in our lives that are of value. But we'll have no time for great things unless we say no to lots of other potentially good things that compete for our attention and energy. An unfocused life can't be a highly successful one. And this is true across all reasonable definitions of success. Great focus makes possible great achievement.

There's a way to put all this simply, summing it up. The best life is a culmination of "no" in abundance, and "yes" in wise measure. One of the great dangers of our day is the burnout of extraordinarily talented and smart people who seem unable to say no. And, yet, there are some common misunderstandings as to what saying no means. It isn't about thinking you're already and infallibly on the best possible path and know everything that would be beneficial for your business or your life. It isn't the inevitable twin of hubris, or excessive pride. And it doesn't mean single-mindedly pursuing your own focal goals in some exclusively self-centered or selfish way that can't allow for any act of turning aside to help another person with their needs, or as they pursue their distinctive ambitions. No isn't about a fixation on the self or a denial of everyone else's needs, although it often appeared in that unfortunate guise in the life of Steve Jobs. And so, this particular misunderstanding of focus will merit a bit more of our attention.

In his interesting book, *Give and Take*, Wharton Business School Professor Adam Grant suggests that there are three dominant styles for interacting with other people: Giving, Taking, and Matching. Givers are always attuned to what they can do for others. Takers tend to approach every interaction with a desire to seek whatever benefits might be available to them, as distinct from others involved in the situation. Matchers are very concerned about fairness. They will give, and sometimes generously, but always with the expectation that in a future situation the party they now benefit will reciprocate and benefit them. Whenever another person does them a favor, conversely, they're eager to even things up as soon as possible by conferring a matching favor. Some think of the ideal outcome of any matching process as always a balancing of karma, where proper resolutions leave a zero balance of personal indebtedness.

The surprise that Grant presents us about these styles is that, while some givers seem to suffer professionally, along various metrics, from the time and energy they commit to others, nonetheless overall, givers disproportionately tend more than others to rise to the very top of their organizations and professions. Grant cites research to show that the most accomplished takers (those who use others) and matchers (those who give only to get, or because they've already gotten) tend to end up, for the most part, neither at the top nor at the bottom, but mostly somewhere in the middle. The givers who suffer burnout or diminished results in their own work because of the time and attention they allot to others can easily avoid these negatives by learning to give in a way that preserves and attends to their own proper self-interests and appropriate self-fulfillment, while still being keen on helping other people. The habit of giving wisely confers benefits on all.

This is relevant to our concern here. To be a person focused on your own goals and interests, and carefully avoiding whatever might deflect you from your path, you don't have to ignore or reject the needs of others. In fact, that would be a very bad idea and a misunderstanding of proper focus. Among your focal goals should be the aim of serving others and helping, however you reasonably can, to improve their lives. A measure of altruistic concern is not only possible for a focused person, but even important for his or her own aims, apart from being morally desirable in its own right. A focused person who generously helps others will normally end up creating a crowd of supporters who will in turn be eager to help him with his goals. As a behavior, this also cultivates in the heart of the helper a sense of meaning and positive impact that then facilitates his overall level of energy and performance as he pursues his own more individually self-directed focal goals.

This is something that Steve Jobs, for at least some of his life, never fully seemed to understand. He apparently lived a stretch of his professional and personal life as a Taker. He very cleverly used people for his own ends. But because of the nature of his ends, however, and the exalted external ideal of what he was trying to accomplish, he nonetheless inspired people enough that they were able to endure his obsessive focus on his own goals, as well as his commonly manipulative behavior. He wanted to make a huge difference. He wanted to change the world. But then, other superbly talented people around him wanted, deep down, the same things. So his taking behavior could often seem to them to be only a minor part of what was, overall, giving behavior—in the pursuit of magnificent plans for the greater good of humanity. He wanted to give something to the world. And he was giving everyone around him a chance to do astoundingly great things together. That's a good part of why, in his case, being naturally a Taker didn't take him down—at least, over the long run.

In a more recent major biography, *Becoming Steve Jobs*, authors Rick Schlender and Rick Tetzeli suggest that Jobs didn't remain a Taker for all his days on the earth. They tell for the first time a story from the man picked by Jobs to succeed him as CEO at Apple. Tim Cook had offered to give the gravely ailing Jobs a part of his own liver to help save his life. He said that it was one of the few times Jobs ever yelled at him, refusing the offer and saying he would never ask for something like that, or even allow a friend or associate to do it. Cook shared the story to put into perspective the character often attributed to Jobs. Over time, and especially in his later days, he seems to have emerged to a remarkable extent from his former thick cocoon of selfish taking, to the point of being able to relinquish such an opportunity to postpone his own death and even, perhaps, renew his health and ability to work and be with his family. His professional focus was unwavering and intense to the end. But his personal focus seems to have broadened and mellowed in healthy ways that have surprised many people to hear.

In fact, even during his exile years away from Apple, Jobs had begun to show some sparks of such a change. Lawrence Levy was the newly hired CFO at Pixar at a crucial time for the health and growth of the company when his physical presence and keen efforts every working hour of each business day mattered immensely. And then, he broke his leg badly while rollerblading. And as a result, he had to undergo emergency surgery. The day after the operation, his boss Steve quietly showed up in his hospital room to reassure him of support, wish him a quick recovery, and offer help with anything he might need. There was no anger, recrimination, or pressure—no "What in the hell were you thinking?" outburst—but, simply, a quiet display of genuine compassion and personal concern. Steve was focused on the needs of his new friend and colleague, and not just the immediate needs of the business.

During the same period of life, Tom Looney needed some time off from his important work in sales at NeXT during the end of a fourth quarter period that was crucial for the business. He and his wife were going to adopt a baby. He had to tell Steve. And Jobs' surprising reaction was to say, "I want to pay for it." He didn't get angry and shout, "How can you do this?" or "Don't you realize what terrible timing this is?" He showed no shock or irritation, or worry at all. He immediately offered to pay what he knew would be the considerable expenses of the adoption. Tom thanked him sincerely and responded that he was being paid enough already, but that he deeply appreciated the support. And then Steve continued to check on the progress of the adoption, along with other things in Tom's life—not at all as a taker, or even a matcher, but as a genuine giver. Focus can have a heart. And the best focus does.

In his book, *Creativity, Inc.*, Ed Catmull, the chief creative force at Pixar who has long served as its president, tells some insightful stories about this time in the life and evolution of Steve Jobs. Early on in the book, he writes the following words in reference to his colleague, John Lasserter, the immensely gifted director of *Toy Story* who had also worked closely with Jobs:

> John once described Steve's story as the classic Hero's journey. Banished for his hubris from the company he founded, he wandered through the wilderness having a series of adventures that, in the end, changed him for the better. I have much to say about Steve's transformation and the role Pixar played in it, but for now, I will simply assert that failure made him better, wiser, and kinder. (58)

To be focused doesn't mean to be stubbornly narrow in any psychologically negative or unhealthy way. It doesn't essentially reflect selfishness, and it never requires being unkind. A balanced life of proper focus should include work goals, personal concerns, family endeavors, and the aim of being useful to others more generally, whenever possible. And that can encompass friends, colleagues, new acquaintances, and of course even strangers in need. The balance that can result will never be static, but will always be a dynamic dance of adjustment and change that can vary from one day to the next, or even from one hour to another. Steve Jobs learned this sort of balance, in fits and starts, and yet never perfectly in his personal life, but in a way that shows we all can improve.

Lastly, having and maintaining a strong ability to focus doesn't mean that there can't be any entertaining or relaxing distractions in your life—what the seventeenth century philosopher Blaise Pascal often called "diversions." The best philosophers in both eastern and western traditions would just advise that when you sip a good wine, focus on it. When you watch a good movie, focus on that. Outside with young children, pay full attention to them and the beauty around you. And put away any device created or inspired by Steve Jobs. When you've selected a great and pleasant distraction from your main duties as an activity that will help you to relax and recharge, don't allow yourself to be kept from fully enjoying that activity or indulgence by any distraction from your distraction. Helpful diversions can recharge us for our most demanding work. Just beware of diversions from your diversions that do exactly the opposite.

People who are scattered and distracted are rarely at peace. Those with proper focus experience a form of inner and even outer harmony that's conducive to many good things. And this is just an application of general philosophical insights about unity and disunity. We've all heard the epigram, "A house divided against itself cannot stand." The disunity of division is healed by a proper focus.

It all just comes back to the perennial Zen injunctive for whoever you are, and wherever you are, and whatever you're doing: Be … Here … Now. Live focused in and on the present. Take it in thoroughly. Bring all of yourself to this moment. Modern life tempts us in a thousand ways to be unfocused and split in our attention, to be scattered all over the place. But that's no recipe for either accomplishment, or fulfillment, or fun. If you can be where you are, and you can do whatever you're doing with your whole heart, then you're way ahead of the game. And that's proper focus. It's inclusionary of its appropriate objects, and exclusionary of anything that would undermine it. I believe that Steve Jobs picked up a lot of this insight and truth when he was a young man and was studying the best eastern philosophical insights. They trained him in the importance of focus. But the value of focus is understood and emphasized by any truly practical philosophy, whatever its origination—east or west. And it's a secret to superior outcomes, in part because of its relative rarity in our time. In a world of the blind, as the old saying goes, the one-eyed man is king. Likewise, in a world of the scattered and confused, the focused individual can rise up and rule.

3. Use the Perspective of Purpose.

How then can you properly be selective in your focus? You can use the perspective of purpose. In his insightful book *Drive*, Dan Pink has gathered some of the best psychological research that demonstrates beyond any reasonable doubt the limited nature of external motivation. Past a certain point, it's hard to motivate people and keep them energized to a high degree by rewards and punishments that are extrinsic, or distinct from and external to their activities—things like money, position, power, or even praise. The real motivators, Pink argues, are internal or intrinsic, and he believes they revolve around three things: Autonomy, Mastery, and Purpose.

We all crave a sense of autonomy. People need to feel that they have some degree of personal control over their lives and even their working circumstances. The pressures and constraints of life abound. We're hemmed in by demands, commitments, and responsibilities. In the midst of it all, we need to have a little breathing room for making our own choices along the way. This inner demand for a measure of autonomy seems deeply ingrained in us. Those who live and work without any sense of relative independence or control never feel thoroughly fulfilled in their jobs and lives. The more of it that can be provided, not only for our selves, but for our associates and colleagues, the better any joint enterprise of ours will fare.

Second, people need to experience some degree of mastery in

what they're doing. All of us want to feel like we're good at what we do. Discernible progression towards a level of mastery is a motivating force for any human being. We like to know that we're getting better. As an ancient Hindu proverb tells us, "There is nothing inherently noble in being superior to another person; true nobility consists in being better than your previous self." And this is a deep, ongoing need. When we feel a growing sense of mastery and we're recognized for it in a way that reinforces our own beliefs, we experience a lot more satisfaction and fulfillment in what we're doing. And that leads, in a virtuous circle, toward further improvements and excellence.

Third, as Pink reminds us, people have a need to feel a sense of purpose in their activities. Why does your business exist? What is its true purpose? Why have you chosen to do what you're doing? And then we can go to another level: What's your personal purpose, or vision, or mission for your life? Without a sense of purpose, we suffer. We wander. We feel hollowed out. And, eventually, we feel lost. One of the bestselling books for a very long time had the immensely engaging title, *The Purpose Driven Life*. This phrase itself, emblazoned on the cover of the book, caused casual browsers to pick it up, and open it with a curiosity that's natural and stems from a need that's universally deep.

I've suggested that clear goals help us to identify and eliminate distractions that would get in the way of our progress. But how do we set the right goals in the first place? By having a solid sense of purpose and mission for what we're doing. Why do we exist as a company or department or institution? What's our purpose? Those should be questions that everyone can ask and answer in their own context. A strong sense of purpose brings with it both a motivation to focus and an ability to do so well.

The most powerful goals are those that are rooted in self-knowledge on an individual level and on an organizational scale. Socrates is widely associated with the most famous philosophical injunctive—Know Thyself! This piece of advice was so revered that it was inscribed in marble at the holiest spot in ancient Greece, the Oracle at Delphi. And as the ancient historian Diogenes Laertius informs us, an emphasis on the importance of self-knowledge may come down to us from even earlier than the work of Socrates, in the thought of the pre-Socratic philosopher Thales of Miletus (c. 624-546 BCE). One story that's often been repeated is that Thales was a bit like the Warren Buffet of his day, as wealthy as he was wise. And so people often approached him with requests for his advice about their work and lives. One day, a man in search of insight asked the great Thales the question: "What's the hardest thing in the world?"

Thales reportedly said, "To know yourself." This is, of course, deep wisdom, even though it might seem paradoxical, for what is closer to me than myself? Yet, we're all masters of self-deception and it can take a lifetime to peel back all the layers that insulate us from genuine, authentic self-knowledge.

The man on a quest for insight thought for a moment about this answer and went on to pose the sage a second question. He asked: "Well, what then is the easiest thing in the world?"

Thales quickly replied, "To give people advice like this." And, Ok, we'll just pass over this one without further comment, since it hits a bit close to home.

The man then asked his final question: "What's the most satisfying thing in the world?"

Thales responded, "True success." And I think that he meant proper success, success that's right for us as individuals, or on target for a group, and that's both deeply satisfying and sustainable in its nature and consequences for ongoing beneficial results.

And then, many philosophers since Thales have suggested that self-knowledge is necessary for true success. But if Thales was right, this means that the most satisfying thing in the world depends on the hardest thing in the world, which may explain why proper success seems to elusive in so many people's lives.

Every process of articulating a sense of purpose or setting goals relevant to that purpose should be an exercise in self-knowledge. It's vitally important to know yourself, whether as an individual or as an organization. And, as philosophers throughout the centuries have clarified, this requires an attention to several further requirements:

Know your strengths
Know your weaknesses
Know your opportunities
Know your limits
Know your deepest values
Know your defining purpose

Two points should be made regarding this short list. Strengths and weaknesses are obviously characteristics of the self, or of an organization, internally. So self-knowledge on an individual or business level obviously has to include such awareness. But opportunities are external things. How can knowing them be a part of self-knowledge? The answer is actually fairly simple. What counts as, or provides, a great opportunity for one person or company may not have the same status for another. Knowing your proper opportunities both reflects, and can be a major path for, knowing yourself. In fact, it's often in learning what counts as a good opportunity for you, or for your business, that you increase your own self-knowledge in a distinctive way. Knowing your strengths and weaknesses, along with your overall values and purpose, can most often help you to spot the right opportunities for present attention, as well as future action and proper growth. But then sometimes, the sudden recognition of an apt opportunity can enhance intuitively, or even transform, your previous sense of self-knowledge and purpose.

And there's a second matter to address. Some people, when viewing this short list of components within the realm of self-knowledge, will wonder about the inclusion of limits. Aren't they already covered by the category of weaknesses? The simple answer is no. Some limits may arise out of weaknesses. But others may exist as a result of prior commitments that are actually strengths. And some may be connected neither to strengths or weaknesses, but just to the availability of time, attention, and power at our command. There is, however, a bit of possible redundancy in this short list of requirements for individual or organizational self-knowledge. Our deepest values ought to provide guidelines, and thus limits, on our choices. And the right values can be considered among our strengths. The same is true, of course, for purposes, if they're appropriate, and properly embodied. But this possible degree of redundancy is useful for the sake of absolute clarity—a quality that's of course closely related to focus.

Goal setting most often arises out of our desires, but our desires are not always worth pursuing. As the French existentialist philosopher Jean Paul Sartre once said, "We are our choices," and so it's important to note that proper choice requires wisdom. Filtered through an understanding of our strengths, weaknesses, opportunities, limits, values, and purposes, our inclinations and desires can be tested and then through wise choice, result in the right goals, and the proper focal points for our actions and energies. Furthermore, there's a sense in which all the other factors we've named culminate properly in precisely our sense of purpose.

Aristotle understood long ago that we humans are essentially purposeful beings. When we have a purpose that we can believe in, one that inspires and animates us, then it will by nature guide our behavior in a way that no external forces or benefits could ever replicate. Buying in to a purpose is just setting your heart and mind to be oriented in a particular direction, and on a specific road—and that process inherently involves the strength of focus.

I think we can say even more. Focus is destiny. And purpose makes it possible. What we focus on determines what we can become, as well as what we can accomplish. Vagueness is the enemy of excellence. Distraction is an adversary of greatness. Focus is its engine.

By all accounts, Steve Jobs didn't want primarily to get rich, or to be famous, or even to attain market domination in whatever he did. He certainly seemed to enjoy all those things when they might come his way. But none was his primary aim. He wanted to change the world or, as he often put it, to make a dent or a ripple in the universe with insanely great products that would act as tools to liberate people to be and do their best—and even to experience real joy in their lives. It was sixties and seventies idealism at its prime: "Come change the world with me." And it worked. Jobs had a great passion ignited by this sense of purpose. And he then recruited and kept great people because of this lofty and contagious mission.

The Monday Morning Orientation Materials for any new hire or intern at Apple have long involved a card, prominently displayed, that says:

> *There's work and there's your life's work.*
>
> *The kind of work that has your fingerprints all over it. The kind of work that you'd never compromise on. That you'd sacrifice a weekend for. You can do that kind of work at Apple. People don't come here to play it safe. They come here to swim in the deep end.*
>
> *They want their work to add up to something.*
>
> *Something big. Something that couldn't happen anywhere else.*
>
> *Welcome to Apple.*

Everyone wants to make a difference, deep down. Everyone wants their work and their lives to matter, and even, somehow, to matter big. When presented with an organization and with leadership dedicated to help make this happen, people respond. It's no accident that employees and customers, and even journalists, have so often become raving fans of Apple and its products. The products came out of and supported a purpose that people could believe in and be passionate about.

A strong sense of purpose can drive business success in a distinctive way. And it can gather people around a central focus like nothing else. This is a secret that Steve Jobs knew and used, for world-class results. And we can, too. Nothing succeeds like a proper and purpose-driven focus.

2

Simplify

I am asking for one simple thing.
Socrates

There is a period of time that we refer to broadly as the middle ages—not in the personal sense of the years between 40 and 60: as a 65-year-old and counting, I assure you that they can continue on a bit longer than that—but in the broad historical sense. During this period of world history, a philosopher named William of Ockham, who lived from roughly 1287 until 1347, introduced a key scientific guideline that has come to be known as the principle of simplicity. When scientists seek to explain an observed range of phenomena, they sometimes have to postulate the activity of some as-yet-unseen particles, or planets, or forces, or entities of another sort. Ockham's principle of simplicity, widely known since his time as "Ockham's Razor," instructs us to: "Never multiply entities beyond necessity." In other words, in the most general sense, don't complicate things needlessly. In its original formulation, the principle was one of metaphysical population control. The philosopher didn't want us postulating, or inferring to, more unseen entities or otherwise hidden aspects of nature than would be strictly necessary for explaining whatever we were investigating. The advice was: Razor away and shave off, or in any other ways cut down, unnecessary complexities. We could even follow the spirit of his own strictures here and articulate his ideal as the basic command: Keep it simple.

In the midst of any apparently complicated situation or problem, there is always a simple core. When we can penetrate down to the essence of the situation, we position ourselves to solve the problem and move forward powerfully. Socrates laid the basic groundwork for this approach long before Ockham. He was always searching for the essence—of knowledge, or justice, or goodness. He stimulated his most famous student Plato to believe that such an essence is always to be found. Plato also came to be convinced that anything's essence is the most important thing about it to know.

The ancient Greek Mathematician Archimedes gave us our deepest understanding of another equally useful principle—that of leverage—when he famously said, "Give me a place to stand and a lever long enough, and I can move the world." Let me quote Jobs on this point. In 1998, he said this to *BusinessWeek Magazine*:

> "Simple can be harder than complex. You have to work hard to get your thinking clean to make it simple. But it's worth it in the end, because once you get there, you can move mountains."

Simplicity is leverage. And it's a place to stand. Complexity can be distracting and confusing, even overwhelming. The focus we talked about in chapter one has to strip away irrelevant or superficial complexities and cut down to the simple core of the situation we face, in order to gain for us the leverage we need.

As a young man, Steve Jobs was powerfully impressed with the aesthetic of simplicity to be found in Zen thought and practice. This strand of Japanese Buddhism imbued him with an urge to simplify his life, his work, and anything he would ever bring to the world. His conception of "insanely great" was always connected to simplicity. And in this, he was a lot like the great Italian Renaissance artist Michelangelo, who explained that, as a sculptor confronting his materials, it was his job to chip away all the marble that did not belong. He saw the beauty hidden within a block of stone and took it as his task to eliminate the surrounding mass down to the simple contours of the perfect shape that was prepared to emerge. Apple products were famous from the start for their simplicity. Jobs urged his engineers to eliminate unnecessary buttons and controls, stripping things down to the absolute essentials, to the extent of realizing at one point that the popular iPod didn't even need an On-Off switch. The engineers working with him often thought he had lost his mind. But as they strove to understand and realize his vision, they came to see the value of the simplicity he sought.

In order to grasp fully what we're dealing with here, there are two negative terms we need to address and comment on—the words: simplistic and simple-minded. These terms are most often, and normally, used in negative ways. A simple-minded person is one whose understanding has not reached a certain level of maturity and sophistication. A simplistic statement or solution to a problem is one that could seem to the careless glance to be true or useful, on the surface, but its failing is that it hides away from the more difficult nuance and precision that alone could make it helpful. This problematic quality is often found in motivational books or talks, or in the form of popular self-help aphorisms that as grand gestures can sometimes strike you as generally true, but that, if they are examined more carefully, turn out to be literally false, and even at times because of this, dangerously misleading. Simple is not the same thing as simplistic. Simplicity is not simple-mindedness. In fact, the scientific principle and the aesthetic urge that motivated Steve Jobs move in quite an opposite direction from any form of simplistic simple-mindedness.

The great contemporary theoretical scientist Steven Hawking has said that it's every ambitious physicist's dream to discover a single law of nature that's so powerful as to explain under one unified understanding all of the physical world, and yet, is at the same time so simple that it could be printed on a T-shirt, a bumper sticker, or a business card. This outstanding thinker isn't praising the simplistic or the simple-minded, but the much different and profound characteristic of simplicity that so moved Steve Jobs, and that can work so potently for the rest of us as well, in whatever we do. As Jobs himself once said:

> "It takes a lot of hard work to make something simple, to truly understand the underlying challenges and come up with elegant solutions." (*HBR*, April 2012, 95)

To get our heads around all this, we need to consider some basic imperatives that are involved in the proper quest for simplicity in business and in life. Putting the essential Jobs to work for us will always involve respecting certain guidelines.

1. Find the Essence. Build Elegant Solutions.

While their contemporaries grope in the dark, great minds tend to shine a light through that darkness, illuminating the landscape in new ways and allowing others to see a creative path forward. The first rule of simplification, when confronting a complex situation or problem is to find the essence of what you face. Peel off the layers of complication you can see and get down to the core. Then, you can build elegant solutions that will work and delight.

As Apple products evolved over the years, paralleling Jobs' own evolution of thought, they became ever simpler and more beautiful, to the extent of being quite striking in appearance and operation. There's a delight to be felt in first seeing them, and then in using them. This reaction arises distinctively out of the Ockhamistic or Zen simplicity of their design and function. Jobs never multiplied features or controls beyond necessity for the full range of expected uses of his devices. And in fact, he was quite strict and demanding about this. Every detail, as a result, was thought through with this in mind. As with the issue of focus, this is an area in which we have to say no a lot in order to arrive at the right yes.

Finding the essence of a challenge or situation may superficially sound easy in principle, but can be quite hard in practice. In principle, we just abstract away from all the details that aren't relevant or germane and isolate the core problem or opportunity. In practice, it can take a lot of insider knowledge, built up over years, and great instincts, along with a dose of actual wisdom, in order to be able to do this well. What seems like a good solution to one problem can end up being inelegant in another way. Superfluity rarely advertises itself as such. We sort through the many in order to find the one.

I was on Twitter fairly intensively for a nine-month experiment several years ago in the early days of this immensely popular social platform. Two friends insisted I sign up for a Twitter account to see what was going on. And in the first weeks, I had just two followers—those two guys. I quickly realized that something interesting was indeed going on at that stage in the development of this social medium: In addition to seeing the tweets of the people you chose to follow, you could go to a general stream with a label like, "Everyone," or some such universal indicator, and see tweets from around the world, from people of all ages and races and nationalities and religious beliefs. As fast as you could read and refresh your screen, there would be a new stream of insights, expletives, commentaries, celebrations, complaints, reports, haiku poems, and questions. From the mundane to the metaphysical, the profane to the profound, everything imaginable could be seen. And, as Heraclitus once said about the world, around five hundred years BCE, you could never step into exactly the same stream twice—the waters were always changing and moving on. The little Twitter bird was flapping its wings frantically fast.

I spent far too much time getting my head around this amazing deluge of information and then doing my own tweeting as a philosopher, about life. Pretty soon, I was tweeting away at breakfast, mid-morning, through lunch, and on and off for the rest of the day, and even until late in the night. I was answering questions, posing new thoughts, and fielding reactions to those ideas. I would seek to be encouraging, provocative, and helpful, in equal measure. I got a few more followers, then a dozen, and then a hundred, and one day, two hundred, then a thousand, and more. And when I got to about five thousand followers, one of them suggested that I collect my tweets as a book. Then someone else asked for the same thing. After several more people had urged this on me, I decided to do it. The result was an extended exercise in simplicity, where I often had the challenge of cutting to the essence of a topic and constructing an elegant epigram or aphorism that could be both useful and true, and sometimes even penetrating and suggestive, at least, according to many of their recipients. The result was a little book called *Twisdom (Twitter Wisdom): A Philosopher Ponders Life in 140 Characters or Less*. And, yes, that last word should be "Fewer," but I chose to follow the Twitter patter, well established by then, that used what grammarians would call the "mass term" in a properly "count term" context. But, then, in the spirit of philosophers immemorial, I digress—so back to my point.

It was a wonderful exercise to learn to think and communicate in 140 character (letter and space) increments. The process began to instill intellectual habits of succinctness—not something that philosophers are known for, generally. And even though the initial experiment of mine ended some years ago, those habits of thought continue to resonate. I still have the skill that I can exercise when appropriate, and it often allows me to cut through complexity and communicate a simple core message in a talk, or a short piece on *The Huffington Post*, or daily in another blog format at my own personal website, TomVMorris.com.

For our purposes here, it may be useful for me to share a few original tweets about simplicity, perhaps to stimulate your own thinking on it. One day, years ago, a Twitter follower emailed me and asked me to reflect a bit in my Twitter stream on the topics of simplicity and elegance. It was a combination of concepts I had never pondered. The request goaded me to think about each of these apparently different things in the context of the other. The tweets I'll display in just a bit are part of what resulted. As I've gone back to them, they have helped me to understand in a deeper way what drew Steve Jobs so powerfully to whatever is properly simple. But first, I want to lay out briefly our second imperative for simplicity. It will be relevant to the content of the tweets I'll share.

2. Master the Complexities. Streamline.

The sort of simplicity we seek for true mastery is to be found on the other side of complexity, on the far side of whatever our challenge might be. We need first to understand and then to master the tangled and knotted details we face in any business endeavor or other context, in order to go powerfully and productively beyond them. And, in case the concept of mastery might seem an extreme one here, consider the way it works in other facets of life. A few years ago, my friend William Powers wrote a book called *Hamlet's Blackberry: Building a Good Life in the Digital Age*. Stripped down to its core, the simple message of this insightful book was that if we don't master our modern communication devices, it's inevitable that they'll master us. As Powers points out, this has been a challenge throughout all of human history. A new technology arises and it's completely up to us how we use it, for good or for ill. Most things in the world can bring help or harm, depending on how they're used and, so, how they function in our lives. It's only when we take control and use them in the best ways that we can depend on more beneficial outcomes. Mastery involves a deep understanding of this, and the measure of control that can come from it.

Complexity is always a challenge. But we can't let it be our master. We need to work hard to untangle the complications that easily confuse us and slow us down. That way, we can begin to see the essence of what we confront, and thereby position ourselves to streamline solutions and processes for greater levels of ease and effectiveness. Let me quote Jobs on this. He told the Mac designers in 1983:

> "When you start looking at a problem and think it's really simple, you don't understand how complex the problem really is. Once you get into the problem … you see that it's complicated, and you come up with all these convoluted solutions. That's where most people stop, and the solutions tend to work for a while. But the really great person will keep going, find the underlying problem, and come up with an elegant solution that works on every level." (*Inside Steve's Brain*, p. 72)

In that one remark, Jobs connects simplicity, elegance, and greatness. It's a nexus well worth contemplating.

Now, we'll look at several of my old spontaneous tweets, in their original order, which I tossed into the Twitter stream just seconds apart, as I ruminated on this issue of how simplicity and elegance might be related.

A friend just asked about elegance and simplicity.

In science, an elegant theory is one that does great work from the resource of a beautiful simplicity.

In modern fashion history, consider Grace Kelly and Cary Grant. Elegance is rooted in appropriate simplicity.

Less is more, within the bounds of good style and our overarching intent.

Elegance never shouts. It whispers with power.

Simplicity and elegance require confidence. When we're unsure, we complicate things.

Undue complexity always bespeaks a lack of command, and a corresponding lack of self-confidence.

The best simplicity requires mastery, and can display it beautifully.

The best philosophy is elegant and simple, not complex, convoluted, and obscure.

Our work should manifest the mastery that produces elegant simplicity.

Work from the heart is simple and pure.

Work that flows from love can be elegant in every way.

In life, we move from simplicity to complexity and, when we do it right, on to the greater and deeper simplicity that can then emerge.

The wonders of elegance never cease to amaze those who can see and understand.

Create, then edit. Do both with your whole heart, and elegance can result.

Simplicity is not a complicated thing, but it can be as hard as anything equally great.

Elegance seduces by enthralling our hearts.

Complexity can hinder and constrain us. Masterful simplicity invites us forth.

Complexity may be a journey, but it's never the destination. Simplicity is the goal that alone can justify it.

Undue complexity confounds. Well-earned simplicity invites.

Those who master are clear. Those who don't know thoroughly cannot explain simply.

We should never shirk the responsibility to understand complexity, but we don't really get it until we've reached the simplicity beyond.

The simplicity that hasn't struggled with complexity is fit for our youth, but maturity requires simplicity to be earned.

I enjoy and sometimes relish complexity on the trail of truth. But I never rest content short of the unified simplicities below.

Elegance is as rare as it is wonderful. Aspire to it in all things.

Simplicity is context dependent, has many contours, and is often hard to define, but the more we know, the better we recognize it.

Wisdom is all about simplicity and elegance. The most practical truths are rarely convoluted.

The English word 'elegance' comes from the Latin, 'eligere,' which meant to select or choose with care. Steve Jobs was always seeking to select with care the precise form or contour of simplicity that produces elegance and beauty. That's where greatness is found. Customers then responded with enthusiasm and delight. And, of course, so did journalists. He could never have bought through normal advertising channels the widespread buzz that his simple and elegant devices created as soon as they were launched out into the world. Fans and reporters alike became evangelists for the products and spread the word as far as it could go. This would happen reliably despite the fact that the first version of a product often had functionality problems and limitations that should have dampened enthusiasm. But the immense allure of simple elegance prevailed. Form eclipsed function quite often in the early reception of a new product and, in a sense, the resulting excitement and praise bought Jobs the time to get the functionality right.

The relentless pursuit of simplicity and elegance had great power. Steve would never stop short of stripping things down to their fundamental and most intelligible essence. The challenge for us is to go and do likewise, within the realm of our endeavors and to the extent that we can. In all things, simplify. The results can be spectacular.

3. Remember: Simple is Beautiful.

Elegant simplicity. It's certainly a compelling concept. But as a philosopher, I have to consider counter-arguments to any claim, reasonable alternatives to any suggestion. What would a skeptic say? I've adumbrated what I consider to be a powerful relationship between simplicity and elegance. But is this in fact universal?

A recent obituary in the *New York Times* reminded me of something from decades ago that made me smile. One of the strangest fads of the past half-century was the "pet rock." Sitting in a bar one night in the mid nineteen-seventies and hearing people around him complain about how much trouble pet care can be—the constant demand of feeding a pet, and sometimes walking them, and always cleaning up after them—an ad man, Gary Dahl, joked that his own pet caused him no trouble whatsoever. He then explained his remark to surprised companions by saying: "I have a pet rock." Their reaction to the silly and even absurd claim led him to find investors and launch a craze that made him a millionaire almost overnight and changed his life.

Dahl bought a big load of smooth rocks for about a penny apiece, drew little faces on them, packaged each in a cardboard carrying case, and sold them with instruction manuals on the easy care of the new pet. The manual said:

> If, when you remove the rock from its box it appears to be excited, place it on some old newspapers. The rock will know what the paper is for and will require no further instruction. It will remain on the paper until you remove it.

People at the time found this hilarious and bought millions of his rocks. And yeah, I know. The seventies were ... different. But I can imagine an example like this being used to argue that simple isn't always elegant, but that it can instead be, as in this case, nothing more than silly, and perhaps even ridiculous. The pet rock is a simple gag that has nothing to do with elegance or aesthetic attractiveness, whatsoever. And if this is true, then there is after all no hard link between simplicity and elegance.

My reply to such a potential objection would be two-fold: If the pet rock is indeed simple, then it's also elegant, after all. And if, in your judgment, it's not elegant, then that's because, to you, it's not simple. In either case, consequently, the example wouldn't show a split between the simple and the elegant. Stick with me for a minute on this and I'll try to say why. If you find yourself initially agitated or excited by my claim, it's been suggested that sitting on some old newspapers might help. And you may then require no further instruction.

Some would suggest that the pet rock was funny precisely because it was the ultimate play on simplicity in its conceptual context, which was the concept of a pet, and that of pet ownership, and our grasp of the core role a pet plays in a person's life. It was clever because it stripped away lots of complications and drilled down to the barest possible essence. And laughter, as a result, or even the inner mirth of finding something funny, is itself an aesthetic reaction just like, but different than, the sense of something as beautiful, or lovely, pleasing, or appealing. There is an elegance that can be found in humor, just as in science or mathematics or fashion. And that's what here made people, at least in their own cultural time, smile, or laugh at the joke.

Others would argue that there was nothing simple about this bit of attempted humor at all. The rock was a simple object, for sure, but it could be funny only in a complex context of assumptions and implications that it both used and controverted. So, for anyone who insisted that the pet rock was not at all elegant, but rather just crazy, or actually stupid, if even in an endearing way, then we defenders of the relationship between simplicity and elegance can counter that any inelegance would be due precisely to the complexity of the joke. And thus again, we'd preserve the link between elegance and simplicity. However, in my own judgment, the concept of the pet rock was indeed simple, and strangely elegant as a sort of performance joke, and that's what made it work to the extent that it became a widespread fad. You can have a beautiful joke that's also at the same time outrageously lame, or silly. A good pun is an example of the same thing. Simple can be powerful.

Steve's wife, Laurene Jobs, has reported that she typically heard Steve laugh the loudest when he was being silly with their kids. Simple jokes can produce big laughs.

There's something deep within us that needs simplicity. A simple and uncluttered vista gives animals in nature a good view and an early warning of approaching predators or prey. An empty horizon provides a sense of safety and repose, and even of peace. It did the same thing for early human beings over very long periods of our prehistory and into our history. As a result, we have, at least most of us, an unconscious default setting in our minds, attitudes, and emotions to prefer the simple and uncluttered. A first sight of the sea, or even such a view after a long absence, can evoke an involuntary sigh of relief and relaxation. The smooth surface of a still pond or a placid lake on a windless day can have a similar effect. The wide vista from a high vantage point on a mountain or large promontory can also be soothing and reassuring at a fundamental level. You can experience a small version of this by de-cluttering a room, or a desk. Zen gardens can have the same effect. And even the act of meditation can be seen as reducing the complexity of the mind to a simple purifying essence that brings peace and tranquility to the soul.

Let me quote the influential American philosopher Ralph Waldo Emerson here. In an essay and talk on beauty, he once said:

> We ascribe beauty to that which is simple; which has no superfluous parts; which exactly answers its end; which stands related to all things; which is the mean of many extremes. It is the most enduring quality, and the most ascending quality.

And then again:

> Beauty rests on necessities. The line of beauty is the result of perfect economy. The cell of the bee is built at that angle

> which gives the most strength with the least wax; the bone or the quill of the bird gives the most alar strength, with the least weight. "It is the purgation of superfluities," said Michelangelo… In rhetoric, this art of omission is a chief secret of power, and, in general, it is proof of high culture, to say the greatest matters in the simplest way.

I've come to believe that there's a deep connection between the aesthetic and the spiritual. We're programmed in our genes and our souls to respond to the simple and elegant. There's even an obvious connection here between the most profound aspect of Buddhist thought that so attracted Jobs and his insistence on the elegance of simplicity. It's to be found in the concept of emptiness. Emptiness is idealized and absolutely ultimate simplicity. Anything that exists is, from this point of view, an addition, or a complication, and should respect the perfect beauty of its stark alternative—the ideally nonexistent, or pristine, untroubled emptiness. Proper simplicity in art, in design, and in the world does that.

Meditation is certainly about a sort of emptiness—emptying the mind of needless clutter: releasing and letting go of what's unneeded, in order to provide for what's deeply required. And in a similar way, emptying your mind of unnecessary assumptions, expectations, and entrenched beliefs, simplifying your approach to your challenges, is adopting what's known in Buddhist practice as a beginner's mind. Socrates didn't pretend to know what he didn't know. He approached topics with something fundamentally akin to a beginner's mind. And so did Steve Jobs. The inner simplicity of open thought then often allowed Jobs to discover or create the outer simplicity of design and function that would so deeply resonate with, and appeal to, others.

Of course, there are contexts in which the overly simple can become austere or harsh, and even difficult, rather than right, proper, and pleasing. Again, an Aristotelian analysis will help.

The intellectual grandson of Socrates has much to teach us. What we should aim for is neither the too little nor the too much that surrounds a virtuous degree of parsimony, but the just right—the beautiful simplicity that ideally can be found in anything we think or do or make.

Regardless of what business we're in, our communications, our packaging, our products, and our solutions to problems are all made more effective by being virtuously simple. There is a beauty in such simplicity that will be evident to everyone involved, and it's something they'll respond to at a deep, unconscious level. If we can evoke this reaction, even sometimes beneath conscious awareness, it will then predispose almost everyone around us to enjoy and form a healthy attachment to what we do.

So we should keep in mind these truths: Needless complexity is not just cumbersome, it's ugly. It's displeasing and off-putting. Properly simple is beautiful. And so it's pleasing, and even delightful. To attain this virtuous simplicity in our processes and products, we need to engage in a form of Socratic questioning, relentlessly examining the unnecessary complexities that easily build up around us, and even within us, and then using the thin clean edge of Ockham's Razor to cut them away.

3

Take Responsibility End-to-End

The responsibility rests with you.
Socrates

Here's the ultimate paradox in the life of Steve Jobs. He had serious problems with empathy in his personal relationships, in and outside of work. He often seemed blind to people's feelings, or else utterly callous to their experience of his harshest words and actions. Emotionally, he was far too often the proverbial bull in a china shop. But as much as, or possibly even more than, anyone else in history, he built his entire business and based the designs of all his products on a profound level of empathy with the end-user, the customer. And he was a master of this. How, then, did he manage it? How could such a seemingly self-centered and utterly self-absorbed person become a world-class master of empathetic concern for the customer?

The simplest solution to our conundrum is that Steve Jobs was always his own most important customer. He designed precisely and almost exclusively for his most highly valued ultimate end-user—himself. He was the quintessential consumer of cool tech stuff. And, fortunately, his aesthetic loves were universal enough that, in most cases, catering to his own tastes meant pleasing and even delighting everyone else. It was the one place in his life where he naturally and perhaps inadvertently acted in accordance with the famous Golden Rule, treating other people the way he would want to be treated.

But the full answer to our puzzle goes deeper. Steve apparently had a visceral need to be great. Whether he felt he had something to prove, in principle, to those biological parents out there somewhere who had given him up for adoption, or to the couple first in line to adopt him who had passed on him because he was a boy, thus inflicting on him what he saw as a second fundamental rejection, or perhaps he had something to prove just to himself, in the light of what he wrongly took to be these deep early rejections. He had to succeed at an outrageous level. He needed to be so great as to change the world. And he had chosen a profession where he could not attain this at the highest level unless his customers genuinely loved what he did. So, he was intent on gaining their love. He deeply needed it. And as a result, nothing could stop him in its pursuit. He had a supreme focus in meeting this need of his. No detail was so small that it could be overlooked.

Jobs was passionately concerned about the entire customer experience. It wasn't enough for him to create great software. He had to design and build the hardware that it would run on. And that wasn't enough, either. He had to create the packaging for the computer, or any other device. He thought of the customer getting his newest tech creation home from the store and opening up the box that held it. The unpacking itself should be akin to theater, a performance of sequential experiences of elegance, beauty, love, and wonder. Everything should be a source of delight. Then, of course, Steve didn't want these things of beauty competing for shelf space in stores that sold any clunky, ugly machines—places whose clerks might know very little about the intrinsic greatness of the Apple product that had been so meticulously created and packaged with care and concern. So he had to design and build his own retail showplaces, the famous Apple Stores that we now know and love.

But even in those stores, where Steve himself had picked out the flooring and the wood to be used in display cases, he couldn't let his customers walk up to any old cash register and stand in line to pay for the purchase in a normal way. Would he want to do that? No, he certainly would not. In fact: Of course not! The Apple Store had to be different in every way. And so it had to be distinctive at the final point of purchase. You wouldn't be in just any normal retail establishment. Jobs had to create and design a special process for you to pay more conveniently and, at the outset, almost magically through hand held devices that could produce a receipt on the spot or instantly send one to your email address without a piece of paper to carry away, keep track of, and eventually file away in a drawer, or lose. There had to be special magic here, just as there had to be magic everywhere. That's what Steve was all about: magic—or at least all the appearances of it. He needed to be a magus, a wizard, a conjurer, as well as a galvanizing figure who might as well be garbed in a long dark robe and carrying a wand. But of course, as he himself would likely say: "No wand. It's not necessary. Nature gives us five wands on each hand. That's all we need." The magic simply had to leap from his brain and each of those hands to every facet of the customer experience.

Jobs wanted to take responsibility for the entire customer experience, as well as for the original process of creating a new product, end-to-end. We can't usually do exactly what he did, but we can certainly find an application of this leadership principle that makes sense for what we do. Examining his actions over the years, it seems to me that there are three imperatives relating to this principle, just as with the two other principles we've already examined—focus and simplicity. These imperatives will help us in whatever we do to take responsibility, end-to-end.

1. Assume nothing. Own everything.

When it comes to the daily ebb and flow of work, easy assumptions are common but can be quite dangerous. Think back through your career to every time you've ever heard anyone use the worlds, "Well, I just assumed …" and recall what the context was. It's my guess that, nine times out of ten, some disaster or catastrophe had just happened and the person speaking was trying to excuse his part in allowing it to take place. He was only making a reasonable assumption, the sort of assumption that any normal rational person would make. Surely, he can't be held responsible for the occasional quirky unpredictability of the world, and so should be exonerated from any untoward result that might have happened by sheer surprise.

In connection with this, there's a grammatically clever aphorism. I first heard it on a reality television show, as uttered by the head of a real estate company to someone who had made just this sort of mistake. He said: "When you ASSUME, you make an ASS of U and ME." Or to tweak another contemporary saying only slightly, "Assumption is the Mother of Mess Up." And don't we all know the truth of this?

But anyone like Steve, and our older guiding light, Socrates, who cares about conceptual precision would certainly want me to point out that the blunt imperative of our guideline here—Assume Nothing—is sensible and useful and even important in so far, and only in so far, as it's applied properly and in a context-relative way to the distinctive behaviors and events involved in the unique pursuit of our business or personal goals and related processes. But this is a complex qualifying condition for a simple insight. So, I should take a deep breath and explain.

Literally and universally, we can't possibly act in accordance with the demand to assume nothing. We're always necessarily assuming many things as we go through the day. We're assuming that our senses are usually trustworthy, that our memories are generally reliable, that the laws of nature will continue to operate as they have in the past, and that the meanings of the words in our language are holding relatively constant as we use them, day-to-day. Let's call such mostly unconscious beliefs as these, "fundamental framework assumptions," without which intelligent life in the world would not be possible. And we can't prove these things to be true. As philosophical skeptics have long relished pointing out to us, any attempt to gather fundamental, non-circular evidence for them will fail. And yet, despite the gleeful suggestion of skeptics to the contrary, we have to take them for granted. They are fundamental assumptions we naturally make, and moreover need to make in order to act rationally in the world. They're partly definitive of what it means to be rational.

And these few examples, of course, just scratch the surface. There are innumerable things we have to assume in order to get going in the morning and make our way through the day. We assume that no one has snuck into our home and reset all the clocks and watches during the night, and so we can take the time they indicate to be roughly accurate. We assume that most of the headline news we get—especially from multiple, authoritative sources—is at least roughly reliable, at least most of the time. We assume that the world is not run entirely and in detail by a tangle of hidden conspiracies that have turned us all into puppets in a play we can't understand or change. You can rightly assume that you're not at this very moment asleep and merely dreaming that you're reading this book—and on and on. Such basic assumptions can't be avoided if we want to live rational, practical, and productive lives. It's in the nature of finite knowers like us to have to make fundamental framework assumptions and hold what philosophers sometimes call "basic beliefs," beliefs whose rationality does not depend on their derivation or support by other beliefs that are taken to be more fundamental. A basic belief is as far down as you can go, and it's a paradigmatic acceptable assumption.

To be effective in our business lives, and in life generally, however, what we should avoid assuming are not, of course, those universal beliefs we all need to take for granted in order to live reasonably in the world. We should shun all unnecessary, careless, or loose assumptions about particular people, promises, and processes, as well as particular events where such an assumption isn't rationally required as a practical necessity. These are the assumptions that we can and should avoid making by simply, like our predecessor Socrates, asking the right questions, checking things out carefully, and then double-checking, most often, and with alternative plans and backup scenarios ready to put into action—taking, in effect, a degree of ownership over the situation. Outside the deep framework assumptions that make intelligent life in the world possible, and inside the circle of people, promises, processes, and particular events at work, we should assume nothing and own everything. That's what our imperative, in its proper context, means.

What then is it to assume nothing and to own everything in the relevant sense? It's simply to take intellectual, attitudinal, and emotional possession of, or full responsibility for, the work or life process in which you've involved. It means, in this sense, becoming engaged intimately in the process, and paying attention to the details within it and bearing on it, rather than blindly having faith instead that others will be sufficiently responsible to get the job done well without oversight or accountability of any kind. Taking ownership is taking personal responsibility, and that means being accountable for what happens.

By insisting that people be responsible and accountable for their decisions, their designs, and the quality of their work generally, Steve Jobs was, oddly, swimming against the cultural stream in his own day and ours. The rise of Apple took place during a time when the concept of accountability in our culture was generally on the wane. In many companies, and in several other human contexts, there was what we can think of as a slow death of accountability on a massive scale. As modern business entities became increasingly more complex, largely in step with the sort of organizational growth and new business strategies made possible by contemporary technology, I have watched far too many companies in the past few decades cross a threshold of complexity that allowed for a huge loss of accountability. Things had become so complicated that, when something went badly wrong, it was hard to see exactly who or what was responsible. We've all witnessed this threshold of complexity problem play out in major corporations, in other large institutions, and in government actions, both domestic and abroad. "Mistakes were made," we're told. And that's about as specific as it gets.

I think this is actually worth a little bit of a philosophical rant, if you'll indulge me, and largely because it's a problem that's just getting worse throughout every domain of modern life. Too many people seem to do everything they can to avoid responsibility for their actions. And we find it almost impossible, as a result, to hold others accountable for what they do. In an increasingly complex world, and on a relentless, 24-hour news cycle, with new stories displacing old headlines before the previous day's events can even sink in, it's tougher and tougher to insist on accountability and get it. And yet, how can a society function without it?

We clearly live in a waiver culture, bred by the litigious trends that we've seen for decades. The other day I was driving behind a dirty dump truck. Huge letters on the rear said, "Stay 200 Feet Back. Not Responsible for Damage." I pulled into a parking lot. A sign at the entrance featured the words, "Not Responsible for Loss, Theft, or Damage." Go in for any medical or professional treatment. The paperwork precedes any other process, and disclaimers and waivers are everywhere to be seen. Or simply take your kids to a water park or skating rink. But before anything happens, first sign all the release forms. I once called down to the front desk in a famous five-star luxury resort where I was scheduled to give a talk and I had to report that the room I had just been checked into had not been cleaned since the previous guest left. There were unmade beds, overflowing trashcans, half eaten food on a desk, and wet towels lying on the bathroom floor. I was being very nice about it all, and just wanted to be redirected to another room—one that was clean and ready. Once I had described the situation, the young front desk clerk responded with a surprisingly petulant tone and the words, "Well, it's not my fault." Ok, then. I guess everything's fine. I'm amazed we don't see people everywhere in T-shirts emblazoned with the words, "Not Responsible In Any Way," on both the front and back.

It seems that almost no one will talk or testify these days about anything dodgy or disturbing without being granted legal immunity first. And then, they'll still often portray events as if things just happened, with no one in particular responsible, and even no agency indicated on anyone's part. "Some unfortunate events took place." We also have a very popular expression, often used to signal the emotional acceptance of a difficult situation: "It is what it is." But the same statement is also increasingly employed to shun responsibility for the nature and consequences of our actions. The attitude seems to be: "Hey, we do stuff, and then the world takes over. We can't be responsible for all the outcomes. Who can?"

Many years ago, Harry Truman famously had a small sign on his desk in the Oval Office that said, "The Buck Stops Here." Although the etymology of the phrase is disputed, everybody at the time knew what it meant and admired Truman for the personal stance it announced. He wouldn't "pass the buck." He would never direct attention to someone else and shirk responsibility for a decision or an outcome that he or his government had created. But lots of people now have come to seem utterly perplexed by this sensibility. They take an opposite stance to be natural. And we need to ask why.

I once had an undergraduate philosophy student from a very small town in Iowa. He told me that growing up, he never got into any trouble because he knew that, as he put it, "If I ever did anything I wasn't supposed to, five people would spank me before my mother even found out about it." Apart from any controversies over corporal punishment, it's an interesting observation. A barbershop in a small rural town in North Carolina never locks its doors. They have people pay for things on the ancient honor system. No one has ever stolen anything. The 85-year-old owner was often asked about this. He liked to say, "Everybody knows everybody. Nobody would even think about stealing, and it's not because they're afraid of the police." There was a small-town, personal accountability for conduct that has come to seem quaint in the modern world.

I know. I'm on a bit of a soapbox now. But this issue is important. It mattered to Steve Jobs, it mattered to the original Socrates, and it should matter to all of us. So I think we need to understand the issue better. Consider the two examples I just gave. Small towns in remote settings can, even now, still harbor lots of relationships with three qualities that strongly facilitate personal responsibility and accountability:

1. **Proximity.** People deal with people they live and work near. Face-to-face interaction is the norm.
2. **Longevity.** Individuals tend to have known each other for a long time, and may live and work together for decades. They will likely stay near each other and continue to interact a lot after they retire.
3. **Density.** People know each other's spouses, kids, friends, and parents. They even know uncles and cousins. They all socialize together and may even work together. They've helped each other in times of need. The interconnections between their lives are many and of various sorts.

Most of human history has involved living situations where relationships tended to have these three features. Village and small town life has always been thick with their implications. It's hard in such a context for people to evade responsibility for their actions. Their chickens always come home to roost. Karma is just down the street and minutes away. But then, a number of major developments in modern cultures over the past century—in so many ways crucial and positive innovations, each and every one of them—have nonetheless individually and in tandem subtly eroded these three qualities in contemporary relationships. Among these innocent-seeming but disrupting developments are such simple things as:

- The telephone and postal systems
- The proliferation of automobiles and modern roads
- Urbanization and suburban sprawl
- Air travel and globalization
- Modern computers, the Internet, smart phones, email, texting, and social media
- The pace of ongoing technological and economic change
- Personal work mobility and a "free agent" mentality across industries

Such developments have all been vulnerable to the famous "Law of Unintended Consequences." Like many other good things, they've had a few unfortunate implications we never saw coming. Some of these have caused accountability to suffer, and even in places to die a slow death in our time. Once we understand how this erosion has taken place, and how it's manifested, I think we can do something to turn it around.

The death of accountability can be seen manifested in various ways, and some of these phenomena date from ancient times, but have been accelerated greatly in the recent past. When a problem arises and we look for who is responsible, we can hear such reactions as:

1. **Denial:** "What problem? There's no problem. It's fake news."
2. **Displacement:** "It wasn't me. It wasn't us. We had nothing to do with it."
3. **Diffusion:** "Who knows? It's complicated. We'll likely never pinpoint the source of the concern."

This third reaction, diffusion, may be the path unique, or at least nearly unique, to the modern world. It's where thresholds of complexity come into play. Once a threshold of complexity has been crossed in organizations or in societies, it often seems nearly impossible to pin responsibility on anyone in particular. And that allows for denial and displacement to work even better. Because of diffusion, people figure they can escape responsibility for decisions that go awry.

When we understand these different moves, we can spot them more easily. In his second act at Apple, Steve Jobs had a way of dealing with them, both through his personal involvement, and through designating for any new project a "Directly Responsible Individual"—referred to internally as the DRI: a person who explicitly and officially was assigned responsibility and could under no circumstances shirk it. Such a person would then be less likely to let others on the project squirm out of accountability for their own actions, or inactions.

Even some immensely popular self-help books over the last twenty years that seem on the surface to hold people accountable at a new level for not only what they do, but also for everything that happens to them in life as well, have also been read, paradoxically, as absolving us of all standard forms of accountability for any sort of damage or disaster we might bring into another person's life. On that reading, any victim of our decisions or actions has actually brought the problems on himself by his long-term attitudes and ways of thinking. According to this viewpoint, the universe, or some pervasive force within it, pays attention and dishes out to people exactly what they deserve. And to many readers, the view in a degraded modern form has seemed to be that if your actions or choices are a conduit for disaster for other people, you can't be held responsible—it was the universe simply having its own way with the victims through something like a new-age version of karmic justice. Of course, the ancient view of karma wasn't supposed to apply only to other people and allow us by contrast the very different possibility of evading responsibility for anything we actually do. It was a view that actually magnified our sense of responsibility. So it's odd to see people who adopt such a worldview selectively claiming credit when things go well but then always shunning responsibility and mumbling about harmful mindsets and the responsibility of others for their own lives when the results of their choices involve damage to those others. The original idea of karma didn't allow for such convenient selectivity.

Steve Jobs was deeply intrigued by ancient eastern philosophies, and viewed their insights as profound. He actually may have been tempted quite often by an asymmetric view of karma—as applying primarily to others, while somehow exempting, or at least allowing for exceptions to, his own actions, in virtue of his deeply benevolent intentions. And yet, he insisted that everyone around him take a full sense of responsibility for their choices and actions as they might impact the business, or others. And he did hold himself responsible for seeing that they held themselves responsible for everything they did.

A big part of the success Jobs experienced was a result of holding people accountable for their work, as well as taking personal responsibility himself for the entire process, end-to-end, of what they were doing together. And this directly flowed from the properly interpreted imperatives: Assume nothing. Own everything.

2. Always Oversee. Never Overlook.

When I was a professor of philosophy at The University of Notre Dame, I once received a phone call from a student organization sponsoring a major event on campus. To raise money for charity, undergraduates from all the dorms would design small boats, build them, and enter them into a fun race across a big lake on college property. The student phoning me asked if I would agree to be an official judge for the event. I wanted to be sure it was something I could take on, so I said, "What exactly are the responsibilities of a judge?"

The student replied, "Oh. Not much. All the judges have to do is to overlook the proceedings." I hoped that she meant, "oversee." And that she hadn't taken all her English requirements yet. But then, after agreeing to the request and arriving at the event itself, I realized quickly that she could have known exactly what she was saying. There was so much craziness going on that day that I indeed had to overlook most of the proceedings, in at least my official capacity. But of course, that wouldn't fly at all for anyone in a business setting.

A leader in a business context needs to oversee every facet of what's being done in the name of the business, at least within his or her broadest scope of authority. And, of course, there's a fine but important line between being thoroughly responsible in that oversight capacity, and being an irritating micro manager—a line that Steve Jobs didn't often recognize or respect, at least in his early years at Apple. Both approaches are based on the same realization, but they implement it very differently. The core insight is simple. Every contact point with your customers, clients, vendors, or the community generally not only represents the business, but in a real sense in that moment is the business to the people that contact touches. When a bank teller is wonderfully helpful, you think of the bank as wonderfully helpful. When a teller is rude and surly, it's natural to think of the bank as a rude and surly place. A big mistake by the shipping department is a mistake made by the overall business. A dirty hotel room gets a bad review on the web for the hotel, and the complaint isn't just for the lax housekeeper who didn't get the job done. Keeping this in mind is vital. A good leader has to oversee and never overlook the many links in the chain, the various stages in the process, and all the contact points by which the overall enterprise will be known.

There were certainly people at Apple who thought their founder and boss was far too much in their face and in their own business. He was known to go roaming around and confronting people about what they were working on and how they were doing it. He would not hesitate to offer a blunt critique, often with an expletive sadly synonymous with excrement, and sometimes he might add a suggestion for improvement. He was often thought of as far too hands-on. But in this, however heavy-handed his methods might have been, he was always showing how much he cared about quality and the customer experience. This care for detail consequently began to take root in the culture generally. When care and concern are shown consistently at the top, these attitudes begin to ripple through the organization. And pretty soon, more and more people are adopting the same mindset and taking responsibility, end-to-end. If we can act on Steve's insight better than he often did himself and avoid the pattern of aggressive micro managing, we can enlist the enthusiasm of others more easily in the task.

Great care in overseeing our process at work, like focus and most other things, can again be viewed through the lens of Aristotle's conception of the virtues, as occupying a midpoint along a spectrum that ranges from the deficit of too little to the excess of too much. Too little oversight is obviously a problem. But as we all know, too much can also create difficulties. The proper virtue is to be found in a robustly balanced concern that's strong without being overbearing.

Jobs always expected other people to be as thoroughly immersed in the process as he was. My friend Tom Looney has told me that Steve once phoned him at 2 AM, and when he answered, trying hard to rouse himself mentally from a deep sleep and focus his thought, Steve started off by asking, "Is this a good time to talk?" The answer, of course, would have been obvious to any half-normal person. It was a question of tremendous superfluity, one that didn't have to be asked. And, in answer, Tom honestly said, "No, it's not—but what's up?" He told me that after this moment of candor, Jobs never called so late again, but still, on that occasion, he went right on into the middle of a discussion they'd been having earlier in the day, picking up where they had last left off, many hours before, at work.

Employees and close associates like Tom could understand now and then such an intrusive approach to work and life only because they knew that Jobs was so focused and caught up in what he was doing, and so sure that others were just as equally obsessed, that it never occurred to him at all that maybe, just maybe, 2 AM was not a good time to ring up someone and continue a work related conversation. In taking full ownership of the process of our work, we don't have to go that far. And, to put it mildly, it's generally not a good idea. But what Jobs was doing at such times was simply a matter of overdoing—extremely overdoing—what would otherwise, in its proper bounds, be a good thing.

3. Honor Demands Honest Accountability.

When I first went through Isaacson's biography of Jobs, like many other readers, I quickly became concerned about the abrasive character and the seemingly mean and even vituperative personality that came through in many of the Apple icon's interactions with employees. And, of course, many other authors who had written about Jobs over the years had also reinforced this portrayal. Why would Steve ever shout profanities at an associate? How could he humiliate a superbly talented person in a public way? The puzzle was just too great. Here was a man so concerned about beauty, and unusually immersed in both Zen thought and the compassionate Yogic wisdom of India, and yet he was often to be seen behaving horribly toward co-workers who were typically struggling hard to help him bring his vision to the world. It just made no sense to me.

Tom Looney worked closely with Jobs during the NeXT and Pixar years. It was his main task to sell state-of-the-art NeXT products to the US government. And he and Steve spent a lot of time together, just the two of them, during those years. When I first sat down with Tom over coffee and snacks to talk with him about his former boss, I had to ask about this particular anger issue, up front. What in the world was going on in these fits and tantrums that Jobs seemed to throw on a regular basis? I confessed that I couldn't make any sense of what I had read. Looney himself, as an affable, manifestly kind person, surely must also have been perplexed by such behavior. I had to get his take on it.

As a former star athlete, Tom had a distinctive perspective on it that I had not anticipated. He at first caught me a bit off guard in the way he began to answer my question. But his remarks immediately gave me a context in which I could start to make a little more sense of what I had been reading. He smiled and said, right off:

> "It always gets me how surprised people are to realize: 'Oh, no! Tiger Woods is a jerk!' 'Oh, my! Kobe Bryant is a jerk!' They're shocked to discover that … the great Michael Jordan can be a jerk. Look, in a high stakes and ridiculously competitive endeavor, where you're up against the best in the world and you manage to fight your way to the very top where the pressure is terribly intense and *everything* matters, you're not real likely to be just a sweet, kind, loving, well balanced, laid-back individual with no real emotional blind spots. In fact, the people who have to go through all the intensive struggle it takes to get that great at what they do most often have huge blind spots as a result. They can't

> be equally good at everything and in every way. Steve just had a very big blind spot when it came to the feelings of people around him, and with many of the people at work. He had a real empathy deficit for any members on the team who, he thought, were underperforming and potentially ruining their chance together to do something historic and game-changing for, literally, the world."

Tom then asked me if I had ever seen a top-flight sports coach yelling at a player in tones of anger or even apparent rage. I told him that, sure, I have, many times. I've seen a good man of modest stature literally hanging from an offensive lineman's facemask, screaming into his eyeballs some very choice language, and at an extremely high volume. Tom nodded knowingly and went on to explain to me Jobs' frame of mind. He wasn't gunning for a conference title or even a national championship in a college sport in one particular year. He wanted to change the whole world for the better. He had the biggest of big plans. He had set his sights about as high as they could be. And he was convinced early on that he had a very limited time on this earth available to him to realize these lofty ambitions. The problem was that he needed the help of other people. And, with big plans, we always do. Without the assistance of lots of people, it would be completely impossible to do what he wanted to accomplish. And he had help, plenty of it. But he worried. At first, it was just Wozniak. Then it was a few others, and then dozens, and then hundreds, and finally, thousands. Jobs knew that any chain is only as strong as its weakest link. He wouldn't hire anyone he didn't think was great and worthy of this noble challenge. But then, if that person ever showed up one day and didn't seem to be producing the best possible version of the great work he had been entrusted to do, Jobs would simply melt down and blow up. The stakes were far too high to tolerate anything less than insanely great work. That was the only way to get insanely great products. Good was never good enough. And so he would be like the coach hanging from the facemask, or the leader of a Navy Seal Team who didn't feel like he had any time for nice, or for solicitous, or even for indirect and diplomatic. The urgency of the situation called for more forceful measures and intense expressions. Anyone who truly got what was at stake would understand what was going on. That's what my new friend explained.

The philosopher Xenophon, reminiscing about his teacher Socrates, began a section in his *Memoirs* by writing: "I shall now describe how Socrates used to help people with honorable ambitions by making them apply themselves to the objects of those ambitions." Looney explained how Steve Jobs was attempting to do the same thing for the people around him. But Tom made it completely clear to me right away that he wasn't seeking to justify or excuse the rough treatment that Jobs often dished out to associates—only to explain it, at least in part. He quickly pointed out that, even though he was Steve's direct report for many years and was running their major effort of federal government sales, he personally never used such harsh motivational and corrective techniques with his own people. He didn't believe in it. And he actually thought of it, appropriately, as terribly disrespectful and wrong. But he was a man with normal empathy, and Steve ... well ... "Steve had some big blind spots and rough edges." His success didn't at all happen because of these tendencies of expression, Tom surmised with a high degree of confidence, but despite them. They're not something to emulate, but completely to avoid. Looney told me that he thought Jobs could have been immensely more effective by taking a kinder approach with much less verbal intensity. He was just trying to hold everyone accountable for their efforts and their results, as he held himself accountable for his own efforts and results. Sloppy wouldn't pass muster. Neither would average or mediocre or even blandly good. Insanely great was the standard that he held himself and all others to in the details of their work and products.

Tom Looney helped toward understanding how Jobs could justify to himself his rough conversations and sudden tirades in the face of disappointing work. But I came to an even deeper grasp of it by reading carefully the most important book in Steve's life. On a pilgrimage to India once, young Steve found himself in an isolated village with nothing much to do. But someone had left a book in the house where he was staying. It was *Autobiography of a Yogi*, by Sri (His Holiness) Paramahansa Yogananda. Jobs reported years later that he read it several times during his stay in that village, and Isaacson tells us that, in fact, Steve found it so important that he reread the book once a year, every year, for the rest of his life.

This fact got my attention and gave me pause. How many of us have done that with any book? How often have you read a book cover to cover several times and then persisted to read it again once every year? How many such books do you have in your life? Likely none. Most of us have never been so impressed by a particular book as to launch an annual ritual like that. You couldn't ask for any more evidence that this one book must have had a tremendous impact on Jobs, and that he considered it very special. With such repeated exposure, it wouldn't be a surprise to find that it was formative in certain ways on the young man's sensibilities, and then on the older man's habits of thought and action. In addition, we have no reason to believe that Jobs had the same sort of relationship to any other single book. Many others had meant a lot to him during his life. We do know that. But this was the one unique book he returned to, over and over. It was even eventually handed out to every person who attended a memorial service for him after his death. It was that important to him and in his life.

Isaacson mentions the book and how many times Jobs read it, but he doesn't then go on to say anything more about it. And I found that to be immensely puzzling. There's also no independent evidence within the biography that Isaacson chose to go read and scrutinize the book himself in pursuit of more understanding in regard to his elusive and enigmatic subject. Of course, in researching and writing such a monumental authorized biography of Jobs, he had a lot on his plate, to put it mildly, with vast amounts of interviewing, video-watching, note-taking, and mountains of other reading to do. I can understand how he had to be selective and perhaps just didn't have time to study this one book himself. But I had to do so. I was too curious to leave such a big hint alone. And I then discovered quickly that it's not only an extremely well written and fascinating book, but also a major key to several things that can otherwise be so perplexing about Jobs.

I obtained a copy of *Autobiography of a Yogi* as quickly as I could and I immediately began to read. It's the story of a young boy who was born in India in the late nineteenth century and grew up to be a Hindu holy man. Yogananda tells of his youthful adventures in search of spiritual growth, and vividly recounts stories about all the holy men and women he met along the way. As it turned out, his main spiritual teacher, a man he studied with for many years, had a distinctive approach with students. While most of the gurus and yogis of the day seemed to take a path of calm inner peace and gracious kindness with their young charges, Yogananda's teacher employed a tougher tone, and continually criticized the young man in their day-to-day interactions at a level he had never experienced. Yogananda says this about his own prior background of receiving stern discipline from his father and his older brother, Ananta:

> "Discipline had not been unknown to me; at home, Father was strict, Ananta often severe. But Sri Yukteswar's training may not be described as other than drastic. A perfectionist, my guru was hypercritical of his disciples, whether in matters of moment or in the subtle nuances of ordinary behavior." (118)

He adds:

> "Whether Master and I were surrounded by his students or by strangers, or were alone together, he always spoke plainly and upbraided sharply. No trifling lapse into shallowness or inconsistency escaped his rebuke. This flattening-to-the-ego treatment was hard to endure." (119)

The revered teacher and holy man was, by nature it seems, rough with his students. Yogananda then reports that his teacher explained the situation to him like this:

> "If you don't like my words, you are at liberty to leave at any time," Master assured me. "I want nothing from you but your own improvement. Stay only if you feel benefited."

The eventually accomplished student then goes on to say:

> "I am immeasurably grateful for the humbling blows he dealt my vanity. I sometimes felt that, metaphorically, he was discovering and uprooting every diseased tooth in my jaw. The hard core of egoism is difficult to dislodge except rudely. With its departure, the Divine finds at last an unobstructed channel."

Sri Yukteswar had also said to his student, about the ongoing and exceptionally harsh treatment he was always dishing out:

> "That is my way. Take it or leave it; I never compromise."

This particular Master, this revered and tough guru, sounds a lot like Steve Jobs, doesn't he? I can imagine a spiritual business card. Steve Jobs, DDS: Oral Surgeon of the soul and hypercritical perfectionist, discovering and uprooting every diseased tooth of mediocrity that prevents maximal organizational health and ideal results.

In the midst of the passages I've just been quoting, Yogananda, as the student, while describing the tremendous difficulties of undergoing all his guru's relentless harshness, nonetheless comments:

> "Under Master's unsparing rod, however, I soon recovered from the agreeable delusions of irresponsibility." (118)

For a long time, Yogananda had chafed under his teacher's treatment and felt hurt by it. It was rough on the young man, and was meant to be. It was the epitome of extreme tough love. And, yet, eventually, the disciple grew accustomed to it, and even came to feel that he had needed it to spur him on to greater heights, and then keep him on a proper path.

In the book's long narrative, it's clear from the beginning that Yogananda had devoted his life to spiritual discipline and development in order to grow closer to God. He desired to be a top practitioner of the spiritual life. He wanted to be, in a modern and somewhat paradoxical image, something like a Navy Seal of the Soul. And to accomplish this, he had to go through the unspeakable rigors and demands of a spiritual version of Seal Training, a regimen that most people can't endure. But he did, and it eventually worked its wonders. As a result, Yogananda arrived at a point of spiritual development where, like his guru, according to his testimony in the book, he could accomplish amazing things and actually perform miracles. Or to put it another way, in the manner that he himself might prefer to articulate it, miracles could then be worked through him. And in this, he became an inspiration for the ambitious young man from California. But, interestingly, he didn't also become a prime role model for Jobs. That place was claimed by Yogananda's own scathingly tough guru.

I've come to realize that we can understand many things about the life and work of Steve Jobs only by pondering what he repeatedly read about in this remarkable book. In his own way, at least metaphorically if not literally, he wanted to work miracles. And, in a sense, he did. I suspect that he envied Yogananda's extensive training and what it prepared him to experience and accomplish in his reportedly wondrous deeds. But as Jobs read and reread the book, I believe that he came to identify more with Yogananda's powerful teacher than with the writer himself. Sri Yukteswar had produced greatness in Yogananda. And I suspect that Jobs wanted to do something like that in the lives of the people around him. He would then seek to take on the role of the guru and be the suitably harsh and effective teacher at Apple, for the greater good of all. He would act as The Master overseeing the spiritual, aesthetic, and technological development of all the seekers after excellence who had chosen to come and work for him. And he, like Yogananda's teacher, would be tough. It was really this tough love, in his mind, that justified his acerbic and critical spirit, his fits of anger, and the public verbal assaults that he often used to correct and motivate his students and disciples—his associates—at Apple and elsewhere. By the use of rough techniques and unadorned candor, he would strip away any shred of irresponsibility in his charges and bring them to a point where they would embrace accountability and be willing, every day, to take responsibility for whatever they were doing, end-to-end.

A lot of other smaller and equally fascinating influences from the book can perhaps also be seen in Jobs' life. At least, before his marriage to Laurene, people would come away from visits to his home shocked that he had very little furniture. It seemed true of him what the philosopher Xenophon had long ago written about his teacher, Socrates: "He was very easily satisfied with very few possessions." In Steve's case, the gurus he had read about in Yogananda's remarkable book had reportedly lived in homes with little or no furniture. It was a sign of where their true attention lay. I suspect Steve saw it as a sign of their intense focus and spiritual strength that they needed so little in the physical realm.

And then consider something that was much more surprising in Steve's life. He refused to see anything as impossible. The various top gurus portrayed in the book he kept returning to seemed to live in a world where literally nothing was out of reach. The impossible might take a little longer, but it could be attained. And, on another and otherwise apparently unrelated front, as I've mentioned earlier, Jobs oddly had taught himself how to stare without blinking his eyes. It was, perhaps even more than tearful sobbing, his single strangest negotiating trick. But why would he even think of such a thing? In the book, we have an answer. There are two distinct passages in the text where it's said that, "When a yogi has attained a state of mental peace, his eyelids do not blink." A Sanskrit verse is also interpreted like this: "He who has attained a state of calmness wherein his eyelids do not blink has achieved *Sambhabi Mudra* (a traditional ritual involving a fixed gaze)." (326)

Jobs wanted to master the physical state of the unblinking stare, perhaps as a sign or token of inner strength and attainment, but without all the hard and lengthy meditative work that it reportedly had taken these revered gurus to achieve the calmness that lay behind their own unblinking states. He could not invest the time they had to invest. He needed to do things in the world that they didn't do. But he wanted at least some of what they had. The unblinking eyelids perhaps symbolically represented something deep and desirable to him. So he trained himself to stare without blinking. He wanted one of the stranger effects of a rare inner state without all the time and work that producing the true inner reality behind it would require. But, without that work, or its resulting tranquility, Jobs came to desire the physical appearance as a technique for power and manipulation, which could not be farther from the spirit of the gurus he so admired. And, did it work? Sometimes, apparently, it did. But it's not one of his finer accomplishments, or something for any of us to emulate.

In his selective imitation of the holy people he apparently so admired, he ironically fell far short of taking responsibility for the full spiritual process they had showed him, end-to-end. He always wanted to hold others accountable to the highest standards. But he held himself honestly accountable only in some things, not in all. Some would call this hypocrisy. But I don't think so. I believe it's more accurate to see this inconsistency as coming from an insufficient level of self-awareness. When Jobs went around like Socrates demanding that his associates attain higher levels of self-awareness and the deep self-knowledge required for the upper reaches of self-improvement, he never sufficiently used the inner mirror necessary to do that difficult work in his own life. And, despite his occasional engagement with spiritual teachers back in his own home country, Jobs seems to have had no one to hold him fully accountable for things in his behavior that easily got out of control.

This will come to be a crucial clue to help us understand many things in the life of Steve Jobs where, despite his great successes, he fell short of what we would ordinarily expect of a highly intelligent and well-informed person who was, through his own actions and with the enthusiastic endorsement of accomplished others, placed in a position of great responsibility and leadership. The spiritual teachers he so admired in the book he repeatedly read were portrayed as individuals with nearly unlimited power, capable of doing the impossible and working miracles of all sorts. And they even reportedly did so in a way that often appeared effortless. Setting completely aside any question as to the veracity or historical credibility of those accounts, one thing is clear. We're told that the sages whose reported powers Jobs admired had meditated eight hours to eighteen hours a day, every day, for decades to get themselves into a condition and position for doing the things that so astonished and impressed Steve. He apparently craved similar results in his life and work, but without all the arduous preparation and inner discipline that it might properly take to get there. And that led to some big problems, one of which killed him.

Ironically, with his professional obsession about taking responsibility over every process, end-to-end, his fixation on what we can think of as short-cut spiritual power may have confused him during the most crucial challenge of his life about how he should apply this paradigm and commitment to his own health, at the precise time when doing the right thing meant the most to him. He apparently thought he could heal himself, like the yogis and gurus he had read about, and he maintained this misplaced bit of faith for far too long.

The many puzzles and perplexities of his life end up having some surprisingly reasonable explanations. And that's important for us to understand. We want to learn from the mistakes that Jobs made as well as from the things he did right. And when we do, we can position ourselves for some astonishing results of our own, as we truly take responsibility for what we do in all things, end-to-end.

4

When Behind, Leapfrog

Which of the two is a better runner—he who voluntarily runs slowly, or he who does so involuntarily?
Socrates

OK, BACK TO BUSINESS. STEVE JOBS HAD ANOTHER IMPORTANT insight. And it's based on a common sense truth. You won't always be first to market with a new idea or product. And that's fine. Sometimes, it's even best. You can learn from the stumbles of those who precede you. You don't have to win every early segment of a race in order to win the overall contest. But when you're not first to market, you do have an extra task.

First to market is great when it's done right. You're the leader, the pioneer. You've blazed the trail. You've created the paradigm. You've set the expectations. Everyone else will have to play catch-up. And everyone who follows you will likely come across as an imitator, whether that happens to be true or not.

I know this, unfortunately, from personal experience. My first book on the philosophy behind satisfying and sustainable achievement in business and life, a book called *True Success: A New*

Philosophy of Excellence, was built around seven universal conditions for success that had been identified in bits and pieces by the most profound practical philosophers throughout history, east and west. In the late nineteen-eighties, I had been asked to give a talk on what the great philosophers had to say about success, and so I researched the topic thoroughly. The talk was itself a success and led to many more on the same topic. People were finding the ideas so helpful that I soon decided to write up my discoveries. The resulting book came out in 1994, a few years after Stephen Covey had published his own pioneering business book in 1989, one that was completely unknown to me at the time, but that had been a major national hit, bringing together seven distinct principles for effectiveness in business and life. It was called, *The Seven Habits of Highly Effective People*. My book and his had in common the number seven, but not a lot more. And yet, in an early review of my book written for *Library Journal*, and sadly available forever and immemorial on Amazon.com, we find the following:

> "Stephen Covey has sparked many imitators, and this is one of them; Morris' ideas are nothing but a rehash of Covey's solid *The Seven Habits of Highly Successful People*."

A rehash? That was very surprising news to me. At the time I researched and wrote my book, I hadn't read *The Seven Habits*, I had never heard anything about the individual habits themselves, and I didn't know anything about Covey. I was an academic philosopher in those days, not a reader of popular books. I liked to think of myself as immersed in the wisdom of the ages, and not the ephemera of pop culture. And so, after being brought to the woodshed by the anonymous reviewer at *Library Journal*, I went out and bought a copy of Covey's book and read it. And I was shocked again. There was very little at all in common between the two books. The fundamental question we were asking was different. The research we used was as divergent as it could be. The conclusions we came to were in many ways compatible and even mutually supportive, but they were very different in both the details and on the big scale. Line up his seven habits and my seven conditions and you may wonder whether the *Library Journal* guy had lost his library card and hadn't even bothered to read at least one of the two books featured in his comment.

A year or so later, Covey and I directed a weekend seminar together for fifty CEOs of large companies. I liked him a lot. He spoke to the group, then I spoke, and we fielded questions together. After hearing me talk about the framework of ideas in my book *True Success*, the ideas that I call "The 7 Cs of Success," and that we'll later consult in connection with our look at Steve Jobs, Covey the very next week wrote me a really nice letter starting with the words, "I like you, Tom Morris!" And then he told me that he had taken extensive notes on my ideas while I spoke and had gathered his family together as soon as he got home to teach those seven principles to them all. It was clear from the note that neither he nor his family thought he was reviewing "a rehash" of the ideas in his own book. But then, why had the reviewer thought so? Covey had come first to market during a particular sweep of cultural and economic history with a business and life achievement book where the number seven was in play, and I felt in the *Library Journal* the sting often experienced, rightly or not, by those who are thought of as second to market. The business and life stuff had already been done.

It was even more of a shame that Amazon quoted only two early reviews, still on my book's page to this day, and that the other one from *Kirkus Reviews*, characterized the book as full of "slick sloganeering" and without any originality of thought. By contrast, the same week that I read those dismissively abrasive judgments on Amazon for all the world to see, a professor of philosophy from the University of Chicago sent me a hand written letter—the old kind with a stamp—expressing his astonishment that my new book was so simple to read on the surface and fully accessible to a broad public audience, but that, in his words, "Beneath the surface and between the lines, there is so much sophisticated philosophical depth and original thought going on, it's incredible." If memory serves, he mentioned echoes of Aristotle and St. Thomas Aquinas, but not of Covey. I don't think the professor had heard of Covey's book, or knew that he was in some sense, "first to market" with universal wisdom for business and life. And he apparently had missed any slickness of sloganeering. But unfortunately, his comments were private and couldn't guide potential readers like an Amazon review.

I still have to smile at the "slick sloganeering" remark. "Know Thyself!" Yeah, Socrates, why don't you just print that up on a bumper sticker while you're at it? "The unexamined life is not worth living." Get a cotton T-shirt for that one. Geez. And forget Descartes, who let us have it with the catchy: "Cogito ergo sum." Very Pithy. And slick. "I think, therefore I am." That's got "*coffee mug*" written all over it—or, maybe, it should be the other way around. But Rene was at least *first to market* with the famous slogan. As indeed was Sartre, with his own Tweet-worthy, "Existence precedes Essence." Nice cosmic sloganeering there. Let's fly it on the flag of existentialism. And he was first to market with it in most minds, so he gets to be the father of it all.

But I digress. It's clear that there are often advantages for being first to market, or for even being perceived as such. But there are also some advantages to be had from not leading the pack. In most businesses, when you've been beat to market with a certain product or type of service, you get to see what happens, what goes wrong, what's right that still could be improved on, as well as viewing how customers react. You can then clearly benefit from all this data in many ways. You don't have to be first to be best. As the philosopher Blaise Pascal once said when accused of using other people's ideas, concepts that others had been first to market with, he replied, "Two tennis players use the same ball. One uses it better than the other." *Touché, mon frère.*

I was once at dinner with Ivan Seidenberg when he was CEO of the telecommunications giant Verizon, along with his top direct reports, all seated at a big, round table. I noticed that Ivan was wearing a very nice, expensive gold Patek Philippe watch. As the evening went on and I casually observed everyone else at the table as they ate and talked and gestured, it seemed that perhaps all of them were also wearing a very nice, expensive gold Patek Philippe watch—and perhaps the very same model. I could notice this only when there was a tug at the sleeves of their suit jackets, which actually looked a lot like Ivan's suit jacket, now that I think about it, At Apple, when Steve Jobs was at the helm, there were a lot of blue jeans and New Balance tennis shoes around, and even a few other black mock turtlenecks. Joshua Strickon, who joined Apple in 2003, told Brian Merchant (as recounted in *The One Device*) that he realized on his arrival that, "Apple is kind of a weird place. You've got people dressing like Steve." He said there were so many Steve look-alikes that he had a hard time finding the real thing. A particularly convincing imitator behind him one day in the cafeteria line actually turned out to be the original. And of course this phenomenon is much more common than Strickon realized. People in various ways seek to be like a highly successful and charismatic leader. Everyone wants to please the boss.

But at the Verizon dinner, at one point early on, it seemed like someone had not pleased the boss. Ivan looked across the table and asked a man sitting there about a new type of product they were launching. He said, very slowly and clearly and with obvious feeling—rather pointedly and dramatically: "Why weren't we first to market?" Years later, I can still hear the steely tone of voice. It was as if all the Pateks then stopped for the world's longest second, and at the end of that expanded moment, the executive being grilled spoke. He quickly explained the reasons that, from his point of view, it had been best for them to wait and get their own product to a certain point of functionality and excellence before releasing it, and then he added, if I recall correctly these years later, some other salient features of the market conditions that made it not only acceptable to be second, but even likely beneficial. Ivan was apparently satisfied with the answer. The boss was, after all, pleased. And he agreed. There are times when it's perfectly fine not to be first to market, and times it's even better to be next. Some great runners find it best to slow down voluntarily at some stages—in order, in the end, to win. Best to market beats first to market almost any day. Except, maybe, when first to market happens to be a truly fine fellow like Stephen Covey. But I promise I'll try to let that go.

So, on those occasions when the competition is out there ahead of us, Jobs believed we should prepare to do whatever it takes to make the most of the situation, and actually to leapfrog over them into our preferred position of prominence. And the general process for this is simple to state, however difficult it might be to implement. Again, we'll explicate it through three distinct rules, pragmatic guidelines, or business imperatives.

1. Look. Listen. Learn. Launch Ahead.

We're born into the world as observers long before we grow to become skillful doers. And throughout our lives, wise action is based on prior perception, keen observational interpretation, and the resultant knowledge that we've processed well. We first reach out to learn. Then we can reach out to do and make. Ideally, that begins a virtuous cycle where proper doing leads to more learning, and so the process continues.

We look to see. We listen to hear. We learn in order to grow and improve, and in business, to create perhaps a better product than already might exist, and thereby gain a new competitive advantage.

We then launch ahead on the basis of what we've learned in order to provide new levels of function, service, and quality. And that provides a new level of success. We can leapfrog in that way over our competitors to win.

There is an art, or skilled behavior, connected to each of our senses. Think first about vision. A painter or a professional photographer looks and sees differently than the rest of us. What I might not notice at all, she may see clearly and in depth. Likewise, a great musician listens distinctively and hears things that you or I likely miss. An expert sommelier can smell and taste more discriminately than I can even begin to experience. And the rest of us can't even imagine the olfactory art of those rare individuals who work with the finest perfumers as consultants and guides. They have a nose that knows beyond anything we can guess.

We tend to think of our senses as passive receptacles for the signals sent out by the world around us. But the true art of seeing or hearing is a matter of action. It's a skilled behavior. And that's a key to something rarely recognized in the world of business. In order to flourish in our work, we need to keep an eye on the marketplace, look at what our competitors are doing, and listen to what customers and critics are saying. And we need to do this not passively, but actively. When someone gets the jump on us and is first to market with a novel product or service in our domain, we're unlikely to leapfrog over it without understanding what they've done, how they've done it, and in what ways it has or hasn't worked. Had I known about Stephen Covey's book when I was writing *True Success*, I could have added a few paragraphs to mine in order to preempt any misguided perception that I was revisiting or repurposing any of his ideas, or in any way doing what he had done, as he had done it. I could have helped readers more explicitly to understand the distinctive originality and usefulness of what was being presented in my book. But as a philosophy professor at the time, trained primarily in contemporary analytic thought and logic, I had yet to come into a full understanding of the "first to market" syndrome and how it might effect someone approaching my book. And that was true despite the fact that I had often been "first to market" in the very different academic marketplace of ideas with my own technical work.

I should have understood this age-old principle from the outset. Socrates was certainly first to market. Cicero once proclaimed that he was the first thinker ever to bring philosophy into the marketplace. And we're still talking about him and his work today, more than two thousand years later. Stephen Covey was in our time "first to market" with a book bringing general life wisdom into the context of work. But then, I was first to market bringing the focused wisdom of the greatest philosophers into our lives in a logically structured and comprehensively universal way. If I had made it altogether clear how my project's originality set it apart, I could have been more widely viewed as "first to market" in what I was distinctively doing. Or I could have made it more obvious how I was leapfrogging over what had already been done, in breadth, precision, and universal applicability. Sometimes, first to market is a matter of fact. Often, it's more a matter of appearance, or what we nowadays call the "optics" of an industry. Whenever we seek to be first, or else to leapfrog whatever competitor was in a sense first, we need to make clear the distinctiveness of what we're doing, and its unique value. Being the first or the best won't get you more market share unless your potential customers realize exactly how you're the first or the best.

Whenever we enter the marketplace, and this is true of any marketplace, we should engage right away in the ancient spiritual practice of paying attention. Philosophers and wisdom teachers across cultures have stressed the importance of attention and the things to which we give it. It's even been suggested that our daily decisions and choices are largely an unconscious result of what we normally pay attention to over time. Philosopher Iris Murdoch has some keen insights about this in her little book *The Sovereignty of Good.* We may think that our conscious deliberations are what settle the issue of what we should do next, but it's perhaps rather the cumulative effect of habitual attention that, below the level of conscious awareness, has already done most of the work of deciding, long before any discrete task of deliberation begins.

When we're not first to market, we need to pay attention to the competitive product that already exists, and to its salient features, as well as to its launch and current position in the marketplace, in all those details. It's important to look actively for information we can use, and listen well to consumers and reviewers—except, of course, for those few reviewers out there who choose to write up their opinions without bothering to go to the trouble of actually experiencing the product. But that should be obvious.

Every top performer in a business context is a lifelong learner and a teacher. When you're an eager and active enough student, you find that there are lessons available all around you. Steve Jobs was always watching his competition and the competitive landscape generally, and constantly was eager to learn anything that could launch him into a position ahead of the pack.

2. In Every Challenge, There is Opportunity.

This fourth of our principles "When behind, leapfrog," requires for its application a resilient positive mindset. People who are discouraged and deflated by the actions or early success of their competitors and see any challenge or setback as a disaster aren't well positioned to come from behind with something better and beat the competition.

If you've watched much basketball or American football over the years, you're familiar with the phenomenon of the second half comeback. It can also be seen in many other sports, but can be particularly clear in these two. A team leaves the court or the field with a scoring deficit, perhaps even far behind their opponent at the half, but then manages to claw their way back and overcome what had originally seemed to be the vastly superior performers, at least on this day of play. The team that's behind at the half clearly faces a challenge. But it's a challenge that reflects a hidden opportunity. The winner-at-the-half tends to relax. The loser-at-halftime tends to regroup.

The team that's ahead mid-game is all too often either already celebrating, at least inwardly, and way ahead of the proper time, or at least they've gone into the locker room feeling far more comfortable and relieved than they yet should feel. Either of these mindsets—the arrogance of premature celebration, or the lapse of alertness and focus that's a result of a dangerous relaxation of thought and effort—can position the leading team for a fall. This is the opportunity that's often provided for the temporary underdogs. Exploiting either of these attitudes, whichever is in play, will allow them to catch the leaders by surprise and mount a comeback that can result in ultimate victory. But this will happen only if the team that's behind will look, listen, learn, and leapfrog ahead with the right attitude and strategies that their early experience has suggested they now try. And of course, something quite analogous is operative in a business context as well. The quick appearance of early success can breed a form of arrogance, or overconfidence, and cause people to celebrate just enough, or relax just enough that the competition can then come from behind and blow past them, using what they've learned and turning it to their advantage.

The original iMac couldn't handle music the way that Windows-based personal computers could. The competition Apple faced allowed people to download music and burn their own CDs. The CD slot on the iMac just could not be used to do that. Jobs later said that, realizing this, he felt like a dope. The irony couldn't have been greater. Steve was a nut for music. He was crazy about it. It was an important part of his life. So, here was a man who really loved music and was providing computers to the world, and his competition had gone first to market with a way to grab and use music off the Internet. He had been completely blindsided by it all. He had to regroup and respond.

But instead of just changing or improving the CD drive on the iMac so that it finally could do exactly what his competitors' models already did, or coming up with a close copy of what they had, Jobs looked, listened, and learned. He saw in this challenge an opportunity to change the game and leapfrog ahead. And so he created the iPod, iTunes, and the iTunes store—and in that way, he revolutionized the music industry, coming back from a bad first half to win the game overwhelmingly. In fact, there's a sense in which his leapfrog actually created a whole new and better game.

Challenges inherently bring opportunities. Any challenge can goad us into adopting a new mindset or a new interpretive grid, or can force us into developing skills we'd never been called on to use before, and then take them to a new level. Here's a trivial example from this week. I've always been a very casual PowerPoint user. I became a public speaker in the day when overhead transparency projectors were all the rage. We didn't have to use whiteboards or slide projectors any more. We could create new images on clear pieces of plastic using colorful bold markers, plop the results down on an overhead projector, and wow our audiences. It makes me feel old even to write that. And when PowerPoint came around, I had little choice but to adopt it. People shouldn't be forced to look at only me for an hour. There should be some form of visual relief. And great PowerPoint slides can reinforce a message. Plus, now I could email my visual files in advance and just show up to an event, with nothing like overhead transparencies in tow. But I knew only the most minimal user facts about the software. I could create a new presentation, but barely. Most of the features were like controls on my car that I still wonder about, after years of driving it.

I had always been proud of my PowerPoint presentations—big, bold fonts on a vibrant, high contrast background, with very few words on the screen, and everything there would serve to focus and punctuate whatever I was saying. Recently, an audio-visual specialist who had seen me speak several times complimented me on the PowerPoint he had seen for the very features that gave me pride. But then he pointed out that adding more vibrant, perhaps photographic visuals here and there would really make the presentation pop and reach people on a new level. I had seen too many PowerPoint slides where the presenter used free access images from the Internet that were bland or silly and detracted more from their talks than they added. So I was reluctant. But the AV guy had seen some other public speakers do it well. So, in a sense my competition was first to market with more entertaining PowerPoint slides. So I was challenged to leapfrog what was already being done. I decided to try it and to use as much creativity in the project as I would in solving a major philosophical problem.

The result surprised me. It was outstanding. So I decided to do the same thing to a different presentation, on my most popular topic. I worked at it for a week. And I was very proud of the result—glowing, in fact. I sent it in to the AV folks who would be running the show for my upcoming audience of about five thousand people. I couldn't wait to use the new stuff. But the AV people wrote back and asked for a version of it in widescreen ratio, instead of the standard format I had used. I had no idea how to transform what I had created into what they needed. Other AV people had made such alterations themselves in the past, but not always with great results. Images could be slightly distorted, or text could end up where it shouldn't be, and we'd have to huddle up on making big changes and small tweaks at the last minute. So this time, to avoid such problems, I decided to take on the challenge myself. Surely, it should be simple. There obviously would be a button somewhere to click and all would be magically altered.

I quickly discovered that my software was two generations old and that I couldn't do the simple translation process in what I had. There was no miracle button to click. For a while, it even looked like I might be facing an impossible task. But I discovered I could create a new presentation from scratch in widescreen by finding and clicking a tab I had never even seen before. I ended up as a result of this challenge gaining ways of controlling things I had never before controlled, cleaning up subtle glitches in my old presentations I had just learned to live with, and improving all the PowerPoint I use. The hours of hard effort I had honestly dreaded ended up working magic. The challenge presented hidden opportunities I had never even suspected and certainly didn't anticipate. And the result elicited one of the longest and loudest standing ovations of my career, from nearly five thousand people who were seeing my new leapfrogging effort for the first time. Another unexpected benefit of the task was the additional example of challenge and opportunity I could cite here in the context of analyzing the procedures used by Steve Jobs—who once said in public, by the way: "People who know what they're talking about don't need PowerPoint." But that's Ok. Nobody can be right about everything. Not even Steve.

I recently watched a PBS documentary special entitled *American Epic: A Journey Through the Music that Transformed America.* In the 1920s, American inventors created a portable recording device that could be taken around the country to capture on discs the many varieties of popular music. Before such recording, people mostly knew their local music and not much more. Four of these devices were carried around the nation, advertisements were placed in local papers, and musicians were recorded for the first time ever. As the records became available nationwide, all sorts of musical performers began to hear and learn from each other, across geographical barriers and styles like never before. Not long ago, one of these recording machines was pieced together from remaining parts of the others, and was put into a studio in Los Angeles. Then, lots of contemporary musicians, across many genres, were invited to come in and record a song the way the first recording artists did. The entire mechanism was powered largely by pulleys and gears run by a weight on a strap, cranked up above the floor, that slowly dropped back down and provided the force to move the recording turntable and other aspects of the very complicated mechanical contraption.

The musicians were excited to have this unique experience. They were told right off about the weight and the pulleys, and that it would take less than four minutes for the weight to reach the floor and the recording to stop. So their songs would have to be less than four minutes long. Then there were severe constraints with the old microphone, and on and on. The performers faced challenges unlike anything they'd ever encountered in a modern recording studio. But as you watch the documentary, you can see how the challenges and constraints of the old equipment ended up providing some surprising opportunities for musical creativity. Some of the results of working around precisely the limits and difficulties are spectacular to hear. Challenges do indeed contain opportunities.

I've actually just completed the manuscript of an entire book on this general phenomenon. You know the old adage, "When life hands you lemons, make lemonade." Everyone says it, but no one explains how to do it. I spent over ten years researching what the great philosophers had to say on the difficulty of dealing with difficulty. And it all turns on peeling back the layers of any daunting challenge to find the new opportunities hidden within it. The book is called *Plato's Lemonade Stand: Stirring Change into Something Great*. Look for it soon. It's been through twenty-four versions, with six different titles, and in previous incarnations has been turned down by publishers forty-four times. Now, that's a history of challenges. But my response to each one displayed the thesis of the book and opened up incredible opportunities for radical improvement and truly sweet results. That's the alchemy Steve Jobs looked for in any problem or difficulty. And he displayed that alchemy in spectacular fashion at times when he had to come from behind and leapfrog a competitor into the future.

3. What You Don't Do First, Do Better.

It's just that simple. Being better beats being first. This is the fundamental leapfrog commitment. Speed is never as important in the end as quality. And a form of game-changing quality is always the best. This is something that Jobs understood, and it's one reason his new products often missed their original ship dates. He typically insisted that things be done right, within the boundaries of the vision he had at the time, and he intuitively understood that insanely great is worth a wait.

Mark Zuckerberg wasn't first to market with a social network site. Friendster already existed. MySpace was being built out. But "TheFaceBook," whose name was later shortened simply to 'Facebook,' improved immensely on what was out there and already being done, and it did so with a cool simplicity, faster loading pages, and other attributes that Jobs would applaud and that allowed it to leapfrog its competition by miles. There are many similar stories in business, even if not of quite such a magnitude.

So, what if the competition is not only first, but also really good? No worries. Good allows for an appreciation of great. It even enhances our recognition and celebration of what can be truly superior. Audi didn't build the first all-wheel drive car. Others were in the market long before. But many of its customers and reviewers in the automotive press believe that it builds the best such car. The iPad wasn't the world's first tablet computer device. But aficionados have acclaimed it as by far the best.

When the competition gets to market first with a product or service, they've become your beta-testing group. What can seem at first to be a major challenge actually provides an opportunity. The opportunity in the challenge is to learn and improve from what you see. And the bigger you can leapfrog, the better.

5

Put Products Before Profit

Wealth does not bring goodness, but goodness brings wealth and every other blessing both to the individual and the state.
Socrates

"He was never in it for the money." I've heard that said over and over again about Steve Jobs. His core commitment wasn't to becoming rich or famous, despite how much he seemed to enjoy being on the covers of major magazines. Deep down, his shrewdness matched his vanity. He viewed publicity as a vital tool he could enjoy using. His commitment was to do something great. In part, he was using the many top magazine covers that featured him to promote his quest for greatness. And it was this ultimate focus on doing something insanely great that attracted other amazingly talented people to Apple, NeXT, and Pixar. The money was never as important as the meaning. Highly skilled and accomplished individuals felt drawn to this value shift. In the world of technology start-ups and take-offs, too many CEOs at the time seemed to be in it just for the next house, boat, or jet—piling up, counting, and flaunting all the loot that the world could provide. Steve Jobs was different. He thought different, and stayed true to that spirit, practicing what he preached. Like Socrates, he lived simply and focused on doing something to help and delight other people in a way that would literally change the world. As he himself once said:

> "The older I get, the more I'm convinced that motives make so much difference." (Scully, *Odyssey*, p. 285)

Our motives determine our focus, and they also tend to bring together like-minded people who will be rowing in the same direction. For peak excellence and extraordinary results, motives matter.

One of the greatest twists in life is that the people who focus well on something other than profits tend to get the healthiest profits. Those who fixate on money never seem to have enough. It's actually a fundamental distortion of business to see it as being primarily about profits, or just money—the most thinly narrow and even perhaps myopic form of return on investment. It's mainly about making a difference, and bringing something new and great into the world for the benefit and enjoyment of others. This was The Steve Jobs Philosophy of Business. With a proper and successful pursuit of the right focal goals, profits accrue as great side effects.

In 1997, I was on a book tour promoting my then latest philosophical contribution to the world of work, the book, *If Aristotle Ran General Motors: The New Soul of Business*. It was a look at the underlying conditions for greatness in organizational life, as well as in our personal experience and drew on some of the most creative minds in history. The book was based around the importance of Truth, Beauty, Goodness, and Unity in whatever we do, reflecting the intellectual, aesthetic, moral, and spiritual dimensions of life. It was, at the time, a new take on what leaders should be thinking about and putting into place in order to create a climate for ongoing excellence.

As you might imagine, in the boom economy of the nineties,

the core message of the book came as a big surprise to people who had become habituated to think only about profits and any business or accounting technique that would enhance the look and luster of the bottom line. For a great many people, the focus of the age was entirely on finances.

During the time I was on an extensive national book tour, I was at one point being interviewed about the ideas in the book by a radio host in St. Louis, and we had just opened up the line to callers. A man came on and said, "Dr. Morris, I've enjoyed listening to the interview about your new book over the last few minutes, and all your talk about Truth, Beauty, Goodness, and Unity sounds great, but we business people have to focus on the numbers, and we don't actually have time for all this touchy-feely stuff that could really be a distraction. The numbers are what count. People in business have got to keep their eye on the ball."

Maybe it was that last image that caught my attention—the mention of a ball. This was happening back when superstar Michael Jordan was dominating not only basketball but the entire world of sports, generally. I spontaneously asked the caller, "Have you ever watched Michael Jordan play ball?"

He said, "Sure, lots of times."

I then asked, "Have you ever seen him look up at the numbers on the scoreboard during the game?" This was something MJ did, like sailing through the air with his tongue hanging out.

The guy replied, "Well, now that you ask, I guess I have."

I commented, "I have too, and actually lots of times. I've noticed that, during games, and especially close games, he'll now and then glance up at the numbers to remind himself about where the game stands and what he needs to accomplish. He wants to know what it's going to take to win. But for most of the game, he's not looking at those numbers at all. He's keeping his eye on the ball, the basket, the other players, his teammates, the movement on the floor, and the overall flow of the game."

The man replied, simply, "Ok."

Then it was time to make my point. "Well, if Jordan didn't pay attention to a lot of things other than the numbers, he'd never see the numbers on the scoreboard that he wants to see. It's the same way in business."

My caller said, "Boy, I've never thought about it like that before. I see what you're saying. It makes a lot of sense."

Steve Jobs was usually thinking about things other than the numbers, other than profits. And by his focused concentration on making the products as great as he could make them, he ended up with fantastic numbers. That's the way it should be—put products before profit, and then profit can happen in a major way, even lavishly and, maybe even now and then, with a super spectacular slam-dunk.

1. Invest in Excellence. Rewards Follow.

Etymologically, the word 'excellence' means a state, quality, or process of "rising out from," or "standing above," the norm or the crowd. In various endeavors or activities where we have extensive experience, we all know the difference between poor, average, good, very good, and truly excellent. Steve Jobs wanted only the higher reaches of excellence for what he brought to the world. His favored phrase was, of course, 'insanely great.' To invest in excellence in pursuit of the insanely great is to do whatever it takes, spend however much is necessary, and work as hard as might be required in order to rise out from and stand above what even very good people are otherwise doing. Jobs wanted excellence to-the-degree-of-the-extraordinary, the rare, upper range of the excellent that can be a game changer for everyone involved. And he was determined not to settle for anything less. Of course, as a fallible and sometimes stubborn human being, he made many mistakes along the way, with a few that were whoppers, and he sometimes thought he had attained his elusive goal long before he had. But we all make mistakes. His edge was that his business mistakes were typically efforts in the direction of the right ideals.

There are plenty of examples of excellence in the arts, sciences, humanities, and technology that did not produce the financial results or other external rewards that would have been commensurate with the investment made in their creation. The best poets rarely profit financially from their work. Philosophers certainly don't have a great track record in this regard, either. Many great painters have died poor. But some of their works have gone on to reap astonishing rewards in later years for owners and investors. And they have had a cultural impact that seems lasting. There are no simple guarantees that any major investment in excellence will have a certain predictable and stable return, measured in dollars, across all fields of positive human endeavor. But Jobs was after something bigger than just the dollars. And the profits did follow. But he had many dark nights of the soul along the way.

There were times when it seemed that it would take all his considerable fortune to keep an enterprise afloat. During his days at NeXT and Pixar, there were long stretches of high anxiety about whether his money would last long enough to make the difference that he wanted to make and reap the results he hoped to see. But he kept investing with what might have looked to an outside observer like a stubborn obsessiveness that could and most likely would generate disastrous consequences. And yet, he prevailed. It took years before Pixar became profitable. But it then led the way in a new kind of filmmaking, reaped all sorts of honors, and made lots of money. NeXT never took off financially, but it created the amazing software that paved the path back to Apple for Jobs and resulted in all his subsequent world-changing success. The NeXT and Pixar years were also crucial for him in many ways. He changed. He matured. Some of the sharp edges were smoothed down a bit. He learned to struggle in order to prevail. He experienced the fruit of proper patience. And he honed his focus throughout that time.

Everyone experiences hills and valleys. Even the best people may go through a form of exile. How we handle those tough times can matter greatly, and prepare us for the success we want.

Do we have the nerve, the persistence, and really the courage to invest in excellence far beyond the norm, or beyond even what seems to be reasonable? If we want results that exceed what's already available, we'd better cultivate that sensibility. It's a mindset akin to the steeliness of some gamblers, but it's rooted not in hope, superstition or a dubious interpretation of statistical fluctuations. It's based in work, skill, vision and hope. And it ultimately comes from inner strength and basic intuition, a human faculty for knowing that we'll look at in more detail, shortly.

I began giving a talk a few years ago that I decided to call "The Four Foundations of Greatness." Initially, some clients seemed reticent to speak of greatness in their endeavors, as if that could be interpreted as a sign of dangerous *hubris*, or a prideful form of overreach. But I slowly began to convince the greatness-shy that, done right, a focus on precisely that is not an exercise in arrogance or pridefulness at all, but rather a noble stretch toward what, ideally, we're here in this world to attain. Whether you think we exist here on earth because of a loving and creative divine providence, or just an immense and random evolutionary progress, it's hard to argue that our full horizon ought to be anything near mediocrity, or poor-to-average performance. On quite divergent cosmic paradigms, it's much more natural for human success to suppose that we're here to rise out from what's come before, to create something new and different and better than what existed prior to our efforts. We're here to shoot at and strive for excellence and nothing less. And excellence is a moving target. What it means changes over time. Yesterday's great can be tomorrow's average. So the quest for the best should always continue.

When your focus is on merely the finances and economics of your business rather than the excellence of your efforts, you're easily tempted to prioritize the wrong things and even to be satisfied with less than your best. As long as it pays, it stays—regardless of quality. But Jobs saw the danger in this approach and urged everyone around him to avoid it in every way. He chose excellence. He aimed at absolute greatness. And his example can inspire us to do the same.

It sounds easy to say, "Invest in excellence. Results follow." But the process being recommended can be arduous, lengthy, frustrating beyond words, and may even at times involve the battle of your life. That's what Jobs was willing to commit to, over and over. And it's the process that eventually produced his spectacular results. But he certainly hit rough spots along the way. And it was his pursuit of greatness without undue concern for price or profit that, in part, led to his initially being forced out of the company he created. But when a subsequent CEO came in and focused on the numbers, Apple rapidly began to decline. Only Jobs could eventually turn it around with his very different values and his personal fixation on greatness.

2. Impact First, Then Income.

Over the years, I've had a number of philosophers join forces with me in my professional effort to spread ancient wisdom and modern insights throughout the world of business and the broader culture around us. I've always shared with them my perspective on professional focus, and I've often used the slogan, "Impact first, then income." The mission comes before the money. Our concern should be to have as positive, broad, and deep an impact as we can for those we serve. If we do a great job for people and bring them revolutionary ideas they can use, then positive financial results will follow.

In 1991, I got a phone call out of the blue from an editor at *Life Magazine* named David Friend. He told me that the magazine was undertaking a two-volume book project on the meaning of life. Volume One would have the simple title, *The Meaning of Life*, and

Book Two would be called *More Reflections on the Meaning of Life*. The first book was already under way. He wanted to invite me as a philosopher, at the time teaching at Notre Dame, to write a short essay for the second book. My assignment, he said, was to answer either of these questions: What is the meaning of life? Or: Why are we here? He then informed me that my essay should be no more than 250 words in length, and would need to be turned in within two days. I was surprised. That was quite an assignment.

David assured me that the task was manageable, and that many had already finished their essays well within the 250-word limit. The network television late night host David Letterman, at the top of his game at the time, had quickly sent in a list: "Top Ten Reasons We're Here." Pulitzer Prize winning author Studs Terkel had also answered the question "Why are we here?" quite succinctly, and his entire essay consisted of the one phrase, 'To make a dent'—four words that actually sounded like something Steve Jobs might say. Just hearing Terkel's terse offering got my competitive juices flowing. Suddenly, I felt that I was facing the brevity and profundity contest of my life. I asked, "Can my essay come after Terkel's? If so, my answer could be: 'To fix dents'—three words. I win." David politely laughed at my lame little joke and explained that my Terkel's short answer would be in the first book and, if I agreed to participate, I'd be in the second. I'd have to come up with my own independent statement of simple sagacity. So I began to ponder. And here's the first part of what, as a result, I wrote:

> "We are here to attempt to give more to this life than we take from it, a task that, if undertaken properly, is impossible. The more we give, the more we get. But that's the point. We're here to discover, develop, and cultivate, in loving stewardship of our world, our neighbors, and ourselves." (97)

It captured exactly what I think and feel to this day.

I'm a philosopher who believes that there's a point to life. In the heyday of existential thought, I could have called for a convention of like-minded thinkers and held the gathering in a broom closet. But now, there are many more of us who are convinced that life actually has a meaning. And I think I know what it is. The reason we're here is all about love, growth and positive impact. If we do all that right, then the income we need in order to pay the bills will be forthcoming.

In the book *If Aristotle Ran General Motors*, written a few years after the project with David Friend, I devoted an entire chapter to meaning of life issues and their relation to business. Summarizing what I consider to be the deepest perspectives on meaning to be found across the world's most sagacious philosophies and religious traditions, I surmised that the meaning of life is creative love, or loving creativity. We're here to have a positive, creative, loving impact on the people and world around us. Connecting our business endeavors with this deeper sense of meaning will give them a deeper direction and lead to better results. If we, however, depart from that perspective, we inevitably undermine the best possibilities for our work.

When Steve Jobs, like Studs Terkel, talked about making a dent in the universe, I believe this is what he was getting at. If we think impact first, then income, we're better prepared to invest in excellence and pursue product quality above profits. And it's only this priority that can generate, in the end, insanely great results.

3. Priority Logic Matters.

What comes first? What comes second? What's our highest value, or our governing perspective? What's ancillary, or auxiliary? What's dominant? What's subordinate? Where is our ultimate touchstone for priorities? What's then a proper focal goal, and what's better viewed as a side effect? People in a great company know the answers to questions like these. There's a deep priority-logic to everything they do. The tail is not going to end up wagging the dog. Incidentals won't look like essentials. People won't go around majoring in the minors. We feel great pressures in every business to get more than adequate financial results. The issue is always over how to accomplish this. Steve Jobs was committed to quality first, in both products and team members. He believed that with this priority, the customer would be served well and the financials would end up looking good.

Decades ago, the prominent protestant theologian Paul Tillich argued that everyone deep inside has an ultimate concern, a value that will override all other values. Implicit in his reasoning was a suggestion that this ultimate value stands at the peak of a hierarchy of commitments. Among the things that we like, prefer, value, or love, among our many and varied concerns and interests, there are relationships of greater and lesser. People who do powerful work and live outstanding lives are clear and consistent about those hierarchies and priorities. They don't allow what's secondary to become primary. They keep the most important things in focus.

When our priorities get out of alignment, trouble happens. After Jobs was forced out of Apple and left, the company's priorities were changed and a very dark period set in. It was only with the return of Steve in 1997 that priorities were reversed and the founding values were re-established and refined and even re-energized, and then implemented in new and exciting ways. And that produced the amazing run of revolutionary products in the Act Two of Apple that did indeed change the world.

Leaders need to make sure everyone understands their proper priorities, and then acts on them consistently. This logic can't be left to chance. The proper emphasis has to be communicated over and over, in words and in actions on the part of executives and managers. Then, the magic can happen.

6

Don't Be a Slave to Focus Groups

But, my dear Crito, why should we pay
so much attention to what most people think?
Socrates

Socrates liked to ask people on the street what they thought about various issues and important matters, not because he hoped to learn the truth from them, but rather it seems, because he wanted to understand all the ways in which people could be wrong. Focus groups often deliver similar results. I know. I've been behind the one-way glass mirror, watching and listening to focus groups debate a product, and I experienced a sort of Socratic amazement at what I was hearing. People can say unbelievably stupid things. And irrational opinions often come wrapped in a shiny foil of extreme confidence.

But the idea of holding focus groups can make so much sense, on the surface. If we want to please people with our products and services, who could possibly be better to ask about what will satisfy customers than a sample of potential customers themselves? But this presupposes something that might seem obvious and yet, on examination, can prove to be different from what we thought. Do we, after all, simply want to satisfy the current wants and perceived needs that people are already able to identify?

The top customer service expert Chip Bell has been saying for years that customer satisfaction is not what we should pursue in our endeavor to do great work. What we need to seek instead, and strive hard to attain, is customer love. We should want those we serve to be delighted and excited, and even awed by what we give them. The goal should be for them to love the product or service, head-over-heels. That way, they'll become our active partners in spreading the word. We'll create through their experience of our work a community of committed believers in what we do, or in what we provide.

Years ago, the pioneering television producer Norman Lear, the creator of such shows as "All in the Family," "Sanford and Sons," and "The Jeffersons," invited me to visit and spend a day with him at his vacation home in Vermont, just talking philosophy. This was the man responsible for producing such movies as "This is Spinal Tap," and "Fried Green Tomatoes," and "The Princess Bride," our all time favorite Morris family film. Norman and I had talked on the phone several times and corresponded quite a bit, but it would be the first time I'd meet him in person. So I was excited about the visit. As soon as I arrived at the beautiful house that previously had been owned by the great American poet Robert Frost, and then the modern artist Kenneth Noland, Lear warmly welcomed me and introduced me to four other guests. Among them were Tom and Kate Chappell, the founders of Tom's of Maine, a major personal care products company with strong environmental values. I was a regular user of their toothpaste, and when Norman told me who they were, along with the name of their company, I spontaneously put my hand over my heart and said, "I LOVE you guys! I LOVE your products!"

Tom gasped and turned to his wife, pointing at me, and

exclaimed, "Look! Look where his hand is!" Then he said to me, "That's what we want to see—someone who truly *loves* what we do! That's real success!" I was indeed a devoted fan of what they did, and an everyday evangelist for their company. In my case, they had true customer love. And what about Norman's own TV shows and movies? Did they "satisfy" viewers like me? Did I cross the country to go see him because his products *satisfied* me? Not at all! I wanted to meet him because I genuinely loved his shows and films. And shouldn't that be something we all want our work to result in—real love? I think that's the proper target. And so did Steve Jobs.

So then, how do we create products and services that will result in not only customer satisfaction, but also the far more important phenomenon of customer love? To most people in business, the answer is obvious: Talk to the customers. Then, listen. If it's a new product, you've got to run it by potential consumers. Survey people. Find out what they prefer, what they truly like, and what they're not so thrilled about. Have a focus group. Have lots of focus groups, and let the customer tell us what to do! Political candidates do this all the time with polls. Lots of companies do as well. Ask the people what they want. What could be simpler than that?

Jobs took a different approach. He loved to quote Henry Ford, who reportedly once said, "If I had asked customers what they wanted, they would have told me a faster horse." This is a tremendously insightful remark, because it captures something deep. Jobs was convinced that people most often wouldn't know what they wanted until he first created it and showed it to them. He hoped to be so innovative and "out there" in a new creative space that the customers whose hearts he was eager to win couldn't even begin to anticipate what they wanted, and would soon desperately need, until he brought it into reality and showed it to them. To play off Henry Ford's insight, Steve Jobs wasn't trying to build a better or faster typewriter, or a quieter adding machine. And that's likely what early focus groups would have wanted. But his aim was much higher.

And yet, that creates a problem. If your goal is customer love and you can't just ask the customer what he or she wants, or in fact would in fact love if it were available, then what's the preferred alternative procedure for coming up with new products, new services, or even new features for what already exists? Here we approach one of Steve's deepest secrets and most important advantages. It's also something we rarely talk about at all, especially in a business context. And that needs to change. So, here's our first imperative for this sixth principle, a way to be free from the confines of focus groups.

1. Intuit What Needs to Be Done.

From his earliest days as a creator of TV shows, Norman Lear had an uncanny feel for what could work on television, even though he was doing original concepts that were revolutionary and had never been tried before. He had great intuition about what could be accomplished, and what might make a huge difference to viewers. Tom and Kate Chappell also had good instincts about what they could do that the world needed. The best and most innovative people in any field seem to have this in common—good instincts, great intuition, and especially a keen sense for what can make a difference.

To Steve Jobs, the human capacity for intuition was always of crucial and central importance. In his youth, he bummed around India in search of spiritual enlightenment, and he later reported his fascination with the different way that so many of the people he met on those adventures used their minds. They weren't as infatuated with linear, logical reasoning as the most of us in the West seem to be, at least since at least the time of Aristotle. They instead drew on a different and distinctive intellectual ability: intuition.

If you had asked Steve what procedure other than focus groups you could employ in order to arrive at an understanding of what your products and services and their features should be, he might have put it as bluntly as this: "Use your intuition. Intuit what needs to be done."

"Ok, then," you might respond. "Exactly how? And, what precisely, or even approximately, is intuition, anyway? How does it work? And what am I supposed to do in order to use it well?"

There are two main views on what the concept of intuition refers to in the human mind. What we can call the simple view is the belief that the word 'intuition' just names an ability we all have to organize and interpret our sense experience, or perceptual data, in such a way as to find or create patterns that can result in new levels of understanding, and that can also provide a form of predictive power beyond the range of our past and current experience. Intuition is just about discovering or producing patterns that can generate new insight. According to this viewpoint, it's not an independent source of information, but is always directly dependent on our normal physical senses for its inputs. It just operates on those inputs distinctively to create usable insight beyond what our basic perceptions on their surface might obviously indicate. Intuition is a way of digging deeper and drawing more from the pool of our experience than what might immediately meet the eye, or ear.

A thought experiment might clarify this. In almost any business or profession, imagine two people in a room. One is a seasoned professional with an exceptional track record of challenges and successes, who has attained outstanding victories powered by wise decisions and creative leaps of contribution throughout many years of experience in the field. The other person is a novice, just starting out. Grant them equally sharp senses and equivalent basic intelligence, measured in standard ways. Then present the two of them with a big range of new raw data relevant to their work, perhaps with the aim of spotting nascent trends, or solving a new problem. On this view of intuition, the senior practitioner, all other things being equal, will have gotten himself or herself into a much better position for reading the data, taking it in, organizing it mentally, and interpreting it properly—by which processes, a new insight may quickly be hatched. And all this can happen while the novice is still trying to absorb the deluge of information, perhaps without even a clue initially as to what it all means. On the simple view of intuition, this human capacity is just a cultivated skill for dealing well with the world, and sifting through all our perceptions to discern quickly what's needed next.

Championship level basketball players have reported that at times during a big game, they will experience a flow of their activities beyond the normal realm of conscious thought or logical reasoning. They will "just know" where the ball is and where it's going to be next. They'll "just feel" what move they're to make and when they're to make it. No conscious deliberation or decision-making is needed. There's absolutely no mental chatter of the sort that, "Ok, Rashid's over there roughly twenty feet to my left and guarded loosely. He's about to get in the clear, moving to his right. If I pass the ball in approximately three seconds, and bounce it off the spot on the floor two feet in front of the toe of his left shoe, he should be able to get it and take it straight to the basket. Now!" None of this goes on at all. The full spectrum of information, in vastly more detail than could possibly be given a verbal representation in the conscious mind, is accessed, organized, and interpreted by the seasoned athlete, and he then acts, intuitively moving in the right direction and performing just the right action at the right time, "beyond thought."

Champions don't attain their best results through riding on a stream of chattering conscious "self-talk." Their heads aren't full of thoughts at all. Rather, there's something more akin to the inner emptiness that many mystics and gurus paradoxically praise. In the flow experience of expert level performance, the rational, conscious mind seems to go into abeyance, or just get out of the way, and the very different mentality of intuition appears to take over and yield superior results. Whoever has the talent and cultivated skill to intuit well can attain the upper reaches of excellence where champions are created.

The pioneering performance psychologist Mihaly Csikszentmihalyi introduced a wide readership to this phenomenon in his groundbreaking book *Flow: The Psychology of Optimal Experience.* I recommend it highly, in case you haven't already had the chance to read it. And if you ever want to ask someone about it, I think we're supposed to pronounce this great researcher's name as if it were spelled something like "Mee-High—Chick-Set-Mee-High." But I believe that people who actually know him intuitively call him Mike. It flows. And there has, of course, grown to be an entire literature on the phenomenon, featuring more books by Mike, as well as others. Some call this "being in the zone." It's an experience reported by top performers across sports, arts, and the sciences. Within such an experience, time seems to pass differently, and excellence is enhanced.

There is also another view of intuition available to us, compatible with this first view and yet going far beyond it. We can call it the subtle view, or even the distinctively spiritual view, of intuition. I can present it best by the use of some preliminary images.

Imagine the conscious mind as a walled fortress. The walls are high and thick and impenetrable. But there are a few obvious entrances through those walls and into the fortress. Those are the known physical senses: Sight, smell, hearing, touch, taste—and some add proprioception, the generalized sense that we have of the positioning, or orientation, of our body and its parts in space. For example, I don't have to look to see where my arms and legs are right now or to establish their position relative to each other. My proprioceptive sense tells me. For this second view of intuition, it doesn't really matter exactly how many physical senses there are.

There can be five, or six, or more. But, in any case, there is a limited number. And they alone are the widely acknowledged portals or doorways in the walls surrounding inner awareness that allow information from the external world directly into the fortress of our conscious minds.

But there's a problem. At each doorway to the fortress, there are sentries or guards stationed to keep out anything unwanted, almost like nightclub bouncers. These guards are our previous beliefs, assumptions, prejudices, attitudes, desires, fears, emotional tendencies, and general worldview dispositions—the sum total of our current habits of thought and feeling. And they're quite powerful. It's actually amazing how well these numerous guards can block things that we don't want to see or hear or in any other way acknowledge. That's how it can happen that you can expose two people to exactly the same things and yet witness in them, as a result, very different experiences and beliefs, leading to quite different emotions, attitudes, and actions. This is also why we have such adages as: "There is no one so blind as he who will not see." We're all blind or deaf or in other ways cognitively immune to some things that we could benefit greatly from knowing. This is a big problem in business, just as it is in life more generally.

And here's a simple truth. The more experience of external reality that we can let in and grasp, the better off we typically are in terms of understanding the world and predicting, or at least preparing for, whatever's coming next. There will always be various uncertainties about what is and what's likely to be, but those who access more experience throughout their journeys are best prepared to anticipate and respond to whatever does come next.

Now imagine that, within the fortress of your conscious mind, in addition to the few, guarded outside doors in the high, thick wall, there's also, somewhere in the middle of the carefully protected edifice, something like a hidden trap door in the floor that can be opened or closed—totally, a little, or a lot. There's a big spectrum of possibilities for how much it can be open or shut at any given moment, and this can change through time. And here's the important fact: This trap door opens into the unconscious mind, a vastly bigger structure than the walled fortress that sits atop it. And this is where things can get really interesting. I like to picture this structure as something like a gigantic basement of the fortress, and I envision it as surrounded by an underground ocean of information on all sides, flowing all around it.

On the picture I'm sketching now, there are three features of the unconscious mind that are crucial for us to understand. One: It's immensely bigger and more capacious than the conscious mind. It's enormous, and perhaps even unimaginably huge. Two: No thick wall of protection surrounds it, as in the case with the conscious mind. Envision it, rather, as bounded and bordered by something that's more like a chain link fence, with big links and large open spaces between the links. This looser containment boundary, because of its nature, lets in a lot more information than the few standard sensory portals for the conscious mind can allow in. It seems to have connections and forms of access that we don't yet understand at all, but from which we can benefit tremendously. Steve Jobs is one person who did. And, Three: On this second view we're seeking to elucidate, the unconscious mind can feed the conscious mind information that's not available to consciousness through the physical senses. This information can bubble up by means of the metaphorical trap door and into the alert awareness of the conscious mind if we allow it to—which, in our adult lives, may take a lot of training. And this form of access to information is what the faculty of intuition is, according to the subtle or spiritual view of intuition. It's the open trap door. Or, to put the matter another way, it's a flow of truth from our unconscious minds directly into our actions, often through our decisions, and sometimes, into conscious awareness.

There is a second image that can be relevant here. Imagine that, even with all the guards at the doorways of the conscious mind, and with all their reasons to keep information out, they still allow in much more than the conscious mind can register and then explicitly contain. The overflow swirls directly into the unconscious mind. The basketball player in our earlier example knows where everyone else is on the court because of his physical senses, but there's too much information being processed for all that data to be itemized and consciously registered. It flows through the senses beneath the threshold of explicit self-conscious attention, or lively conscious awareness, and ends up in his unconscious mind. It gets processed there quickly and then, nearly instantly, directs action without any need for mediation through anything like deliberative thought. The main job for the great athlete, or the top performer in any complex endeavor, is to keep his highly trained senses open and as fully functioning as possible every moment, while keeping his conscious mind out of the way, so that the understanding of the unconscious can flow, intuitively, into the decisions and actions that are needed.

On this expanded conception, much of the content of the unconscious mind originates from sense experience. But the precise view of intuition that we're seeking to understand now, the second view—what I've suggested that we can call the subtle or spiritual view of intuition—allows the possibility that information can also come into the unconscious mind by means other than the sense experiences of the body. On this view, the soul or the spirit of a person can be directly affected by truth—unmediated by the bodily organs of physical sense. This spiritual view of intuition allows for the organizing and interpreting activities of intuition that are recognized by the simple view, but it goes beyond that account and also acknowledges a phenomenon of enlightenment that in a profound way bypasses the senses and thus results from truth moving through the metaphorical chain link fence surrounding the unconscious mind and entering that larger sphere of our interiority more directly. This can then spark action, as well as consciously available insights, discoveries, creations, and innovations that can otherwise seem to come out of nowhere, as if almost magically.

On this second view, the mind has access points that aren't straightforwardly physical in any known way or form. They allow for what some religious believers refer to as divine guidance, and others think of as just a spiritual knowing—whether it shows up as a conscious thought or merely as doing the right thing at the right time, or being in the right place when you're needed, without any sufficient measure of conscious knowledge that led you into that position. This is a view that articulates what a great many people think to be possible, and primarily because they believe they've experienced it. It also may be a mode through which apparent coincidence, or what's often called serendipity, operates. Perhaps there's even a sort of communication, person-to-person, that can take place through this spiritually intuitive capacity.

On the first view of intuition, it's just a mental ability we all have to organize and interpret our ordinary experience—however, sometimes in extraordinary ways. On the second view, intuition can also access more than just what comes to us through normal sense experience. It has a more direct contact with truth through the depths of the unconscious mind and what it may be able to receive apart from the operation of our normal physical senses. It's still an organizing and interpretive modality of information processing, but its sources are deeper and at times more mysterious than we otherwise might imagine.

I'm fortunate to have seen this second view of intuition in action through the lives of people I've known well and trusted completely, including my father and his mother. They occasionally seemed to have access to information that was not available to their physical senses, or to anyone else around them. And without enjoying any form of normal perceptual contact, they would have an uncanny reliability in their experience of what we're calling intuitive knowledge. I've pursued this issue more and have told some of their stories in my book *Philosophy for Dummies*, as well as in some of my more recent novels, so I won't rehearse it here, despite its immense intrinsic interest and potential relevance to our understanding of Steve Jobs and the ways he worked in the world. Such knowledge is more widespread than you'd think.

This is most likely the view of intuition and its use that was seen in action by young Steve during his time in India, while in pursuit of his own grasp of spiritual wisdom. I suspect that it's a major key to his immense creativity. He fed his conscious mind voraciously. And as his unconscious mind was fed, as well, he kept wide open, as much as he could, and much more than most people do, the doorway between the two. Out of that inner flow came his many insights and innovations. And he then touched us all deeply with them because he knew, intuitively, what we would want and need before we did.

But how can you then go and likewise do this? That's the question. How can the rest of us manage to intuit like a genius? I'll provide some thoughts on that in a minute.

2. Let the Customer Teach, Never Dictate.

HERE WE DESCEND FOR A MOMENT FROM THE METAPHYSICAL and back to the mundane. Jobs would not tell us to ignore our customers completely. We can, of course, learn from them. And we certainly should. They can be our teachers and guides. But they should never become tyrants, dictating to us everything we do and provide. As Henry Ford and Steve Jobs both understood, we can't serve our customers in the best ways unless we pay attention to, and yet somehow also transcend, or go beyond, what they are able to tell us now. We can do that by beginning with deep attention. We need to pay attention to our current customers and potential customers in a way that allows them initially to teach us, but then also will provide for the possibility that we can, in turn, teach them.

On the first view of intuition, we watch and listen and then organize and interpret what we see and hear. With our intuitive abilities, we can go beyond the surface inputs of what's manifestly said and shown, and we can manage to discern deeper patterns that point the way forward. On the second view of intuition, this process can still take place, and it can be a very important procedure, but there is also the additional chance of our accessing even more truth, and vastly more interesting possibilities, far beyond anything customers might be able to tell us.

What does a great teacher do? The wrong answer is that a great teacher conveys a wide range of well-selected information in such a way that it can be easily remembered and used. The right answer is that a great teacher stimulates and inspires us to go far beyond anything he or she says to us, or even shows us. A great teacher's main job is to spark our interest, elicit concern and curiosity and even a hunger and thirst for understanding, and perhaps also to enlighten and guide us, but not to dictate to us the relevant contents of our minds. Good students may be nothing more than accurate human video and audio recorders, simply able to play back what they've heard and read with relatively good fidelity. But great students are much more than that. They are potential adventurers, explorers and pioneers, eager to launch out into their own journeys of risk, courage, and discovery, led forward by the teacher as their guide.

The tyrannical pedant does indeed merely dictate. You'd better memorize his sentences and phrases or you won't do well on his test. But this teacher gets no more than he gives. The great teacher, by contrast, creates far more than can be imagined. How then can you make sure your customers will be not just adequate or good, but even great teachers? By being a great student to them. It's Yin-Yang process, a dynamic flow, even a mutual interdependency. Approach your customers properly to learn from them well, hint at the magic of what you might be able to do together, and then they can perhaps become extraordinary teachers, sparking your own creativity in many ways, and positioning you to intuit well what needs to be done.

Those among us in the world of business who slavishly follow focus groups and even the most expert opinion research can't expect to surprise and delight customers the way Steve Jobs was able to do, and to accomplish repeatedly through his career, but especially during his later years. His imaginative ability to enter into the lived experience of his potential customers and intuit both what they would want and how it should work for them was a clear marvel and an example for us all.

Yes but, again, how? It's one thing to be told to intuit the way forward, and it's quite another to get a grip on how that might be done. It's not like a skill we all learn in school or in our families growing up. It's not a major subject in business training. Where then are we to go to get a grip on this remarkable skill that we need to use, and even master? In order to limn the possibilities here, I want to give you another example from my own experience and tell you a story of what is perhaps the most important aspect of the most remarkable intellectual adventure of my life. It will suggest a few interesting conditions under which intuition may flourish, and you can be empowered to create beyond any normal, reasonable expectations.

3. Give Yourself Time to Think Different.

In February of 2011, I finished a normal breakfast and pushed back my chair, prepared to go upstairs to my study and work on a book about difficult change, a project I'd been working on for many years. It's the only book I've ever rewritten twenty-one times. And I was ready for version twenty-two. But before I could get up out of the chair where I had just enjoyed toast and coffee,

I had a moment of complete relaxation and suddenly began to undergo what would be the most unusual experience of my life.

A movie started playing in my head. There's no better way to say it. In the Foreword of her soon-to-be-famous book *Frankenstein*, Mary Shelley called her own experience of its story, "a waking dream." That about captures it. I suddenly had the most vivid daydream imaginable, but much more complete and detailed than normal daydreams. An old man and a boy were sitting in the sand under a palm tree, talking. The conversation was great. I felt I needed to write it down. So I ran upstairs as quickly as I could, taking the steps two at a time. I rushed into my study, sat down at the computer, and typed as fast as possible to catch up and continue. It took me two years from that day, about twenty-four months, before I could even think about doing version twenty-two of the change book, because the gripping film of my inner theater had continued to run.

There were days when my mental movie would play for an hour or two. And on some rare days it would show for six or eight hours, or even ten. Sometimes, the projectionist would take a day off. Occasionally the theater would be shut down for a week, or two, or three. Then, it would start back up where it most recently left off. And now, I think, maybe it's finished. But I could be wrong. For the past year I've just been editing the novels that have resulted from my transcriptions. And there's been nothing new. We just might be on a hiatus where my job is to get it all into print and e-book form. Then, perhaps there can be more. I sure hope so. It's my favorite story ever. My attempt to capture all this in writing has led so far to eight novels, totaling over a million words.

The story of the mental movie, and subsequent series of books, is set in Egypt in 1934 and 1935, a place and time about which I had very little conscious knowledge when this remarkable experience began. The story I was given is a coming-of-age tale about a thirteen-year-old boy and his friends, as they're guided through various unexpected adventures by the boy's seventy-year-old uncle, a man of surprising wisdom and power. There are mystics and warriors, criminals and revolutionaries, legendary objects and mathematical puzzles. There are poisonous snakes, deadly spiders, gun battles and bombs. There are creative people whose ability to know seems to go far beyond what would be physically possible in our world, and there are miraculous looking actions that appear to defy explanation. More than one hundred named characters populate the stories within the epic tale as it plays out in the desert, across the city of Cairo, on the Nile River, and up in Alexandria, with mysterious side adventures in such places as Giza, Tripoli, New York, and Berlin, in ways that have amazed me. As the first few books have been published, many early readers have said that they're "*The Alchemist* Meets Indiana Jones in the spirit of Harry Potter" or that they're "Part *Temple of Doom*, part Dan Brown, and part *The Hardy Boys* Meet Aristotle." They've been compared to *The Little Prince* and *Lawrence of Arabia* and even to aspects of *Star Wars*.

After I had watched this extended inner film during the day and written it all down, I would then read the stories aloud to my wife at night. She would say, "Where are you getting all these Arab names?" I'd answer, "I hear them in the movie." At the end of each day of watching and writing, I'd research all the details I saw and heard in the story—a certain sort of car, or watch, or animal, or store. Did these things exist in Egypt in 1934? The answer would always be yes. But when this experience began, the sum total of my knowledge about Egypt was: The desert, Cairo, Alexandria, The Nile, camels, the Pyramids, The Sphinx, Giza, and, yes, some Pharaohs. My total knowledge about 1934 and 1935 can be fully captured in this phrase: "Between the world wars." That's it.

So, where were all these details coming from? Where was I getting this rich wealth of information that checked out as historically true—apart from, of course, the fictional elements of the storytelling—from targeted research I engaged in only after I saw the relevant things happen in this protracted and exciting movie? Where was I getting not only the many Arab names I had never heard, but in many cases, names that were perfect for the personalities of the individuals involved, given their original meanings—which, of course, I also didn't know at the time, and learned only much later?

If there is one continuous underlying theme to these books and within the stories they tell, it's the power of the unconscious mind to bring us knowledge of things that would otherwise seem impossible to know, and to allow us to do things that might appear impossible to do. The nice irony is, of course, that I've been living this theme of the stories in the process of giving birth to the books. I should add that I had no idea how to write fiction, either. I had never learned any of the things they teach in creative writing programs, such as the matters of structure and story dynamic and point of view, and so many other elements of the craft. But my path was made easy, because the film played in my head in such a way that I didn't have to know any technique. I just had to write down what I saw and heard as it unfolded.

Starting with the events in the short prologue to the series, *The Oasis Within*, the old man in these tales shares with his nephew, and then with the boy's new best friend, many insights about the power of the mind. And he makes clear that he's not mainly talking about the conscious mind, with all its clutter and constant chatter. He's referring to the bigger and more powerful unconscious mind—that massive resource that we ordinarily don't even try to use. It's almost like we're desperate for water and merely fill spoons now and then from a slowly dripping faucet while there's a vast underground river easily accessible to us instead, if we would just dig. But accessing this river takes time. And that's the one thing we tend not to give ourselves. We all need to take time to cultivate a free access to our unconscious minds. That, I suspect, was the path of Steve Jobs.

In my own experience of peak creativity, in order to keep up with the movie I was seeing and to keep it playing, to find out what would happen next, I learned quickly that I had to devote some time each day to sitting quietly and waiting. I came to realize that if I could calm the normal chatter of my conscious mind and just be still and patient, the inner movie would start up. I could see how a lifetime of hard work in philosophy was also paying off and feeding into what I was seeing and hearing. But the details of the story and the ideas percolating through it also went far beyond anything I had ever studied or even briefly reflected on. And that's the creative combination: what was coming to me, and what was coming from me, intermingled in deep and literally novel ways. I had to learn to make the time to allow it to happen. I had to learn how to get out of my own way, empty my conscious thoughts, and open myself to what could come to me from somewhere beyond my own familiar resources.

Those of us who aspire to great innovation and superior service to others routinely work hard and gather as much information relevant to our aspirations as we can, learning as much as possible about all the areas of our work, but we often forget to give ourselves time to process it all and organize it and interpret it, and perhaps, go far, far beyond it. And that always does take time. You can't "think different," in the mode of Steve Jobs, without the time to do so, and something like the enjoyment of an occasional meditative state to allow you to access what's beyond the norm. The conscious mind must be emptied to make room for something deeper to enter. Nothing that's full can be a receptacle to more. Emptiness is key. And so again, we encounter the importance of emptiness in the realm of creativity. But to turn down the volume and get beyond the chatter of the conscious mind always takes a measure of time and peace.

The best of innovative greatness lies far beyond what can be accessed amid the normal demands of life, unless you've worked hard to keep open the trapdoor to the unconscious on a regular basis. With time to think, or even, to put it more accurately, time to clear the space for the thought beyond thought that's available to us deep in the heart of our unconscious minds, we touch things that are otherwise unavailable. And that's the paradox. To think different, and in this way to be like Steve, we have to learn to cease to think at all, now and then, and to be open, and simply to allow the truths and beauties and connections and unities at the core of it all—the great good things of which we're capable—to penetrate our mundane worldly shells and spark our hearts to something new and insanely great.

Before the age of fifty-eight, I had only hints of this—bits and pieces of insight about the creative process at its depth, and how sparks of insight from somewhere beyond the norm can enter into our lives. But the extended novelistic experience of the past six years has taught me things I never could have guessed. It has allowed me to write things I never could have imagined and, by this process, to understand a little more how someone like Steve Jobs was able to create so many wonderful things that the rest of us never could have envisioned before we saw them presented to us.

Perhaps accessing and using intuition is, at its best, an art, or finely skilled practice. We have to work hard to learn all that we can through our conscious minds, and then work equally hard to get out of our own way. We need to learn to be quiet, and even peaceful, if just for a moment, to meditate and attain a higher awareness. What then results from such a process, done well, could never be duplicated by a focus group behind a one-way mirror, drinking coffee and answering questions, or through surveys, however extensive. We can all intuit, I suspect, if we'll just do the hard work to make it possible. And then, when the magic happens, incredible rewards can flow.

7

Bend Reality

I admit the appearance of inconsistency, but there may not be any real inconsistency, after all, in this.
Socrates

The American philosopher Henry David Thoreau said it first and best: "The world is but a canvas to our imaginations." With that perspective, he captured an important piece of the operating philosophy that would later catapult Steve Jobs to the top of several industries. One of Steve's best-known qualities was a trait he seemed to share with the famous adventurer, Don Quixote. They both had a capacity to see what they wanted to see and believe whatever the romance of their imaginations presented to them, rather than accepting the straightforward evidence of the senses and the consequent stubborn, mundane realities that everyone else so clearly recognized.

Over the years, I've read a number of interviews with some of the most famous living authors. They were often asked what they thought was the greatest novel ever written. Many of them independently picked the same book, *Don Quixote*, written by Miguel de Cervantes in Spain and originally published in two volumes, in the years 1605 and 1615. The full original title was, in English translation, *The Ingenious Gentleman Don Quixote of La Mancha.* The story, in its high concept, is simple. A non-titled nobleman named Alonso Quijano reads too many chivalric romance novels about knights rescuing fair ladies, and these popular tales begin to inflame his imagination. He finally decides to go out on his own quest. He takes on a new name and recruits a simple farmer, Sancho Panza, to come along as his sidekick. They set out together on a series of wild adventures inspired by the noble Don's exciting, idiosyncratic vision of what's real. This whippet thin, energetic idealist leads his short, chubby squire into one insane situation after another. And literary greatness ensues.

I had never read this highly praised book earlier in life. So, several years ago, I went out and bought a new translation by Edith Grossman and in a few days devoured it with enthusiasm, cover-to-cover. I was astonished, and could see what all the great authors were saying. This sprawling tale is the portrayal of a man who is either the rare adult, the metaphorical unicorn, who manages to revive within himself the fantastical imagination and boundless vision of childhood, and perhaps in doing so becomes the paradigm of an amazing visionary—the sort of person who could lead us into realms as yet unseen; or else, he's merely a sadly deluded and dangerously deceptive madman whose beliefs and actions can terribly mislead anyone crazy enough to follow him. But, which is it? Which is he? Is he an apt object of longing admiration, or rather pity? Should we seek out such visionary individuals, cherish them as creative souls, and avidly follow wherever their imaginations might take us—or are we much better off to avoid such people at almost any cost? There are many such errant knights loose in the world these days. How can we take their measure?

The translator Grossman herself says that, in her youth, she read the story repeatedly, and cried every time. In her adulthood, she continued to read it and laughed every time. Does Don Quixote carry within himself the image of a hero, or a clown, a lost soul, or a troubled madman? Is his story a terrible tragedy or an outrageous comedy? Is it a glimpse of the best, or of the worst, in human nature? Or is it all this together? The persistence of these questions is, in part, a powerful testimony to the greatness of the story.

Some of the people around Steve Jobs thought that he was in fact at least slightly crazy and simply unable to deal with reality as it is. Did he just stumble into an industry at precisely a time and a place where such craziness could succeed, both because of its excesses, and yet also despite itself and on a ridiculous scale? He would not accept anyone's judgment that something he wanted was impossible. He saw what he chose to see and, with his kind, genuine, simple-hearted, and slightly rotund Sancho Panza-style companion, the scientifically brilliant but perhaps in other ways naïve Steve Wozniak, he set off on a series of adventures that often seemed, in their initial stages, plain crazy, or just insane, and not at all insanely great. The question that we should ask, then, is what was behind all this for Jobs and, most importantly, how did he so often make his alternative vision of reality work?

The stories are many. Isaacson recounts an early episode when, before the founding of Apple and while as a young man working at Atari, Jobs wanted his good friend and squire Sancho Wozniak to create a certain kind of computer game. Woz said it would take him several months. Jobs gave him what was later to become the famous unblinking stare and told him that, no—to the contrary—he would be able to do the task in four days. Wozniak later said that he really knew it was impossible, but he bent to the unfazed ironclad will of his friend and got it done in the exact, absurd time demanded. Isaacson also reports that, at a much later date, Jobs wanted an engineer at Apple to cut down the boot-up time for the Macintosh computer by ten seconds. The engineer said it was simply impossible. Jobs would not accept that verdict and convinced him to try. Within a few weeks, the associate had figured out a way to shave off twenty-eight seconds.

The third story Isaacson tells about such things involves a time, years later, when Jobs called Wendell Weeks, then the head of Corning, and asked him to supply a certain sort of special glass for a computer model in great quantity and within six months. Weeks told Jobs it was impossible. And, again, he refused to accept that judgment, insisting to this highly accomplished man, who was in a vastly better position to know, that it could indeed be done. And, as had so often happened in the past, the sheer unstoppable confidence that Jobs seemed to have in his own possibility beliefs moved whatever mountains were in the way and the task got accomplished, again, on time. Because of that challenge and achievement, Corning has had an unprecedented run of producing in America every piece of glass that's to be found on an iPhone or iPad ever since.

Jobs seemed completely convinced that whatever intuitively should be done is actually possible to do, however obviously crazy it might appear. People around Jobs called this mindset and attitude of his, "The Reality Distortion Field," using a concept from an old Star Trek episode where aliens create an illusion, or alternate reality, through the use of mental force. Employees would try to keep each other from getting caught up in it and losing their own sense of reality. But, as at least one Apple employee has explained, it was in the case of Jobs somehow normally a self-fulfilling distortion. And through the state of sheer will power that it managed to produce in him, it became contagious and spread and often ruled the day, even in the minds and lives of those who otherwise were sure they knew better.

No biographer that I know of, including Isaacson, explains where this Reality Distortion Field came from or how it worked. And it's likely far too simple and superficial to suggest that it was just the ultimate wish-fulfillment needs of an extreme narcissist that were operative beneath it. I suspect that much more was going on. And I think it's important to venture a guess as to the source and true nature of this outlandish and yet repeatedly successful phenomenon.

To get our bearings, and perhaps our answers, I believe we should go back to the seminal and, for Steve, formative book, *Autobiography of a Yogi*, the one text that, as we've seen, he read and reread throughout his life. A salient feature of the book is that it's chock full of outrageous sounding miracle stories—accounts of wild and seemingly impossible deeds performed by holy men and women within the relatively recent past in the nation of India. These narratives encompass healing miracles, instant travel without physical conveyance, mind-to-mind communication at a distance, and even the dramatic extreme of apparent resurrection from bodily death. Most modern, scientifically minded Western readers will find themselves either cynically dismissive of these accounts, or else struggling to know what to make of them—written, as they were, about identifiable figures known to many at the time, and recounting acts that were widely accepted to have happened, at least within the circles of people and the culture involved.

I think Jobs found the holy men and women featured in this book to be utterly compelling in their austerity, asceticism, discipline, and connection with greater powers than most of us ever access. In the narratives of the book, it's explained that the crucial link the miracle workers had with divine power came from years and even decades of devoted meditation, many hours a day, to the exclusion of any worldly activities that might prevent the required level of devotion and power for such actions. I suspect that Jobs deeply wanted the elevated state of mind and spirit that resulted, according to these stories, and especially the powers it reportedly conveyed, but without having the time, inclination, or dedication for all the extensive hard work that reportedly had been required in the lives described, in order to get the purported results. He was, after all, a man in a hurry to make his own dent in the universe. You don't even have to accept the stories of the book as in any way precisely accurate or even remotely true in order to imagine the effect that repeated exposure to them may have had on the young spiritual seeker from California, and throughout his adult years, as he discovered and explored the new technologies that could seem, in their own way, to be nearly miraculous.

It's my suspicion that the portrayals of spiritual power in Yogananda's book wove a spell in the heart and mind of Steve Jobs, just as reading chivalric romances had affected the fictional Don Quixote. And they deeply convinced the young man that such power is indeed available in our world to bring whatever wonders the intuitive imagination can project down into the dimension of reality we all share—and even in many cases along the way, to make the seemingly impossible possible. Whether I'm right in thinking this and, if so, whether Jobs was right to believe what I ascribe to him, I think we'll be able to see how this imaginative man could so often escape his own version of the worst results of a superheated imagination that were felt by his quixotic counterpart.

There are three things each of us can concentrate on and accomplish that can give us some of the magical edge that Jobs apparently enjoyed. We can think of them as three requirements, or rules, for bending the contours of reality in our favor, as we work to accomplish true good in the world.

1. Create New Possibilities.

The actual reflects the possible. Nothing can become fully actual and existent in our world unless it was first possible. This is a basic and fundamental starting point for what philosophers call modality, or the logic of the possible and actual. But the converse of this proposition is also true. The possible springs forth from the actual. There are actual truths that underlie the full array of options for what is possible. In philosophy, we learn such things from a detailed study of both the logic, metaphysics, and epistemology of modality—which encompasses such primary notions as the possible, impossible, necessary, and actual. In the past half-century, a huge literature and understanding of modality has arisen. And despite the great complexities to be found amid it all, there are a few basic points that are simple to grasp and powerful to know.

How do we handle what's actual? How do we treat it? How do we see it and properly infer what it might lead to? A creative possibility thinker like Jobs is always looking for new angles and ways to develop actual things for the greater good. There is a sense of practical modality in which we can create new views of what's possible through the use of our intuition and imagination. This is a deep source of innovation. And it's an important implication of Einstein's famous allegation: "Imagination is more important than knowledge." Knowledge is primarily a relationship between the mind and what actually is. Imagination is a relationship between the mind and what possibly can be. Innovation happens in its highest forms through the use of intuition and imagination working on what's actual, to conjecture and realize, in the fullest sense of the word, what may be possible. The view of someone like Steve Jobs is that present reality is like a pliable potter's clay to be bent and molded into something strikingly new.

Whenever Jobs was told that anything was impossible, it didn't shake him in the least. It probably gave him an inner thrill. It indicated a new doorway of discovery. Jobs likely thought of himself as a creator of new possibilities. He wanted to be a maker of magic. He was certainly a pioneer of the possible. And this gave him a sense of self that both ennobled him and empowered him with a degree of confidence that's not often seen in the world—and especially among people thought of as at least mostly sane and rational. His certainty that something deemed impossible could be done, his utter and complete conviction in the availability of his vision to become an actual reality, amazed and often captivated the people around him, undermined their own felt certainties, and created instead new and powerful uncertainties, adumbrating otherwise unimagined options, and sometimes easing their anxieties, sparking their curiosity, and often stimulating them to try things they would never ordinarily have attempted.

When you think of yourself as a creator of new possibilities and communicate that well to others, then if they work hard and see results, it may happen that they, too, will eventually come to think of themselves in the same way, as well, and will take a pride in pioneering work that they otherwise could never have accomplished or experienced. Confidence can be contagious. Possibility thinking is powerful. When Jobs bent people's minds in new directions, he did so with such a sense of his own certainty as to crack through theirs, and introduce them to new and otherwise unseen horizons.

The potential future is always waiting for its moment in the spotlight of the actual present. Those who create the path to new possibilities will shape and bring forth the future that seems right to them, whether anyone else shares that vision or not. And that was something I believe was an immensely exciting, personal passion for Steve Jobs. He decided to become a creator of the future actual through broadening our sense of the present possible. And that's exactly what the greatest innovators in any field do.

2. Don't Let the Past Determine the Possible.

WHAT'S PAST CAN PREPARE US FOR WHAT'S POSSIBLE, BUT should never completely define it, or be assumed to determine it. Most people do today roughly what they did yesterday and the day before. They'll then do tomorrow a version of what they did today. Habit, or inertia, will rule. This is as true of companies as it is of the people in those organizations. The prominent twentieth century philosopher Ludwig Wittgenstein once remarked that the limits of your vision determine the limits of your world. If you spend your time looking through the rear view mirror, you can't see any place you haven't already been. You won't tend to do anything that you've not already done. You'll be trapped in a time that no longer exists except through its echoes in your heart and mind.

Any number of facts about the young Steve Jobs could have put the brakes on most people. High school grade point average: 2.65. College dropout. Sloppy smelly guy that pretty much no one wanted to meet with, or help to start a business—notably excepting, of course, the ever-trusting good friend and teddy-bear sidekick, Woz, the introverted nerdy guy down the street. Dreaming and hatching plans in his parents' garage with no money or means for getting it, and no real connections at all, his past did not predict a rosy future. But Steve refused to be defined completely by his past.

And yet, aspects of the past certainly stuck to him. From his personal history, and his emotional life in all contexts, it looks like he harbored deep down an unnecessary sense of parental abandonment stemming from the fact that he was given up for adoption as a baby. From everything I can tell, he wound up with wonderful adoptive parents and enjoyed a normal childhood. But, when he learned the full story of his start in life, he grieved. His birth parents didn't want him. They threw him away. They didn't believe he was worth keeping. That was how he seemed to have interpreted it. And this unfortunate way of thinking created a wound in him that would not heal. Because of it, he suffered deep and acute self-esteem issues. He had lingering fears of unworthiness. He felt a need to prove himself to the greatest degree possible, and even to a point that everyone around him would have called impossible. He had to bend reality to his will, for his ends, and to show that he was here in the world for a great reason— to make a huge positive difference like no one else. Because of all that, he became in many different ways monumentally self-absorbed, to the extent of what seems to have been extreme, malignant narcissism. A childhood narcissistic wound is always surrounded by a sort of inner scar tissue—psychological and emotional defense mechanisms whose purpose is to prevent certain forms of suffering from happening ever again. But the sad irony is that they just create new forms of suffering, both for the wounded individual and others around him. In this respect, Jobs could not and did not shake his past.

But the exceedingly strange alchemy of narcissism, at least as it operated along certain stretches of its spectrum, when combined with innate talent and opportunity, launched the drive that propelled Jobs in nearly all other ways to not let the past determine his future. This drive became almost magical, as it infected other people around him and caused them to join him in doing more than anyone would otherwise, at the time, have thought possible. Then, the more success he had, the more compelling the drive and the displays of confidence that went with it became in the lives of others. Doors opened. And new possibilities were in fact created and exploited for good.

Too many of us allow the past to hold us back in various respects, rather than using it to propel us forward in new ways. Steve was not immune to that, either. His origin story haunted him. And his first success at Apple for years restricted what he thought he could and should do. At Apple, he made and sold computers. He then founded NeXT to make and sell computers. He also bought Pixar, to make and sell computers. But he had to loosen the grip of the past in order to move into what would be his unexpected next forms of success with amazing software, incredible animated movies, and small new devices that took new technology into the flow of our lives in revolutionary ways.

Life is supposed to be a series of adventures. Despite the strong gravitational pull of the past, Steve Jobs certainly lived that view, from one adventure to the next. He had plenty of big setbacks, failures, and scares along the way, but until the very end he always bounced back to launch out into the next creative adventure. In his business vision and work endeavors, ultimately, he did not let the past determine the possible.

3. Expand Your Vision to Change Your World.

The book of Proverbs in the Hebrew Torah and the Christian Bible says, "Without a vision, the people perish." With too small a vision, we can easily stagnate and atrophy. With none at all, we can indeed simply fail. And with the wrong vision, we can pursue all the wrong things, waste our energies, and squander our time on earth. So therefore, in the light of this, some vital questions need asking. What's your vision? Is it really right for you? And is it big enough? Is your best vision for the future, and for what's possible, shared by the people who work with you? Does it drive and inspire what everyone does? If you lead an organization of any size, or any group of people, this can be crucially important. Do you communicate your best vision vividly enough and often enough and with sufficient passion? Do you reinforce it in as many ways as you can? Are you making sure that it's shared and deeply felt?

And let's even forget work for a second. What's your vision for your personal life? Do you have a vision for your family, or your closest circle of friends, or your community of neighbors regarding the good you can do together? How about your health? Does the past indeed determine the possible? Or are you launching out into new seas of potential and growth?

A few months after my fifty-eighth birthday, I decided that I needed to get into better physical shape. I wasn't in terribly bad shape at that time, but I was a little overweight, and it occurred to me that it would be nice to see if I could get stronger, in preparation for the coming years when such things would just be tougher. I had seen too many older men around me who seemed barely able to walk anymore. And so I began to hit the weights harder in my neighborhood gym. I had always worked out three or four days a week, for maybe twenty minutes at a time. But now I got serious. I worked out for two hours a day, every day, through an entire year and then cut back to an hour a day. And I expanded into exercises I had never before tried. For example, in my entire adult life, I had never done the classic exercise called "bench press," where you lie on a flat padded bench with a perpendicular horizontal bar above your chest, weights on each side, and gripping the bar, un-rack it, lifting it slightly up, and then you lower it down to your chest, and raise it up again until your elbows are straight—one repetition. The gym where I've exercised for over twenty years, whenever I'm home from speaking, has a Smith Machine for bench press: the long bar moves upward along a vertical guide, tilted slightly backward, and with a degree of resistance in addition to the weight of the bar and the additional weights that are on the bar. Unlike a free weight bench, you don't have to use as many small muscles to balance the weights, and you're tightly constrained into one and only one position for raising the bar, which is a countervailing consideration of difficulty. I'm going into all this detail for a reason.

The first day that I noticed someone benching, as we insiders say, it was a man about my age. He had thirty-five pounds of weight on each side of the long bar, and the bar itself on that machine weighted fifteen pounds. So he was lifting eighty-five pounds, total. I watched him do five or ten repetitions and thought, "I should try this." Then I did. And it felt good. So the next day, I did it again. Then I did it the next day, as well. No one had told me that it's best to take a few days off between sessions, or that you shouldn't really do an insane number of reps. So, very soon I was doing fifteen to twenty sets at each session, or more, and at least ten reps per set. But finally, I started pacing myself better and benching just two days a week. I quickly increased the weight to a hundred pounds, then a hundred and twenty, and then to a hundred and fifty. Within four months, I had younger guys working out with me, encouraging me and cheering me on, and I was up to two hundred pounds. One day, a friend who was also a trainer insisted that we put two hundred and forty pounds on the bar, and it felt like a house. If I had been asked on that day, or any previous day, "Will you ever lift over three hundred pounds?" my answer would have been, "Absolutely not—Are you crazy? That's impossible." I would not have hesitated to use the extreme concept of the impossible. And I would have had an ironclad confidence in that judgment. But at age sixty, I did it. I benched three hundred. And every few weeks, just to make sure I could still do it, I'd do it again. And in the years since that age, I've gone even higher. And now I don't know what my exact limits are. It's been a revelation. I worked hard. I didn't let the past define the possible. I bent reality, as I knew it. And as I write this, at age sixty-five, I'm stronger now than at any time in my life. That's another thing that, in past years, I probably would have thought utterly impossible, and maybe even absurd. And I would have been wrong.

I'm lucky to have a regular workout partner who helps me expand my vision of what's possible, and that's changed my world. Don Sharp is a younger man by over ten years, and is a lifelong surfer and skateboarder as well as a nearly lifetime serious weight lifter. I met him when he heard me across the room grunting, groaning, and even, at times, yelling out under the weight. He came up to me one day in the middle of my workout and commented, "You make more noise than anyone else in here."

I said, "You should hear me when I first get out of bed in the morning and walk to the bathroom." I was kidding, of course—a little. I had been through a few years of overall muscle stiffness in the morning that seemed it would never go away. But at a certain stage in life, you have to decide where the noise will be made. And in the gym is better. My heavy workouts totally ended the morning stiffness and pain. This man then said to me, "You're the only guy in here really pushing it, really trying. I want to be your workout partner." And so we started lifting together most days. And ever since, Don has pushed me to do things I probably would not have tried without his encouragement and confidence. "You're looking strong today. Let's go higher." His confidence would make me try a weight that I know I would never have done without his firm and eager suggestion.

One day, I got down on the bench with a particularly heavy weight on the bar and said, "I don't think I'll be able to do this one, but we'll see."

He shot back, "Well then, don't even try. You've got to have the right attitude or you're wasting your time." He was right.

Another day, we had just finished a heavy workout and were grabbing our gym bags and getting ready to leave the building. He said, "Well, I'll see you here tomorrow."

I was too tired to think about doing it all again the next day, and terribly bad weather was forecast. So, looking for an excuse to take a day off, and assuming I had a great one available, I said, "Well, I think it's supposed to rain really hard tomorrow."

He said, "Not in here." I had to laugh. That's an attitude that will not treat an excuse seriously, that always pushes forward and won't let up. And that's the attitude Steve Jobs always had at work. It's one I've now gained myself from my time around my friend Don. With that sort of approach, you redefine what's possible and get to places you'd otherwise never think of even trying to go.

My now extended experience in the gym has led me to realize that we all need such people as Don in our lives, professionally as well as personally. So then, here's a question: Do you have regular contact with someone who can help you to expand your vision of what's possible? You need it. Find such people. And here's another question that's of equal or even greater importance: Do you serve in this capacity for anyone else? Do you help your colleagues or friends to expand their sense of the possible?

I love it that my workout partner is named Don, which is a British term for a teacher, a tutor, guide, or mentor, at such places as the Universities of Oxford or Cambridge. We all need dons in our lives. But even more, we all need to be dons in other people's lives. We can help others as they help us to pioneer the possible.

I've come to think that it's fundamentally important to have both these things going on in your experience. And that was the position Steve Jobs was in, throughout most of his work years. He certainly served to expand other people's sense of the possible, with his famous Reality Distortion Field. But I believe that he also sought out people who could do that for him, through their books, and in person. In particular, a number of Hindu and Buddhist spiritual practitioners lured him forward into realms of unanticipated possibility that stretched him and inspired him and allowed him to do the creative, innovative things that he accomplished. When we don't have that going on in our lives, we artificially limit the good we can do. Whether you're a Christian or a Jew or a Hindu or Buddhist or Muslim, or an adherent of any of the world's other religious traditions, or whether you're just an open-minded seeker of truth, it's important to find people who can inspire you to broaden your sense of the possible, because only then can you properly approach the actual in such a way as to change our world for the better.

8

Impute

And the same is true of all other things; they have, each of them, an end and a special excellence.
Socrates

In 1979, a man Steve Jobs greatly admired, the engineer and early Apple investor Mike Markkula, wrote Steve a memo in which the odd and almost quirky word 'impute' was used as a directive, or even an imperative. And it lit a fire in him that would never go out.

Impute. It can take a bit of thought, initially, to get your head around this strange sounding one-word philosophical guideline. First, a rather prolix way of explaining it: To impute a quality or characteristic or attribute to an item or person or organization is to represent that thing or individual or company as having that quality, by implication or association. Or, in a related sense, it's to act in such a way as to imply that the quality in question characterizes that entity. For example, if you've praised a hotel at which you've stayed as perhaps the greatest in the world, you don't then need to comment explicitly on the quality of their room service—you've already implicitly imputed excellence to it, as it's generally known to be a salient component of top lodging quality. And, typically, in such a hotel, every employee realizes that everything they do in the sight or hearing of a guest "imputes" a level of quality to the establishment as a whole. So they're always on top of their game, never wanting to impute anything less than stellar excellence to their hospitality enterprise. One dictionary defines imputation as the assigning of a value to something by inference from the value of the products or processes to which that thing contributes. And this at least hints well at what we need to understand.

So what exactly, then, could Mike Markkula or Steve Jobs mean when they tell leaders and associates in a somewhat oracular way always to impute? They're seeking to remind us that everything we do says something, signals something, and so *imputes* something about the overall quality of our enterprise, our business, and our products. We should then take charge of this reality and use it with intention.

1. Always signal greatness.

In the smallest things we do, we should remember that we're imputing a level of quality to other aspects of our business, to our overall endeavor, and, indeed, to our individual and organizational brand. And we should therefore proceed, in every detail, in such a way as to do this both deliberately and well. Every aspect of the packaging of an Apple product had to be designed to speak of high quality, drama, and elegance of design, and had to contribute in the right way to the customer experience, if even when simply getting the device out of its box and setting it up at home.

Whether we're aware of it or not, we send cultural messages and value signals in everything we do—in what we wear, how we act, where we go, what we say, and in our choice of associates. Little things can convey big messages. And that fact is exploited all the time by advertisements for luxury watches, cars, homes, and clothing. My wife and daughter were talking not long ago about an unusual schoolyard scene they had witnessed in recent years many times. They said that some of the young preschool mothers picking up their five-year-old children at the end of the class day seemed dressed more for clubbing than for kindergarten. And a small subset of those would occasionally show up looking more like off-duty, high end escorts, than preschool moms. Their choice of clothing was sending signals, and perhaps they were acutely aware of this—but then again, maybe not. Extremely bright, skin-tight shorts paired with sky-high heels and barely-there blouses definitely attract a degree of attention in an elementary or pre-school setting. They impute. You can certainly be a fan of any of these items in the proper context without necessarily admiring the imputation that takes place in quite a different and contrasting set of circumstances. A form of dress imputes. The packaging of a product, or the presentation of items within a retail store, imputes. The way we control imputation can vary with circumstances, and sometimes has to be extremely sensitive to the matter of situational context in order to operate appropriately, and in accordance with everything we desire to stand for, communicate, or espouse.

Steve Jobs believed that absolutely everything about Apple and his other ventures, NeXT and Pixar, should in every detail, however small, impute the highest quality, and in fact, nothing short of maximal greatness. Less would never be acceptable. In addition, he always wanted his consumer-friendly computers at Apple to signal exactly that: their comfortable friendliness. Everything about Apple would be great, and fun, and cool. Everything would be exciting and world changing. Even the smallest thing would impute.

2. Remember: Everything Matters.

One of my favorite movies in the nineties was *Flatliners*, a film starring Kiefer Sutherland, Julia Roberts, Kevin Bacon, William Baldwin, and Oliver Platt—quite a winning array of young actors at the time. The story was that a group of medical students were hearing accounts of near death experiences reported by people who had undergone cardiac arrest and then had been resuscitated after several minutes without a heartbeat. Many of these patients talked later about leaving their bodies, moving down a long dark tunnel and emerging into a beautiful setting somewhere beyond, where they felt great love and acceptance, and then they experienced a sudden realization that it was not yet their time and they had to return to their bodies. The med students were fascinated by these tales, but were equally bothered by the fact that the patients reporting such things weren't scientifically trained observers whose perceptions and descriptions could be trusted for accuracy and clarity. Was there real evidence for life after death to be gathered in such a way? One of their group, they decided, should go under and seek to have such an experience, with his or her heart stopped for the maximal amount of time possible, short of permanent damage, and then be brought back to see if there would be similar observations made that they all could trust at a new level.

You know how these things then play out. Kiefer Sutherland's character was the volunteer, and the procedure went as planned, except of course for last second dramatics leading us to doubt whether the others would indeed be able to resuscitate him or not. Spoiler Alert: He comes back. And he has had experiences while dead, by all typical physical standards, and presumably in a state when he should have been unable to experience anything. Later in the movie, if I recall correctly, the character played by Kiefer is talking on a phone, and someone makes a remark to him, presumably about something not really mattering, and his response is a completely urgent rejoinder and exclamation like: "*Don't you realize that … EVERYTHING MATTERS*?"

In an era of "Don't Sweat The Small Stuff, and: It's All Small Stuff," we have here what can seem to be a very different perspective. But appearances can be deceiving. I think the popular advice about remaining sweat-free, at its most insightful, is an encouragement to not let things get to us, bother us, worry us, or unnecessarily keep us awake at night. It advises us to calm down, avoid unnecessary anxiety, and so treat everything, in this respect, as if it's small, inconsequential, and even, in the cosmic scheme of things, trivial. After all, the biggest of perspectives can make almost anything look small. But it's one thing not to allow small matters to unhinge us—a piece of advice that Steve Jobs would often have done well to follow—and yet, it's another thing altogether to think that details don't matter, or that there is anything in this world that's of absolute insignificance. It would take much more than a breezy slogan to even begin to justify that view. And I rather suspect that Kiefer's character was right.

Steve Jobs seemed to believe that in the arenas of design, product quality, and the customer experience everything matters. His life would have been much better, I think, and the lives of those around him would have been much easier, if he had also allowed this philosophy to guide his own actions, attitudes, emotions, words, volume and tone of voice, especially as they impinged on the feelings of others. Whenever he lived this insight, he saw wonderful results. Wherever he was blind to it, he created problems. And these problems, I believe, actually reduced his effectiveness and success as a leader, and as a human being. Imagine what he could have been. Or perhaps that's one of those extreme possibilities that can be nearly impossible to envision.

3. Details Communicate How You Care.

People notice details. We especially tend to pay attention to the small things in commercial transactions. The more expensive the transaction is, the most alert we tend to be. If something done in a business setting, even the least little thing, implicitly says, “We don’t really care about what we’re doing; we’re just going through the motions,” then, as potential or actual customers, we take notice. And then we most often do anything we can to avoid giving any more business to those people. But, of course, if little things declare instead, “We really care about details,” and, “You, as a customer, matter to us,” we notice that, too. And because it’s so rare these days, this will likely help turn us into raving fans.

Ultimately, caring about the details in a business matter, and especially in reference to a customer experience, means caring about the people affected. And it’s a universal rule of human psychology that people are attracted to people who care. If we care about our customers, we should make sure to show that in all the details of what we do. And if instead we don’t care, we should be in a different business altogether. And meanwhile, to add something that many of our mothers would have said long ago, we should be ashamed of ourselves.

Experts in communication have concluded that the vast majority of what’s conveyed through a communicative interaction isn’t the content of whatever might have been explicitly said, but is rather the signification of all the behavior involved. For our own survival and best interests, we have had to become carefully attuned to what behavior conveys or imputes, beyond the manifest content of what people say to us or we say to them. And it’s never a good conclusion to reason, “Well, if people pay that much attention to details and need to see in those details that we care, we should at least contrive ways to manipulate the details well enough to make it look as if we care, even if we don’t.” Most people can tell the difference. Deceptive contrivance tends to become glaringly obvious. And in addition, you would have added the sin of deceit to that of indifference, which is a great way to make people genuinely angry and resentful.

Real care, real passion, and real commitment come across with all the hallmarks of authenticity. This is not one of those matters where you can fake it till you make it. If the details are suffering in your business, or in your own work, you need to go back and relight the flame of real care and genuine concern for what you're doing and for all the people you serve.

My wife puts vegetables into sauces, soups, and stews that no one will ever see or identifiably detect by taste. But they add to the great depth of flavor we'll enjoy, and they provide an extra layer of nutrition and thus a boost to our health that we can always use. Her attention to every aspect of a dish imputes her care and concern. And that same imputation is to be detected in everything else she does, as well. Love imputes by habit. And so does greatness. People who know how I edit a novel are typically amazed at the time I spend analyzing commas and word choice. And still, I'm far from perfect. But I try, because I know that every detail matters. And I want each word and punctuation mark to impute my wholeheartedness in care for the story and the reader.

My daughter is a great photographer and book cover designer. The smallest tonality of color matters to her. And it makes a discernible difference. Vic Gundotra, a man who has worked at Google and helped get the company into social media, has told an interesting story about such a detail. He says that one Sunday morning, during a religious service he was attending on January 6, 2008, he got a call on his cell phone, which vibrated for his attention, but he didn't answer. He later saw that the CEO of Apple, Steve Jobs, had left a message that he had something urgent to discuss, and asked him to call his home number. Gundotra says he returned the call right away. And here's what he writes about the conversation that transpired. I'll let him tell the story.

"Hey Steve—this is Vic," I said. "I'm sorry I didn't answer your call earlier. I was in religious services, and the caller ID said unknown, so I didn't pick up."

Steve laughed. He said, "Vic, unless the Caller ID said 'GOD,' you should never pick up during services."

I laughed nervously. After all, while it was customary for Steve to call during the week, upset about something, it was unusual for him to call me on Sunday and ask me to call his home. I wondered what was so important.

"So Vic, we have an urgent issue, one that I need addressed right away. I've already assigned someone from my team to help you, and I hope you can fix this tomorrow," said Steve. "I've been looking at the Google logo on the iPhone and I'm not happy with the icon. The second O in Google doesn't have the right yellow gradient. It's just wrong and I'm going to have Greg fix it tomorrow. Is that okay with you?"

Gundotra reports that this conversation taught him something important about leadership and passion and attention to detail. "It was a lesson I'll never forget," he wrote. "CEOs should care about details. Even shades of yellow. On a Sunday." (Blog post on Google+, August 25, 2011) As the groundbreaking German-American modern architect Ludwig Mies van der Rohe famously said, "God is in the details." And as others have added: So is the devil. And so was Steve.

The best craftsmen are known for their apparently infinite attention to detail. A fact that always impressed young Steve was that great cabinetmakers care as much about the back of the cabinet as the front. They expend effort to finish a side of the piece of furniture that most people will never see. The same is true of the best watchmakers. They will finish the inner components of a fine watch with great care for aesthetic detail as well as for function, even if the owner of the watch will never have the opportunity to take off the back and look at the parts of the mechanism. To a master craftsman, everything matters. There are no unimportant details. Everything imputes the concern for quality that governs the entire process. You show how much you care as an expression of who you are.

And that reveals a truth about imputation. Whatever we do sends signals, even when no one seems to be recognizing or receiving those signals. Masters put quality into every detail, because they are masters, whether any given detail is noticed or not. And that's the level of concern for greatness that Steve Jobs wanted everyone around him to embody, all the time. Imputation isn't a simple matter of marketing, but of inherent care. It may even be that in lavishing the best attention on every detail, the signal we send that's most important is the one received in our own hearts.

If you ever purchase a well-crafted Swiss or German watch, or any high-end timepiece that's crafted here in America, you'll likely discover to your delight that all the packaging is lavishly beautiful and of very high quality. It imputes the care, superior craftsmanship, refinement, and even greatness to be found in the product itself. Go to a top hotel or spa. You'll most likely find their version of the same principle on display all around. Everything imputes quality at its best. This is a principle that Jobs understood deeply, and that he used throughout his work life. You can't expect your customers to care about you unless you're clearly communicating, in all the details, that you care about them and are always giving them the very best you can. And then, great things indeed can happen.

9

Push For Perfection

When he's serious, he sows in fitting soil and practices husbandry, and is satisfied if, in eight months, the seeds which he has sown arrive at perfection.
Socrates

It was a remarkable time for ancient Athens. Other places would later go through such periods—Rome, Alexandria, Florence, Paris, and perhaps even Silicon Valley. In that first hotbed of world changing creative thought, Socrates seemed to be everywhere. He would go around relentlessly examining other people's opinions to razor away falsehood, confusion, and imperfection. He would test ideas, ferret out ungrounded assumptions, and seek to dig deeper. He inspired some and aggravated others to no end. But his quest seemed noble, regardless of his occasionally frustrating methods. His aim seemed to be uncovering the hidden ideals behind any vitally important concept for living well. His student Plato made that quest even more explicit. In connection with any flawed reality in our world, his developed view was that there is a perfect version conceivable, a flawless counterpart, form, or ideal model that can be an object of contemplation and proper desire. From this point of view, the philosopher's mindset seeks to find the ultimate ideals, the true perfections behind the rough actualities of our world, and to focus our thoughts at that lofty height. Steve Jobs was on a roughly analogous quest with any product he envisioned.

Great products arise when lofty ideals inspire creative and practical real-world solutions. Jobs was known for interrupting and delaying a project launch at the last minute if he wasn't completely satisfied with the item in all its contours, features, and functions—or, to put it in his own words, if he didn't love it. At least one person who worked closely with him has said that he had a keen and even extraordinary ability to spot defects. If he was in any way haunted by a sense that something wasn't right, or that there was some sort of a flaw, even if he couldn't at first pinpoint the exact problem, he learned never to ignore his intuition, but to take his concern seriously and continue to ponder the possibilities until he could hit on precisely the change that was needed. He was a firm believer that we should strive never to allow the merely good to supplant the ideal best.

In the cultural folk wisdom of our day, we're most often told that perfectionists never get anything done. But Steve was a perfect counter-example to that claim. Aspirational perfectionists who are sensitive to the realities and demands of their context tend to invest the extra energy, creativity, and care that it takes for truly spectacular results.

Of course, there are times when a job or a specific task is constrained by various limits of time, energy, financial resources, need, and available contributors. And time is often the ultimate pressure. Something has to be done now, or in forty-eight hours, or within the week. Otherwise, a disaster will unfold. People have told me that, under such constraints, they don't have the luxury of perfection. But I would suggest to the contrary that Steve's approach can still find a suitable application in a fully context-relevant way. Under whatever pressures you face, you have to adjust and try to provide, within the restricted sphere of possibility you confront, not a mediocre solution, or a merely good enough one, but still one that's great, or best, or even perfect for the situation.

Perfection is, by its very nature, an ideal or limit concept that must be applied properly, like any other idea. And it was the conviction of Jobs that it should always be used in our work. He was convinced that nothing short of this lofty aspiration was ever acceptable. Ironically, he was often far from perfect in his pursuit of perfection, but it was still an absolute ideal that drove him and goaded him to the great things that he indeed was able to do all through his career.

"Wait," you might be thinking. "Slow down. Perfectionism is itself a real problem. It's not a tool to solve problems or create great things. And it can be such a big, persistent personal difficulty as to require intensive psychological therapy." Ironically, on this common view, perfectionism is itself a flaw, or imperfection in human attitudes and motivations. If this is anything like your first thought in response to the topic of this chapter and the principle we'll be examining, I want to assure you that I understand your concern, but I also want to suggest that attending to a simple distinction here can make all the difference. And the distinction in question will be just the particularization of a general move in philosophy.

The proper response to this common concern is to start out by noting that almost any "ism" in human life or thought can be a problem. But because sexism is bad, we shouldn't therefore have a problem with sex itself. Right? Again, racism is bad. But race is perfectly fine. Perfectionism, as a problem, is a misplaced or improperly enacted pursuit of flawlessness that causes the perfectionist to hesitate, refrain, and freeze up with anything short of the envisioned ideal he carries in his head. It's not a mindset that elevates, pushes, and ennobles, but one that tyrannizes and oppresses its sufferer.

There was another ideal that always impressed Steve Jobs: Great companies ship. They don't just envision and design and forever tinker. They actually bring new products to completion and ship them out to consumers. Companies like Apple aren't just intellectual or artistic think tanks. They can't encourage idle ideals, or any psychology that gets in the way of real accomplishment. The attitude that we call perfectionism comes about when a healthy ideal spins out of control and becomes onerous, and even a source of fear and loathing. And that's not what we're talking about here at all. The philosophical principle most relevant to our concern is that of functionality: The value of anything in our lives is related to how it functions. A push for perfection can function in such a way as to create a company like Apple and its many astonishing innovations, or it can function very differently in the pathological way that shuts people down. When we do it right, the Steve Jobs push for perfection can lead to amazing results.

1. Good Enough Never Is.

Jobs often said of competitors that their problem was that they were good, or that their products were good, and that's never good enough. Great was always his goal. And as we know, the phrase "Insanely Great" conveyed his top guiding principle and ideal.

If you look at the history of his work on product design, and even at how he played a crucial role in radically revising the movie script of *Toy Story*, taking it from the dark place where executives at Disney apparently wanted it and moving it to the fun, light-hearted, entertaining, and engaging film that it eventually became, you can begin to see how the classic Jobs push was always for a version of perfection. And perhaps that should be our own push, as well.

"But," you may say, "Nothing's perfect!" Or: "Perfection is impossible!" Or: "We simply live in an imperfect world!" Or even: "The very concept of perfection is a metaphysically idealized, tyrannical, and alienating abstraction"—in which case, you've obviously taken too many philosophy courses. But this form of objection in at least a simple form is common, and it's understandable.

In order to evaluate this very natural form of pushback, we need to draw a clear distinction between two statements:

(A) Nobody's perfect.
and,
(B) Nothing's perfect.

I submit to you that in the world today, (A) is true but (B) is false. The word 'perfect' comes from two Latin roots that together mean, "thoroughly complete; fully made." It's normally used, as a concept, with the implication that the thing deemed perfect has no imperfections, no flaws, and no untoward rough edges of any sort, physical or metaphorical that could, even in principle, be improved on or removed to attain a result better or greater than what it already is. The perfect item does not in any way fall short of its ideal realization. That's what perfection is.

In order to know that Proposition (A) is true, which we can call The Doctrine of Human Imperfection, we don't need to examine every human being on earth and everyone who has ever existed. And that's a good thing. Who would have the time? A survey of wives, and probably the female gender generally, would be enough for us to conclude that at least half the human race is imperfect—and, yeah, not that half. They'd tell us plenty of stories about the men they had known, and universal patterns would soon develop. But: What about all the other human beings out there with pretty impressive qualities? There are surely saints among us as well as sinners. What's to prevent some people from having attained the pinnacle of perfection?

The simple answer to this question is: The possibility of further growth. No human being can be perfect because every single human being, and certainly all married ones, however exalted and far along the growth curve that any given individual might be, each and every one of us is still a person who could grow some more, learn a bit more, become wiser, and in principle if not in practice, be more. That's why none of us can ever be complete or perfect, in the most comprehensive and literal sense.

And when you ask the real saints, should you ever come across one, they'll be the first to admit it. They feel their imperfections. They know their flaws. They realize how far they have yet to go. They look forward to more growth.

So, proposition (A), the Doctrine of Human Imperfection, let's allow, is true. Nobody's perfect. But I think that, by contrast, Proposition (B)—what we can call The Dogma of Universal Imperfection—the statement that nothing is perfect, is just false.

If you're tempted to think otherwise, then let me ask you a simple question. What's wrong with the mathematical number two? If it's imperfect, it has to have some flaw, some mar, or some incompleteness. But what would that be? Does such a question elicit a quick answer? I hope not. There's no such feature that the number two has. It has no flaws. It's perfect just as it is. If you're more clever than necessary, you might be thinking, "Well it could be three, and greater." But numbers are essentially what they are, and thus such an alternative of growth or greatness is logically and metaphysically impossible. And if just one thing is perfect, The Dogma of Universal Imperfection is false.

"Oh, but that's just because the number two is an abstract object," you might protest, if you're a little more sophisticated than the average Joe. And then you might go on to doubt the propriety of even saying literally at all that such a thing as a number exists, voting with the Nominalist camp rather than the Platonists on this issue. Whether you have such doubts or not, it can still be a good thing to voice at a cocktail party, right before you take your leave to go get another drink. I tend to think that numbers do exist in an appropriately robust way, as do other abstract objects, and are therefore just as much to be counted in the inventory of reality, so to speak, as rocks and trees and people. Perhaps they have even more of a right to be counted. But we won't fight that battle here. We can just go to another example.

What's wrong with a given pure water molecule, a simple sample of H2O? What could be its flaw, or imperfection? I don't think this question admits of an identifying answer. A pure instance of H2O has no flaws, for what it is. It's complete, or fully made. So, it's perfect. But again, this example is about as far from a business context as you might imagine, unless, of course, you bottle and sell the pure liquid of life. So I have a much better example.

Have you ever been struggling with a business problem and someone came to you with a solution and you smiled or even laughed aloud and said, "That's perfect!" You may have had such an experience many times. I certainly have. Were you always and inevitably wrong? Surely: not. I submit to you that, in a particular context, at a particular time, and for a particular purpose, a form of perfection is possible, and that it's sometimes attained, however rare or uncommon this might be. But the frequency or relative commonness of perfection doesn't matter, only its occasional actuality does. One instance of it is enough to prove that The Dogma of Universal Imperfection is false.

And here's an interesting thought. How often have you heard people say, "Hey, nothing's perfect"? I'd guess that you've likely heard this said quite a few times in your life. And it's ordinarily an attempted excuse for something's being less than what was wanted or expected. "Nothing's perfect." But I invite you to think about this for a moment. We have here what may actually be the most common excuse there is. "Why get on my case? Nothing's perfect." Or: "Hey. Cut me a little slack here. Nothing's perfect." But now, contemplate the matter a bit more deeply. If The Dogma of Universal Imperfection were true, then this excuse would be—wait for it ... and let's have a drum roll, please—*the perfect excuse,* in which case, something would indeed be perfect, namely it, as an excuse, and therefore it would be false, and not true—which is certainly an imperfection. So, if we try to assume that it's true, it flips on us and ends up false, which, in the logic of truth and falsehood means that we've shown, by a method call *Reductio Ad Absurdum* ("Reducing To Absurdity") that it can't possibly be true. And, yeah, sometimes it's super fun to be a philosopher. You're welcome.

Bonus Philosophical Reflection: Why stop now? People throughout history have often contemplated a deep question when considering in a metaphysical mood the night sky, or the wonders of creation more generally. The question is this: Why is there something rather than nothing? The philosopher Martin Heidegger called this wonderment the most disturbing metaphysical enigma. The best recent book on the question, in my opinion, is a study that looks at it from every angle, and is called, *Why Does The World Exist?* The author is Jim Holt.

Maybe we have a new spin on Hamlet's "To be or not to be—that is the question." Why should there be anything? Why indeed is there something rather than nothing? Why is there Being rather than universal Nonbeing? Why is there a universe, or perhaps a multiverse of universes, rather than an infinite all-encompassing void? And there's an implication of Hamlet's question, as it's applied on this biggest of scales, that may be surprising. When you pose this great and haunting metaphysical query, you appear to be assuming that, at least in principle, instead of a vast cosmos full of entities and forces, particles, waves, and laws, there could have been the option of uninterrupted nothingness, instead. And, given that assumption, you want to know how in the world, or out of the blue, we got our current and ancient alternative of apparently profuse existence, rather than the other theoretically available and totally empty option zero, in which scenario even the number zero itself would not exist (*per impossible, horribile dictu,* alas and alack).

But if The Dogma of Universal Imperfection ("Nothing's perfect") is false, and moreover could not possibly be true, then it's necessarily false—false in every possible set of circumstances. But if "Nothing's perfect" is always false, then "Something's perfect" is always true, or true in every possible set of circumstances. Now, hang with me for a moment and one more question.

We have to revisit our underlying assumption here. Could, in fact, nothing ever have existed? Only if nothingness was, or could be, in itself, perfect. And this is because that, remember, something perfect would have to exist in every possible overall set of circumstances, as we've just seen. So if nothing existed, it—the nothingness itself—would have to be perfect. And that seems odd in the extreme to suppose, or to conclude. Remember, in the case of The Doctrine of Human Imperfection, we ruled out any normal human being enjoying a state of perfection, on the grounds alone that, in every such case, there is always a possibility for improvement. If no universe or even a single particle of matter had ever come into existence, and universal nothingness alone prevailed—no things, no forces, nothing—then wouldn't there at least be a possibility for improvement in that state of affairs—for example, if one good thing were to exist, instead of just nothing? And if there is a possibility of improvement, the state of nothingness is not perfect, and so it could never have even possibly been The Full Story. We philosophers like to use capital letters, the famed upper case, for Extremely Profound Insights.

To put it another way, perfection is completeness, lacking nothing. So if nothingness were perfect, it wouldn't lack anything. But nothingness is precisely the state of lacking everything. So it would not be perfect. But as we have seen, in every possible total scenario, there has to be something perfect. So, on this simple reasoning, there could not have existed a universal condition of nothingness. Therefore, there had to exist at least one thing. And it had to be, of course, perfect. Why? Because, again, if "Nothing's perfect" is always false, then it follows that "Something's perfect" is always true. That's where we get the conclusion that there would have to exist, in reality, at least one thing. But if there were in existence only one thing, then it—that thing—would have to be perfect. But then, would it have to be perfect in only one way, or in many ways, or in all ways? The latter possibility would be what theists throughout the centuries have referred to, at the height of their conceptual sophistication, as a Maximally Perfect Being, or a God of the highest sort.

There is no simple deductive argument here that would compel a theological conclusion from all rational people. There are, however, hints regarding perfection that can lead us in a certain direction. And no, it's not the conclusion that "There is a God and He Was Steve Jobs." But these are deep waters that I think both attracted and perplexed Steve himself. And even though this is perhaps a little bit of a tangent for us, it's a philosophically illuminating one, so let's go with it for a moment more.

Jobs rejected the reality of a creator God, as traditionally depicted in the West, when he was a teenager and the classic problem of evil first occurred to him: How could a good and powerful creator permit all the evil and suffering in the world? Of course, young Steve wasn't the first person ever to ask this question. And many other very smart people throughout history have not only asked it, but have strenuously sought answers. And, as a result, they've come up with some deep perspectives that likely never occurred to the teenage Jobs. But, despite his adolescent rejection of classic western religion and theism (the belief in an ultimate creative source of all, or a maximally perfect being), he also seemed haunted throughout his adulthood with the issue, and could not quite settle into an easy embrace of the atheism that once had appealed so strongly to his young mind. Did his fundamental attraction to the idea of perfection, at least in design and technology, play any role in what appears to be a subsequent lifelong wonderment as to whether there is perhaps something more than our physical plane of existence? Such a wonder or curiosity seemed to be manifest both in his reading habits and in at least a few occasional conversations, especially during the time of his final illness when he felt confronted with the great unknown and the vast uncertainties that surround us. But really, we don't know much about his final inner attitudes and suspicions regarding such an ultimate philosophical issue. And it would be a stretch to speculate on this, as much as I would otherwise like to do so. I will say that it clearly seems Jobs was so impressed with the power of mind or spirit, as he experienced it, and with its ability to form and mold physical things, bringing new creations to be, that he was haunted with a sense of a creative Otherness beyond our physical domain that could perhaps form and mold on a more fundamental and grand scale. He may even have seen worldly perfections as hints or signs of greater perfections that are now mostly beyond our ken. And some say that in his very last moments of life, he may have caught sight of where he might eventually find his answers to such questions. We'll comment some more about that later.

But the fact that's relevant to our current position in the examination of what sort of philosophy Steve Jobs operated from is that perfection as an attainable ideal loomed large in the sensibilities of this creative genius and goaded him on, guiding him to the great results that he wanted—again, and again. It was a deep conviction in his soul that perfection should be sought. And he insisted that everyone working with him share this vital quest.

2. Perfection Takes Persistence.

Unless you're the number two, a pure molecule of water, or a divine creator of all, perfection doesn't come easy. And that's one reason Jobs pushed himself and everyone around him so hard. The highest aims require the most arduous efforts. Perfection takes commitment. And often, it takes commitment at a nearly crazy level. But one of the greatest slogans of highly successful people is: Do what's right, not what's easy. As the Roman poet Horace once said, "The greater the difficulty, the greater the glory." Persistence matters. Apparently ridiculous levels of persistence can pay off in ridiculously wonderful ways.

The English word 'persistence' comes from two Latin roots—a verb meaning, 'to stand' and a particle, *per*, meaning, in this case, "through." To persist is to stand firm and unbowed through problems, difficulties, and confusions, to keep standing and fighting or working through any challenges you face. It's a strong continuation concept. Its embodiment takes determination and the quality often called grit—a characteristic recently found by psychologists to be one of the most important personal attributes for attaining success at anything hard and worthwhile. We have catchy sayings like "Winners never quit, and quitters never win," because they capture aspects of a truth most of us have experienced it in our lives. Steve Jobs wanted to win, and he refused to quit working at something, or to even allow anyone else around him to quit working at it, until they had attained the insanely great results he was always stalking.

Barry Lam, the Chairman, CEO, and founder of Taiwan-based Quanta Computer, an Apple laptop supplier, once wrote of Jobs:

> "He was very demanding. Best product, best design, best quality, and best delivery. He wanted perfect product, perfect quality, and perfect operation. We had to improve a lot to meet his requirements. In this way he improved the whole operations because of his tough requirements."

A drive for any sort of perfection can be a powerful force in an organizational context, and deployed properly, can lead to all sorts of improvements, even in ways never intended or even anticipated.

A persistent quest for perfection has consequences. If it's implemented well, it can enrich and enliven everything and everyone around it. But of course, if done badly, it can also be a perversely tyrannical thing. In accordance with what I like to call "The Double Power Principle," we can say that like almost anything in business or life, such a commitment can have great power for good or great power for ill, depending on how we use it. Functioning properly, a quest for perfection can yield amazing results.

For Jobs, winning wasn't ever a matter of money or market share. When reminded of the competition's market dominance in desktop computers or software availability, he'd often say, in his endearing and poetical way, "I'd rather lose than suck." He didn't want to win the wrong game. To him, what mattered was the greatness of the software and the hardware and, ultimately, equal greatness in the retailing of it and any servicing of it—in short, all things having to do with the customer and the customer's experience. And here's the irony of it all: The more progress you make in giving the customer insanely great products and experiences, the more you set a new standard for competitors and, in the customer's mind, for your future endeavors. You will then have cultivated a customer base that will always expect more and better, and even what's newly astonishing.

And that brings with it a big challenge. You have to keep getting better. It's an ongoing quest that never ends. "But wait," someone could object. "If you've already done something perfect, how can you set the bar higher? There's nothing greater than perfection." But there is always the challenge of perfection in some new or bigger, or more audacious product or service. There's always another new challenge of greatness, or of perfection. You have to persist in doing more great things and, in fact, increasingly greater things. It's one sort of challenge to perfect something small, or to attain perfection in a task easily completed. It's another to create the same quality in something big or complex and daunting. The key, though, is to see this dynamic of ascending expectations not as a burden but as an exciting challenge and call to adventure. And that's why it's important, again, to have a vision you're passionate about, like changing the world or making life better for people. You need, in an ongoing way, and as a sustainable commitment, an inner drive to continue to set the bar higher, and then to rise up to the new level of expectation that you then still keep raising—which leads to our third point.

3. Yesterday's Great is Tomorrow's Average.

Here's an image I love and a story I've told many times in different contexts. It conveys a universal insight for our adventures in life. Imagine you're out in the woods on a hike and that you're leading a group of people. Suppose you're in very hilly area and that, as a group, you set it as your goal to get to the highest point around you, from which you'll be able to survey all the surrounding terrain. From where you stand, one hill looks to be the highest—let's call it Hill A—and so, you climb it. You lead the group up the side, you trip, you fall, you help each other, you struggle some more, and finally you reach the summit, from which vantage point you can now see a much higher nearby Hill B, a peak that previously was blocked from view. At this juncture, let me ask a question. If you currently stand atop Hill A, and the highest spot around is now clearly the top of Hill B, what's the first thing you'll have to do in order to attain your true goal of getting to the highest spot? The answer, of course, is simple: Go downhill. And when you as leader suggest this to the group, what's everyone going to say? This is almost universal. They'll say, "What do you mean, we have to go downhill? It took us a long time to get up Hill A! We can see a lot from where we already are! Hill A is great! Why don't we just stay here and enjoy the view we have?"

There are so many people and companies, and even families, stuck on top of Hill A because no one wants to go downhill—which metaphorically represents changing what you've most recently been doing, leaving aside your current state of success for a new challenge, and getting out of your most recent comfort zone. I love the verticality of the image, because if your goal is to get to the highest point and, in order to do that, you now have to first go downhill, it will initially look, in the first stage of your progress, as if it isn't progress at all and you're getting farther from your true goal. But this is a great representation of a universal movement that's involved in going from good to better to best—a necessary transitional stage from a first success to a greater one, by way initially of a big downhill segment in between. There are valleys between the hills, where your skill set may suddenly seem outdated, your sense of competence may fall off, or your confidence, or the familiarity that's often involved in the efficiency that can accompany the known. Something will drop off when you leave a known success for a newer challenge, and you'll have to adjust as you hope eventually to move higher. Those who are not willing to go downhill and insist on staying at the level of their first success—in effect, thereafter confined to Hill A—are inevitably destined to be passed by and left behind by competitors who are eager for the new challenge.

The story's scenario can also be taken as the starting point for a nice illustration of the truth that in changing times, with many in the market striving to be better, yesterday's great will be tomorrow's average. The imperative implied by this is then that of continuous improvement, innovation, invention, and discovery, spurred forth by a quest for peak excellence and even perfection. If I were ever asked what my single most important life realization has been as a philosopher, I would probably offer the simple perspective encompassed in one sentence: Life is supposed to be a series of adventures. Each one should lead on to the next. And in the world of business, these adventures should be about growth and improvement from good to excellent, and always in quest of what within the context is perfect.

The pace of biological evolution is in most respects extremely slow. Cultural evolution is vastly faster, by a huge difference. Technological evolution, of course, is much more rapid still, by an even wider margin. In a time when technology centrally and crucially affects us all, we need to keep going, growing, and adapting, all the while setting our sights on greater attainments, loftier aspirations, and continually raising the bar on our own expectations. When there is no going back, we need to embrace going forward in all the best ways.

There's probably no more important lesson from the innovations made by Steve Jobs and his associates than his relentless efforts to make the product better. He was not always successful at every stage along the way, and struggled with many obstacles on each path he traveled, with more than a few of his own making, but he was persistent. He eventually knew when to step away from a device that he couldn't perfect and sell at the level needed, and when to turn his attention either to a new product, or to new features and changes for an existent product. He wanted to dazzle and delight. And he did everything he could to surround himself with other people who shared that same commitment—which is the concern of our next principle, and next chapter. The best work comes only from the best contributors.

10

Tolerate Only "A" Players

For which are the greatest and best?
Socrates

This is going to be a very short chapter. And that's because the principle we need to explore here is so straightforward and simple. Any business leader who is concerned with hiring people and partnering up with others has one thing always to keep in mind, what Steve Jobs called "A" players. The imperative was to: Find them. Hire them. Put them in the right places. Keep them on the team. Those are the demands of excellence. Nothing else will work, without the right people in place. It's all, in the beginning and in the end, about "A" players. This paragraph alone could be the chapter, but I do have some stories and philosophical principles to mention that can help.

1. You Deserve The Best. So Do They.

In his excellent book, *The Second Coming* of Steve Jobs, Alan Deutschman writes about what happened to Jobs when he was forced out of Apple in 1985 and started the company that he called, simply, "NeXT." Deutschman writes:

> "Steve was *fanatical* about hiring the best people. He said that they would interview one hundred people for every one whom they finally chose." (45)

Deutschman goes on to say that Steve would often fill positions with ridiculously overqualified candidates, mentioning the example of a brilliant Harvard graduate named Alex who was an art collector and highly esteemed by his colleagues. He had risen to the middle ranks at Apple, but was hired at NeXT to be a receptionist. Jobs could do such things because people wanted to be a part of The Legend in its next phase. They somehow came to understand in the orb of his presence a truth that we often miss. It's actually a philosophical insight. Our jobs don't make us. We make our jobs. In the end, our roles don't define us; we define our roles. Nothing is a constraint. Everything is a platform. It's up to us to endow whatever we do with the highest levels of excellence and importance. That's a part of our creative challenge and joy, when done right. Steve wanted to surround himself with people who understood this and lived it, day-to-day.

One of Steve's favorite words was 'Bozo.' It connoted an unfunny clown, an unacceptable underperformer, or a human irritant to be avoided at all costs. He never wanted bozos in the operation, but in fact only the opposite. And I can relate. In the early eighties, without knowing anything at the time about Steve Jobs and his policies, when he was enforcing this perspective at Apple, I put up a poster on my office door at Notre Dame featuring a classic photo of Bozo the Clown in a red circle with a red slash through his face and the words below: 'No Bozos.' Life is too short. And for Jobs, it wasn't just the worst workers who were to be avoided, but even the average and mediocre. He would often say that if you hire

"B" players, they will attract other "B" players and eventually even "C" players. But merely average and even basically good employees won't get the job done when you're on a quest for perfection, or the insanely great. If you're trying to do anything extraordinary, you need and deserve the best colleagues you can possibly find. And when you bring such people on board, they will also need and deserve to have the best people around them that you can find. It's human nature to rise or fall to the level of the people who are close to us, however subtle the changes might seem. Excellence needs to partner with excellence for the most amazing results.

I've experienced this, first-hand, and I've benefitted greatly from it. Fresh out of graduate school at Yale, I was hired by the University of Notre Dame's Department of Philosophy. I was told that they wanted to become the best place in the world for my specialty at the time, the philosophy of religion, and what's known as philosophical theology. They already had some amazing people in place, and then hired other top experts in the field. We got the best graduate students in that subdomain of philosophical study, and often had top visiting scholars in the field from around the world to come and spend time with us on their vacations or sabbaticals. We were chock full of "A" players. And we constantly made each other better, stimulating each other to think in new ways, and even inspiring each other to tackle new topics as we tried novel, innovative paths in our area. Average wasn't on the horizon. Good enough never was. We sought always to be radical pioneers, blazing new trails that others could explore, opening up new areas for thought and research. We wanted, in our own domain, to change the world.

Any "B" or "C" player would have been completely out of his or her element. And the rest of us would have suffered from having a colleague who could not participate at the highest levels and play an equal role in the demanding and exciting adventures we were on. It was a magical time, and a period of great progress. We did insanely great things. And we did them because of the amazing people we had in place. We stimulated each other. We set each other standards. We goaded our associates on to great things.

But there's a cautionary note here that's important to acknowledge. If you're old enough, or film savvy enough to remember the popular movie "10," starring Bo Derrick, you may recall all the surrounding hype for rating people on their level of attractiveness. In those days, you couldn't escape comments like "She's a good nine," or "He's a six, max." Of course, this was morally and culturally problematic in several ways. But it was astonishingly popular. One prominent news show at the time got carried away and surveyed all top actresses and models of the day for "the best nose," and "the best mouth" and "The best eyes" and on and on, displaying a picture of each physical feature. Then, when they photographically combined all the results, they didn't get exactly what they had intended, although they seemed not to notice that their result fell far short of "the perfect ten." It wasn't exactly a distorted Picasso-style visage, but it demonstrated in its own way a famous logical fallacy: The Fallacy of Composition.

The fallacy in question involves reasoning that if all the parts of a whole have a certain property, then the whole entity composed of those parts will have that property as well. But the problem with this reasoning should be obvious. You can use nothing but large cement blocks to build a fairly small house. In such a case, all the parts are rightly deemed large, but that attribute does not automatically transfer to the entirety, the house, that's composed of them. All the parts of a complex machine can be good, but that same quality is not guaranteed for the machine itself unless all the parts are put together properly. And even then, the machine may be of a flawed design, despite its fine parts.

It's also well known that you can easily make a comparable mistake in your search for excellence. Imagine that you're trying to put together the best sports team. You hunt for "the best" at each position, and then bring them all together. You may or may not get the best result. Why? The answer is simple. If in making your selections, you focused just on individual excellence in a position, you may not have taken into account the additional element of collaborative excellence, or the ability to work well with others. A gathering of prima donnas doesn't necessarily make for a well-oiled machine or a superbly functioning team. It's all in how we define the "A" players. We shouldn't just consider excellence in isolation, without any concern for interpersonal skills. We need great people who can work together greatly.

Every leader should aspire to have that sort of group of fellow travelers. It's a job of crucial importance to gather such people. You get the results you need only by bringing in the best in all the relevant senses, and then lavishly encouraging them to new forms of excellence together.

2. Customers Want The Best.

If you have any doubt whatsoever about the claim just made in the title of this section, "Customers want the best," then do a casual survey. Actually, the survey is so informal and simple that you can do it in your head, as an easy thought experiment. Imagine asking your customers what they would prefer, at roughly the same cost:

1. A Lamentably Poor Product
2. A Barely Adequate Product
3. A Very Good Product
4. A Truly Great Product

There shouldn't be a lot of variation in the answers you find yourself anticipating.

Poor quality causes problems. Adequate is unexciting and uninspiring. Very good is nice, except when it's clear how it could be better. Great is, of course, the best of all. And the conclusions here are utterly obvious. Sometimes, philosophy is indeed just common sense in dress clothes—or a toga, or even a black mock-turtleneck and jeans, paired off with New Balance sneakers. But it often pays to call to consciousness and reposition something that's obvious so that it becomes top of mind and we can use it to guide our decisions.

Do our customers want the best they can get? Or would they prefer to pay for mediocrity? To pose such questions is to answer them. Customers typically do want the best. In the coming years, they will more and more demand the best they can afford. And this brings us back to a further and deeper vital truth.

3. Only the Best Can Create the Best.

Good people do good things. People of excellence typically do excellent things. Truly great people accomplish truly great things. There's most often a harmony between cause and effect. Astonishing results don't come from average, partially disengaged causes. Water doesn't by nature run uphill. Neither does creative innovation. We know the way the world works, in at least this respect. If you want certain results, you have to assemble the right causes. If you want to change the world, you'd better gather some high potential world-changers. Why did so many incredible inventions come out of Bell Labs? It was for the same reason that so many great products have come to us from Apple. Great people can do astonishing things together.

I was talking to a neighbor in the gym recently. He was the founder and CEO of one of the world's top reinsurance companies. On an earnings call not long ago, a shareholder was on the line, in addition to all the analysts who were busy asking their standard financial questions. This man then spoke up and raised a very different sort of concern. He noted that, with the flourishing of the industry, many new players were getting onto the field.

How, he asked, could my neighbor keep his great talent pool from being raided? Surely, he said, as the best in the industry, everyone would want some of his guys. The CEO fielding the question said he was glad that this wasn't coming up during annual salary discussions, because he knew that his top people on the call were sitting in their seats at that moment grinning like Cheshire cats. He then went on to answer that it's a lot more than great compensation that keeps great people together. He has always hired very carefully, and been keen not to include any jerks in the mix, regardless of their intellectual acumen and other talents. The consequence is an unusually strong and engaged team of top, innovative performers. They love working with each other. They really enjoy just being around each other. The overall level of excellence on the team is deeply satisfying and highly motivating. The executives and other team members know they can do great things together that could not be accomplished in other contexts. From everything my CEO friend told me that he had said in answer to the caller, it sounded like the people in his company have formed a strong sense of community, and this always involves ties that bind in a powerful and thoroughly positive way. Life is about much more than just money. And that's something both Socrates and Steve Jobs knew.

How did Jobs elicit such a degree of loyalty among his people? I've heard several of his long-term associates say that they regularly turned down much higher salaries from other places trying to poach them from Steve, at even double or triple their level of pay staying with him. Most of them just deeply wanted to work with Steve and change the world together with him. They truly believed in what he was trying to do. But another important part of their tie to the enterprise was that they wanted to work with the others on the team he had created. They admired each other tremendously. They hoped to change the world together. And they were convinced they could. In addition, they believed that no other place could replicate what they had with Steve and the overall group of truly great people he had brought together into a community of collaborative excellence.

Great people know that they can do together what they could not have done alone, and could not accomplish in a very different, and more mixed, context. Great people who get along well together and have fun in their work aren't quick to jump ship in response to a financially more lucrative offer. One friend who long worked with Jobs has told me that, during his time with Steve and the people he had brought together, he often got offers to leave that involved much more money. But there was a lot more than money keeping him in the position where he felt like he and his comrades were going to make a dent in the universe. They were so charged up that they couldn't easily be split up.

Let me tell you another quick story. A couple of years ago, I sat next to a company founder on a flight across the country, and he excitedly told me about a reflective exercise that a psychologist friend had asked him to do. He was instructed to take a sheet of paper and draw five columns vertically, and five rows horizontally, with room enough for several words, or a couple of sentences, in each resulting block. The vertical columns were to have the headings: (1) Physical Health; (2) Economic Health; (3) Social Health; (4) Moral Health; and (5) Spiritual Health. The horizontal rows were supposed to be labeled Friend 1, Friend 2 and so on through Friend 5. He was told then to write in the names of the five people he spent the most time around. Friend 1 could be his wife, but the rest should be outside his immediate family. He was to fill in brief information about all these people, estimating or characterizing their overall personal health in the various dimensions labeled. The psychologist then left the room for a few minutes while he jotted down his impressions, as requested.

When this man's wise counselor returned and read the chart, he said, "Ok. This is your future. We can predict pretty accurately our own personal health along these five dimensions by looking at the people who are closest to us. So carefully consider what you've just written. Take note. And then you would be well advised to take whatever action you need to take."

I was fascinated. I asked the gentleman what had happened in his life as a result of this exercise and this information. He was obviously very keen about it. His next words to me were surprising, and actually made me laugh out loud. He said: "Well, the divorce was easy." Then he added, "Dissolving my business partnership was much more complicated." He had decided that some of the people closest to him were having an effect on him that he did not want. He took this little exercise seriously enough to make huge changes in his life and work.

The idea behind such a chart and exercise is ancient. We tend to become like the people we're around. Social contact is contagious. Human nature is amazingly malleable. And, as the most insightful philosophers have always insisted, that makes it important for us to choose our friends well, and our colleagues, to the extent that we can. When we have the chance to get to know great people, wise and virtuous individuals, we should never pass up the opportunity. And we should cultivate such intimates in our lives. In his play *Henry IV*, Shakespeare wrote, "It is certain that either wise bearing or ignorant carriage is caught, as men take diseases, one of another; therefore, let men take heed of their company." Cervantes even added to his great novel *Don Quixote* the adage, "Tell me what company you keep and I'll tell you what you are." This is why, when Socrates was accused of corrupting the youth in Athens, he quite reasonably retorted, "Why would I want to make the people around me worse?"

There's a good book relevant to all this called *Connected: The Surprising Power of Our Social Networks and How They Shape Our Lives*, by Harvard researchers Nicholas A. Christakis and James H. Fowler. They add to the famous sociological claim that only "Six Degrees of Separation" stand between each of us and almost anyone else on earth their own additional and distinctive conclusion that there are "Three Degrees of Influence" by which our behavior affects, and is affected by, others. The actions of friends of friends of friends can raise or lower the probability of good and bad things in our own lives, whether we know the people separated from us by all three degrees or not. My favorite line in the book puts it like this: "You may not know him personally, but your friend's husband's coworker can make you fat." But then again, by their reasoning, you can do the same or perhaps the opposite to him as well. We always hope that influence will flow in a positive way, but that's not always how things work. So we should do whatever we can to follow the ancient adage that advises us, in all things to, "First, do no harm."

The conclusions I draw are two-fold: First, that it matters even more than we have ever realized in the past who the people are that we meet and socialize with on a daily basis. We need to have as close acquaintances individuals whose good judgment we can count on to choose as their other friends and associates people who will not abuse the privileges of all-you-can-eat restaurants, lest we all as a result have to loosen our belts. And then, every time you put down that second Twinkie, you may be affecting public health on a much broader scale than you might ever have imagined. Hence my own favorite enjoinder, and actually an inference: "You be wise; and I'll be, likewise." And with that, many may gain as a result, as our actions propagate through our social networks of surprising influence.

Steve Jobs seemed to have an intuitive understanding of something like this, long before any of the confirming research. He always sought out the best and the brightest, starting with the friend of his youth, Steve Wozniak. And then he continued this habit at Apple and NeXT, and at Pixar. He surrounded himself with the very best people he could find. And so, he placed each of them, likewise, in a laboratory of excellence. Then, he could push for perfection with all the right people. He even said that he thought his greatest product ever was the team he eventually assembled at Apple.

Hiring at its best involves the forming and sustaining of a community. Done right, it creates and perpetuates a great, thriving, creative team of lively minds engaged in a noble purpose together. And, as Steve Jobs understood, this is the sort of workforce that can be responsible for insanely great results.

II

Engage Face-to-Face

I have been benefited by conversation with both of you. For I think I know the meaning of the proverb, "Beautiful things are difficult."
Socrates

Sometimes, simple things can have astonishing results. But it can take a rare flash of genius to spot that one simple factor that might make all the difference. Fortunately for all of us, Steve Jobs had, in his own way and at least at several crucial junctures in his work, such flashes of genius. And because of that, he saw something very simple and yet extremely powerful that we all need to realize and act on.

The best instigators of creative innovation have understood a fundamental principle. Bring together a group of smart, well disposed, talented, diverse and yet, in some ways, like-minded people—ideally between two and twenty individuals—put them in an environment where they can focus, pose them a problem that requires a highly creative solution, and then encourage their candid and free flowing interaction over the issue. Let them play with ideas and explore possibilities. Encourage them to goad each other on, and gently but carefully challenge each other's thoughts. Fill the room with the fresh air of "What if?" and "Maybe" blended with keen analysis and genuine focus. The high level activity that often results from this can be thought of as a collective form of concentration, or a meshing of minds in real time and space.

There's something basic and yet deep about this distinctive process. And here's the big surprise. You can't replicate the elevation of thought that can emerge in such a setting by any means other than the give and take of face-to-face conversation. You can't do it by email, e-chat, text messages, or conference calls. It won't work the same way with Apple's own Face-Time, or with Skype, or through any other sophisticated video and audio conferencing service. These are all greatly useful supporting tools. But the best cauldrons of creativity require physical proximity, face-to-face—at least, at the start, and then periodically, afterwards, as well. That's why such gatherings, done right, can be the engines of innovation.

1. Others Spark Us. Talk In Person!

Steve Jobs understood what I like to call The Proximity Principle: Nothing can replace face-to-face conversations. People spark each other in person in a wholly distinctive way. Of course, many forms of creative collaboration can take place through any means of communication. And the more complete and instant the communication channel is, the better the results will typically be. But there's a special phenomenon of creative thought that can arise only when people are physically present with each other, spiritually attuned, and mentally engaged with a shared focus.

But still, of course, there's a big caveat as well. You can't pack a bunch of obnoxious jerks into a room and expect great results. And even one obstreperous grump or clearly contemptuous soul can torpedo the process. The proximity principle done right requires that the people involved, or at least as many of them as possible, share some important common values, attitudes, and emotional dispositions. High regard all around the room is a great facilitator.

And that's certainly encouraged by having just the best "A" players involved—as long as they also have a good dose of emotional intelligence. Great experience and high intellect helps most when blended with real respect and kind regard. Shared commitments will also drive the process. But differences can come into play in vital ways, as well.

In too many organizational contexts, people cluster exclusively in functional teams and by selective affinities. Like attracts like. We gravitate toward what we know and what makes us comfortable. And yet, that's too easily a formula for habit, sameness, and ultimately mediocrity, which hardly makes any person who cares comfortable at all.

More companies than ever are nowadays encouraging people to get to know colleagues across functions, in other parts of the organization, and with very different skill sets. Jobs famously insisted on designing office layouts so that people would run into each other during an average workday and meet others in the company they might not otherwise know in settings that could facilitate a moment of pause and conversation. This tactic to allow the proximity principle to work informally as well as formally then spread to many other tech companies. And as people across industries have now learned, architecture and office design can either help or hurt innovation in an organization. If your space doesn't facilitate face-to-face meetings, you just have to work a little harder to orchestrate them. And it's work that can pay off, big-time.

This can provide some perspective on Yahoo's publicly controversial ban a while back on people working regularly from home, requiring them instead to come into a shared office space. William Powers, an avid student of technology and author of the insightful book I mentioned earlier on how to use technology well, *Hamlet's Blackberry*, recently told me about a successful business he helped launch in the Boston area that was subsequently bought by Twitter. He wrote me this interesting comment:

> Last year I collaborated on a technology project with a Cambridge, MA start-up called Bluefin Labs. I tried many times to organize my team so we could work together remotely, using Skype, conference calls, Gmail chat and other means. It never worked—not for the creative stuff that really mattered. We had to be physically together for the magic to happen. So most weekdays, I did a five-hour round-trip commute from my home to Cambridge. It was arduous but necessary.

As Socrates realized, "beautiful things are difficult." Great things are hard. And pursuits of creative excellence require the most and best of human interactions.

The real magic does seem to require physical proximity. Another man I know also works in the tech industry, in a job that requires him to travel fairly often to faraway places and meet with remote team members. It takes a lot of time, trouble, and expense to make the trips. They're exhausting. I asked him recently how important those face-to-face sessions are. Do they justify all the time and cost? He said he's sure that the team accomplishes three to four times as much together, in the same room, face-to-face as they could achieve remotely, by phone and video-conferencing and email or text. A recent Op Ed in the *New York Times* entitled "Engineering Serendipity" described how even basic productivity can be enhanced by the chance conversations and expanded social networks that result from people sitting at larger tables in a company cafeteria during lunch times. Something that basic can make a positive difference. Steve was right. Proximity pays off.

2. Collaboration Takes Conversation.

An email exchange isn't real conversation. Online chat or texting isn't, either. Even a lively give-and-take session over the phone or by Face-Time or Skype typically lacks the total experience of body language and other nonverbal communication within the atmospherics and dynamics of physical presence that's such an important part of real conversation. The deepest and best collaborations require full engagement. And that's really no mystery, because face-to-face conversation can be in itself a form of collaborative thinking. We spark each other in person in ways that can't otherwise be replicated. And it's not just about what we hear the other person say. Sometimes, the creative spark comes in what we hear ourselves say or in what we feel in response to our physically present conversation partner.

The philosophical background for this is simple. The fact that we are beings with bodies is no accidental feature of our existence in the world. Not even the currently wild dream of downloading our minds and personalities as software into new hardware can avoid the fact of embodiment, in however different a form that might be envisioned. Even for the most distinctively mental of activities, the full particulars of embodiment need to be respected. And we've developed, over millennia past, our abilities to read the features, postures, tones, and movements of others for what they might convey. We're exquisitely sensitive to such signals and we respond, whether consciously or not. Bodily propinquity, as a result, creates a matrix for collaboration and creative thinking that's unique. Physical presence has no substitute. It's a basic fact that can't be ignored. There's an engagement and an energy arising from personal presence that can't be produced in any other way. There's something almost like an interpersonal chemistry to being within the radiant zone of another human being that we don't yet fully understand, but frequently experience.

Socrates philosophized on the streets of Athens and at dinner parties with other individuals and groups of people, rather than just retreating into an isolated place where he could have enjoyed quiet solitude and uninterrupted time to think. And, as far as we know, he didn't ever write down his own thoughts. He talked to others to spark ideas. He asked and suggested and objected. He played with ideas through personal engagement with the people around him. And through the interaction, insights arose. So did new perplexities. But then, they in turn provided the possibility for even deeper interaction. As his example proved, face-to-face conversations can be educational, disruptive, inventive, surprising, and enlightening.

It's no coincidence that the greatest flourishing of philosophical thought in Western history was to be found in ancient Greece, in that city of Athens where many creative thinkers knew each other personally and talked together, daily, face-to-face. The renaissance artists of Florence and the later impressionists of France provide other vivid examples of this. They did new and innovative things not just because of the personal contributions arising from their individual distribution of creative genius, but in and through their interactions with each other.

This was also to be seen with the Royal Society in England, whose far-reaching group impact basically launched much of early modern science. The Founding Fathers of America, in their own time, produced new and powerful forms of political innovation that's simply unparalleled in history, and the ways in which they challenged, stimulated, and encouraged each other in person mattered deeply for those results. A further example of the same phenomenon would be the array of writers in Paris between the late nineteenth century and the Second World War. They learned from each other in cafes, over strong coffee and plentiful wine. They competed. They argued and loved. They inspired new things across disciplines. Consider as well the historic breakthroughs of the physicists who lived and worked together at Los Alamos. The more recent hotbed of creativity in Silicon Valley is just another storied example, far beyond the impact of Steve Jobs and Apple. And Steve certainly benefitted in many ways from the first wave of these technological collaborations and conversations. Many more such cases could be cited. It matters when great people work and even live close together. Jobs called it "The Beehive Effect," and thought of it as responsible for a great many good results.

Camaraderie, fellowship, friendly association, and the conversation made possible by physical presence can cause something to happen that can't be replicated by even the best individuals working in isolation and thinking within the confines of their own minds. We certainly need private time, periods of quiet, and a chance to get away and ponder in isolation. A measure of solitude can feed the soul and allow the mind to wander down new paths and explore new territory. There come times when individuals have to process what they've seen and heard and thought. It can't be all face-to-face, all day, every day. But without that lively face-to-face interaction, the greatest things don't happen. The best individuals don't fully blossom.

One philosopher whose work sheds light on this phenomenon is Michael Polanyi, in his books *Personal Knowledge*, and *Tacit Knowing*. He points out, for example in the sciences, how many Nobel Prize winners have been the personal students of former Nobel Laureates who worked with them in the lab and may have hung out with them outside of work. And Polanyi argues that it isn't just about politics and connections. He claims there are important matters that can be communicated, master-to-student, and that can never fully be put into words. There are ways of working, habits of attention, and other orientations within the space of a discipline that can't be adequately described, but can be modeled and picked up, or "caught" like a benign and helpful virus. It's almost like something passed around a lab. And it can be contagious throughout a workplace. The history of art displays the same phenomenon, and so does business.

One of my best teachers at Yale, the philosopher Paul Holmer, told me long ago of his worry that, in our time, we're in serious danger of losing the greatest model for teaching ever devised—the master-apprentice relationship, where Polanyi's personal and tacit knowing has a chance to be passed on to the next generation. It isn't about texts or manuals, or even about hearing talks. It's about working together and being together, face-to-face. This has a distinctive, and even unique power in what it can create.

3. Brainstorming Creates Breakthroughs.

THERE IS AN OLD AND OFTEN CITED PROVERB: AS IRON SHARPENS iron, so one man sharpens another—and, of course this is a process never confined by gender or race, or age. The results of this principle can be seen in the best sports teams, military units, local neighborhoods, and even families. It can be found in creative, progressive businesses, and in the various professions. A proper form of interpersonal stimulation leads to a greater level of excellence through what we might think of as combinatorial creativity. There can even come to be a friendly competitiveness in such contexts that spurs people on to new levels of thought and contribution they might never have attained otherwise, in solitude.

Brainstorming conversations that take place even in casual settings can spark major creative leaps and novel, important innovations. The same interaction can also, at the same time, generate the inspiration or motivation to put those ideas into action, guiding their implementation, along with providing what is then also the sort of network of partnerships that alone can help bring great new things into the world.

How does this work? We all have different experiences and distinctive perspectives on the world. Our minds work differently and process things in their own ways. In most of the sciences and humanities, we tend to focus on commonalities that can be abstracted from all the particulars, but it's often the idiosyncratic variances that can make all the difference. When I was a professor and had large lecture classes, I often enjoyed the great experience of telling my sea of students about a new thought I had hatched, and then listening as they processed the idea and added to it in ways that might never have occurred to me. One student from Nebraska would see it one way. A young scholar from Mexico, or Argentina, might notice a totally different facet of the idea. The differing backgrounds and experiences represented in the room could result in a tumbling kaleidoscope of insights that I might never have attained all alone in my study.

One of my favorite technical essays I wrote and published during my years of academic philosophy came out of a lively conversation one day with a young man, Chris Menzel, who at the time was an advanced graduate student, and who would go on to have a great career in the logic, mathematics, and metaphysics side of philosophy, teaching and producing groundbreaking work to this day. Just hanging out one afternoon in an informal setting, we began to discuss a major issue that was relatively unexplored in modern times. We sparked ideas off each other. It was a wild, wide open, and free wheeling discussion combining creative speculation with the highest levels of precise analysis. I conjured up a crazy story. Chris spotted various vital elements and implications. I saw others. We wrote up the results together and the essay was quickly published in one of the top philosophical journals as an article that's still read and debated to this day, more than thirty years after that lively and engaged conversation. Most readers over time seem to think that our ideas were totally outrageous and must be wrong, but can't quite manage to prove they're wrong—and in the process, they're thinking hard in new ways about important matters at the core of philosophy. That's just like what Steve Jobs wanted to see every day at work in his own domain.

It seems to be a standard recommendation, and even received wisdom on the art of brainstorming that during such a free wheeling session productive of creative ideas, the only thing that's not allowed is criticism. We're supposed to just conjure and record as many suggestions as possible, and without any analysis or critique. But I've found this common restriction to be off the mark. Criticism is fine and can be powerfully helpful during such brainstorming if its intent is positive. In any critique of a new idea that's been proposed, the critic as a collaborator simply needs to seek to revise the original idea in a way that accommodates the criticism. And from that, all can benefit.

In productive brainstorming conversations, the free flow of ideas allows for new connections and novel conclusions. One thought sparks another. And a cascade of insights can easily overflow the boundaries that have otherwise contained our thinking. An odd angle on a problem may create a new approach to a possible solution. Sometimes, just listening to yourself in such a lively exchange will help you as much as listening to the others who are present. You find yourself spurred to new insights, or novel articulations of old insights that may help you or your conversation partner on to see the one elusive thing that's needed. Face-to-face conversation at its best is both a dynamic performance art and a creative endeavor. It's a form of thinking that's unique.

So, talk to someone new today. Go to a meeting with an open and expectant attitude. Hang out with a colleague for a bit and ask what he or she might be working on or thinking about recently. Orchestrate some physical get-togethers. Use the ancient conversational energy of face-to-face brainstorming to create new breakthroughs in the problems you face and with the opportunities you have. Even the most casual of conversations may generate a spark or plant a seed. Take advantage of the powerful possibilities of proximity in this ancient and innovative way. Steve Jobs, the man who brought us so many of our wonderful technological alternatives to in-person, face-to-face conversation, would heartily approve, and perhaps even be proud.

12

Know Both the Big Picture and the Details

There is an ancient saying: "Hard is the knowledge of the good."
Socrates

At a casual glance, it can seem like the world of highly productive individuals is divided into two groups: The Big Picture Thinkers and The Detail People. It's when they get together that the big magic happens. But the real truth, especially when it comes to people in leadership positions, is more often quite different from this, as the example of Steve Jobs showed us. He was the biggest of big picture thinkers, but he was also more immersed in the details than his professional expert associates in design and engineering had ever seen. His embrace of both levels offers us a simple, and yet difficult, formula for our own success.

1. Be Bifocal. Think Big and Small.

I've known plenty of people who were exciting big picture thinkers but never got anything done. Either they didn't know how to get their hands dirty with the details, or they didn't want to. When I was a first year graduate student at Yale, I wandered into a dorm room party and met a guy who told me he was an undergraduate architecture major. I said, "So, I guess you have to know all about materials and stresses and stuff like that."

He first looked surprised and then scowled and shook his head and replied, in a tone of clear disdain, "No. I'm at Yale. I'm an artist. I'll design the cityscapes of the future and just hire guys from the state universities to figure out how to make it all work. They learn the engineering stuff. I make artistic statements." Oh. Ok.

This attitude is why so many artistic statements in the cityscapes of the recent past and present have fallen apart or tumbled down. The creator who dreams the big stuff needs to learn how to sweat the small stuff in the right sort of way. As some other artists—a group of painters known to the word as pointillists—saw quite well and showed to the rest of us in a revelatory manner, the big picture emerges from vastly many small points of choice along the way. Details add up.

The effective leader can't just be a man or woman who announces, "Here's The Big Vision—Make It Work." Nor can a good leader simply be a person who whittles away at multitude of details without having a clue where it's all going. We like to say that an effective leader has to multitask. But as psychologists increasingly tell us, there really seems to be no such thing as literally simultaneous multitasking. The only thing that's actually available to us is toggling back and forth from one task or dimension of focus to another. The most effective leader then needs to be a master toggler, adept at switching focal points, back and forth, big and small.

The leader also has to be adroit at contextualizing—at putting all the details into the proper perspective. Wisdom is always, in some sense, about perspective. And so is leadership. But we can't put things into their proper perspective without having a big picture clearly in mind as our context. Just as a leader has to think on various levels, he or she must be a doer as well as a thinker. And doing always ties us to the details. Talkers can stay at the blue-sky level. Doers have to descend into the tricky particulars. There's no such thing as a purely vague or general action. Steve Jobs managed to operate with both the big and small, and at least most of the time, it seems, in an effective way.

2. Never Pride Yourself on Half the Formula.

The Yale student in the Department of Art and Architecture I met long ago was making a basic mistake. He was priding himself on half the formula: "I'm a big picture guy. I don't have time for the petty little details." And, of course, it can go the other way around. Former US President George H. W. Bush liked to say that he wasn't really into "the vision thing." He prided himself on being a more detail-oriented person.

It's a common psychological defense mechanism: Whatever lack or weakness we have, we rationalize it into being a personal strength instead. But that's a prescription for trouble. Rationalization is by definition a departure from reality. When we're honest with ourselves and acknowledge a weakness, we can often do something about it. We can build new skills and habits, cultivate new and perhaps much-needed qualities, and thereby diminish or even eliminate the flaw or limitation we had. Or, if none of that works sufficiently, we can hire others to partner with us, complementing our strengths with their own different virtues, and making up for our weaknesses and blind spots.

We do, however, need to make one distinction. What may hobble us as a weakness in a particular context can actually become a form of strength in a very different setting. My friend David Rendall has argued this convincingly in a great little book called *The Freak Factor*. The thing you were criticized for as a child may end up being the key to your adult success. Dave likes to say that when he was a kid he was always being told to sit down and be quiet. But now, as a public speaker, he makes his living by standing up and talking. Sometimes, what needs to change isn't you, but your immediate environment, or situation. You can find a context where what was otherwise a weakness becomes a strength. And doing so can change your life. But this won't always help the leader whose weakness is that he or she can't be bifocal, and is blind either to the big picture, or to the details. The change of context that would be required to turn that into a form of strength would necessitate abandoning any major leadership role at all. And yet, this is sometimes exactly the change that a person who has been thrust into a leadership position needs to make, getting back to what he or she does well, perhaps on the front lines, making a contribution that no one else can make as effectively there. But when that's not an option, leaders need to augment whatever scale focus they do best, and learn the other as well.

We sometimes have to work on our weaknesses, in order to diminish or correct them. Of course, you may have read in recent years how winning coaches and students of peak performance have been saying that enhancing your strengths is generally far more important for outstanding performance than fixing all your weaknesses. And that seems to be true, especially for people in front line positions. It may even hold as a general rule of thumb for those in managerial and leadership roles. But there are many gold medal Olympic athletes and champions across sports who will tell you that it's only by working hard on correcting some of their weaknesses that they could maximize their strengths and attain the results they so deeply wanted. The great dunker has to learn to shoot those free throws, after all, and figure out how to move better and quicker on defense, whether that comes naturally or not.

The popular advice to enhance your strengths and forget about your weaknesses can only go so far in most environments. And here, in thinking about the competing strengths of visionaries and meticulous detail people, we come to a clear exception to the rule. If you're in a leadership position and your weakness is that you aren't bifocal, you're simply going to be limited in what you can accomplish. If clarifying the big picture is a weakness, you need to fix it. If a concern for details is the weakness, you need to fix that. These are flaws that can't be ignored, because they are both areas crucial for the role you play. A quarterback can be a weak blocker. No big problem there. A defensive tackle can be limited in his abilities to catch the ball and run with it without fumbling. He might even be a bit slow on long runs, even without a ball. But that's Ok. He doesn't have to get these skills up to the level of what's most closely involved in his primary role. But a leader's chief role in any organization has to involve both the large and the small. Any problem in this regard, any weakness in managing both scales of concern, should be fixed so that there can be a form of inspiration and oversight forthcoming on both levels.

3. Excellence Requires Dynamic Balance.

There's no such thing as perfect balance. When we think of balance as a static thing, perfectly poised and steady in absolutely every relevant respect, we misunderstand its basic nature. Google the word balance and look at the images. Several rocks are stacked up, one on another. Stillness results. A ballerina is on her toes, poised and perfectly unmoved. But these images can be very misleading. Let's try another approach. Imagine yourself as a tightrope walker. You're moving along the rope. You can feel the constant adjustments your muscles are making as you inch forward. And you know. Balance is a dynamic flow of movement, awareness, and adaptation, played out in cycles. It's sometimes a dance of adjustment. We're always a little out of balance, even in our best times, but as long as we're aware of what's going on, and adjust and adapt properly when that's called for, we never fall off the tightrope completely.

Walking a tightrope is actually a very good image. An expert tightrope walker with amazing balance is still always a little bit out of balance, on however small a scale. His legs wobble left, then right, then left, then right, constantly rebalancing and adapting. That's why he doesn't fall. Balance is an extended process, and never just a fixed point of stillness and poise. Steve Jobs worried about the big picture, and he immersed himself in details. He could adjust his mind to whichever level was most appropriate at the time or in the context. Some would complain that he got too much into the details of engineering and design, interfering and micromanaging great people who knew what they were doing. But I think an interpretation of his actions that's a bit more accurate and closer to being fair would describe him as never overlooking anything that could matter to the customer, paying close attention and giving his distinctive feedback, based on his sensibilities and his intuition. Even those who were initially irritated or frustrated by hearing that they needed to go back and fix or change some tiny flaw or defect that he had noticed were, for the most part, soon won over by the results.

What balance requires can change, moment to moment. What doesn't change is that an adaptive process always is needed. When we learn to balance the big picture with the details, dynamically and adaptively, we put ourselves into a position of power that can't otherwise be attained.

13

Combine the Humanities With the Sciences

Surely, I said, knowledge is the food of the soul.
Socrates

Even if you're otherwise familiar with every other philosophical principle in Walter Isaacson's list of fourteen keys to the leadership success that Steve Jobs lived and used during his life, this one may take you by surprise. And it's a principle that's deeply embedded in Steve's entire life story of bringing together the humanities with the sciences. Steve was a poetry reading, music obsessed, Zen focused, big picture thinker who studied calligraphy, but also loved the scientific details of engineering. Most people think you have to choose. You can follow the path of the humanities to a life of enlightened sensibilities and high-minded culture, characterized as it often is by the recalcitrant phenomena of underemployment and relative poverty, or you can take the steep road of the sciences to a real job with solid compensation and a tangible contribution to society.

As a philosopher, I personally understand this point of view. And, if you'll indulge me for a moment, I'd like to share my own story about it. My greatest challenge at a fairly young age was that

I wanted to immerse myself in the humanities and, in particular, the study of philosophy. I actually wanted to be a philosopher. What was the challenge, you may ask? Well, if you've ever read Kant or Hegel, you know half the problem. Even in English translation, they can give you such a throbbing headache that it may take a bottle of aspirin for you to get through it all. But my worried mother put the real challenge of the humanities quite succinctly when she asked me many, many times: "Who's ever going to pay you to know this?"

And my clearly concerned mother surely wasn't the first to think of such a thing. I'm guessing that even Aristotle's mother likely had much the same worry. Her son had promise. He was very smart. He could do great things in almost any field. And I can imagine that she was thinking, maybe, real estate. But he studied philosophy instead and still did pretty well for himself. He invented logic, which helped. Not that anybody wants to use it anymore, but still. It was impressive.

And I'm suspicious that Aristotle's most famous student may have had a mother with the exact same concern. But that young man also studied the humanities and focused on philosophy, and still did amazingly well for himself ... in real estate. His name was Alexander the Great. Can you even begin to imagine the pressure? "Hi, I'm Alexander the Great." Mediocrity was not in the cards. Average was out. But, as I say, he flourished in the broad area of real estate. At one time, his portfolio of properties was described as "the known world." Not bad.

But my challenge was how, in my own life and time, I could turn an expertise in perhaps the most esoteric domain of the humanities into an opportunity for gainful employment. I didn't live in ancient Greece. And, let's face it. Forbes has never done a cover story: Hot Job of the Year—Philosopher. I had heard about one philosophy Ph.D. who had a real job outside a university context, but he was a loquacious cab driver in New York City. My driving ambition, however, was not an ambition for driving. In my own case, I pursued an undergraduate degree, along with a couple of Master's degrees, and a double Ph.D. in the humanities, and ended up driving quite a lot, after all, to get from my home and education on the east coast to South Bend, Indiana, where I taught for fifteen years at the University of Notre Dame. I played the technical, abstruse game of academic philosophy there for many years with great energy and joy, and successfully, writing in the top journals and publishing ideas in books that perhaps a hundred and thirty-seven people in the world would go on to read and understand. But I eventually wanted to get beyond the traditional classroom and be a philosopher out in the world. How could this possibly work? My mother's worry came back to haunt me.

I had to get creative, and distinctively innovative. I began to rediscover the practical side of philosophy, the stream of thought that had been almost completely ignored in too many American universities for a hundred years. I also realized that I needed to study the various sciences of human behavior for the light that they could shed on life in the world. And, in addition, I often read in the natural sciences for more indirect but often fundamental insight into the existential human side of the equation. I found myself combining the humanities and the sciences in new ways. And what I discovered as I went along this new path launched me into the broader world as a public philosopher, speaking and writing on issues of success, excellence, leadership, change, creativity, ethics, happiness, and partnership, among other things. Now I get to study individuals like Steve Jobs and speak to people at the top companies in almost every industry in the world. I'm actually making some progress in taking philosophy from unemployable to unavoidable, and perhaps even indispensable. And if that ever changes? Well, I realize there's always real estate. And it's something else I enjoy. I even already have my broker's license, just in case.

I discovered first-hand and came to understand deeply the

combinatorial principle that Jobs espoused. Creativity can often best be found at the interface of very different disciplines, distinct realms of knowledge, and quite diverse activities. How then can we combine the humanities and the sciences in whatever work we do? And, then, again, why exactly should we? There are some interesting answers to these questions.

1. Read Widely To Innovate.

Obviously, I'm having a little fun with this, based in my personal experience. But I've actually discovered throughout my own life history some new perspectives on how Jobs was right to urge us to be more comprehensive and diverse in our interests, and at a time when so many people want to keep the arts and humanities on one side of a very high wall, with the sciences, mathematics, and technology far away on the other side. They think of the humanities and the sciences as comprising two very distinct worlds that can, and probably should, be separated.

The twentieth-century British novelist and scientist C. P. Snow saw this issue very differently from most people around him at the time. In a profoundly important lecture he gave at Cambridge University in 1959 entitled, "The Two Cultures," and in a related, widely-read little book by the same name that followed, Snow pointed out that there is indeed a modern split between the sciences and humanities, but he argued that this desperately needs to be overcome for the future good of the world. In his own time, he saw legislators and other political leaders in England who were, more likely than not, trained exclusively in the humanities and law, being called upon more and more to make decisions regarding public policy that centrally concerned the sciences. The politicians were intellectually unprepared to even understand what they were supposed to decide. Likewise, too many scientists were working hard in their sometimes very narrow areas without any sense of the implications of their work for humanity, or the human condition, generally. There are striking ways in which Mary Shelley's short novel *Frankenstein* models the ongoing danger that this presents. A narrowly focused science can easily produce something it can't control and that has monstrous implications for us all. When either science or technology outstrips ethics and a clear and imaginative psychological grasp of its implications, terrible trouble can result. A split between the humanities and the sciences can become problematic in many ways.

The philosopher Immanuel Kant once spoke of "the starry sky above and the moral law within," and in that phrase encapsulated elements of the two-fold focus that, according to both C.P. Snow and Steve Jobs, we all need. We must seek to understand the external world around us—the subject matter of the sciences. We benefit greatly from the new technology and the useful techniques bequeathed to us by mathematics and statistics and engineering, for example. But we also should ground ourselves in the most important aspects of our own common human nature, often best understood by and through the humanities in poetry, art, history, fiction, and philosophy generally, as well as in the many deep values that some of the finest minds before us have discovered and discussed and explored to great effect.

The best people I've known in science have been avid readers and fans of the humanities. The most insightful people I've met who live and work in the humanities have also done their best to keep up with crucial elements of modern science, and infuse their own work with its fundamental principles and perspectives. I think Steve Jobs at some level wanted every leader and business innovator to understand the importance of this. The more widely we cast our own intellectual nets, the better thinkers we can be, and then the better leaders and creators, as well. I think he might want to ask us all: Why should we ever settle for anything less?

My best thinking about leadership has been stimulated by such divergent figures as Aristotle and Harry Potter. And this is a good example of how insight can come from unsuspected sources. When I first began to read the famous Harry Potter novels, I expected to encounter just simple and entertaining tales for children. I had no idea that I would find in those lively stories some incredibly deep wisdom about leadership in any context. This has led me to caution CEOs about stocking their night tables with only the most popular recent leadership and management books. When you read what everyone else is reading, you end up thinking what everyone else is thinking and then doing what everyone else is doing. But how then can that help you to stand out in a distinctive way and become your most innovative and best self?

One of my favorite recent emails was from a man who had been in one of my business audiences and told me that, because of what he heard me say, he now had the Anglo-Saxon epic *Beowulf* on his bedside table for nightly reading. I was thrilled. Reading widely encourages innovation. Why? For this simple reason: The paradigmatic creative moment has the form of uniting divergent perspectives, or drawing from diversely juxtaposed conceptualities in a new way. The broader our experience of the world and of disparate ideas in our world, the better positioned we are to have that creative experience and innovate. New points of view spark new ideas. A novel can turn on a light. A poem can light a candle. Suddenly you see clearly what's been dim or hidden, just a bit out of view. Variety invigorates and redirects our thinking in new ways. It's just that simple.

2. Stock the Mind. Stimulate the Imagination.

Jobs told Isaacson that his favorite reading assignments in high school, the things that had the most impact on him, included prominently *King Lear* and *Moby Dick*. In Shakespeare's play *King Lear*, the title character wants to decide which of his daughters should inherit the lion's share of his fortune and kingdom and, to this end, he tries to determine which of them loves him the most. In order to judge that, he then asks each of them to speak of her love for him, as powerfully and eloquently as she can. Two of the sisters play the game well. One refuses to try it at all. And tragedy ensues. Madness, death, and despair abound.

You would think that the story might be enough to prevent a future corporate leader from ever fixating on whether his employees, or even the broader world, might love him, or profess their love, or to what degree. And yet, Jobs seemed to care very much about his image, and would go out of his way to court and woo potential employees and business partners in a quasi-seduction, as if in loving his ideas, and influenced by his abundant charisma, they would be attracted enough to him to join him and work beside him loyally, regardless of any rough treatment they might receive through the emotional outbursts and tirades almost inevitably to come. Perhaps in fact, while using his apparently boundless energy and famous charm to weave a spell around anyone who could be useful to him, he nonetheless after all may have taken a cautionary lesson from the king and then moved forward without any undue concern about personal love and affection from the members of his work family. And yet, even so, I suspect that, deep down, he was conflicted. He expected his charm to work permanently, and was surprised when it didn't. He really wanted the love but couldn't stop the outbursts that came from another deep place in his complex personality. This is something we'll have the opportunity to consider a bit more, and later on in our philosophical explorations.

In Steve's other favorite high school book, Melville's huge novel *Moby Dick*, Captain Ahab is running his whaling vessel not for the proper profits of its owners, as he should have been, but rather in service to his own monumental obsession. As a result, the ship is lost and nearly everyone dies. You might think that this would serve a future business leader as a cautionary tale about obsession.

But, throughout his career, Steve was clearly a man obsessed. Perhaps the lesson he took away from the seafaring classic was not that obsessions should be avoided by people in leadership positions, but rather that our obsessions need to be positive rather than negative, and oriented around creation rather than destruction. Then, everything could perhaps work out just fine.

Or did Steve learn his main lesson from Ahab's first mate, Starbuck? This was a man who saw what the captain was doing and could have stopped him, but didn't. When Steve was forced out of his role and responsibilities at Apple, and began to watch it gradually drift toward an abyss, he eventually took action to intervene before it, like a very large and damaged ship, could go under. He didn't make Starbuck's mistake. Classic texts can teach lessons that anyone in business can benefit from pondering and applying in their own spheres. Let me give a few other simple examples to further indicate the importance of what someone like Jobs might recommend, concerning the relevance of the humanities to science, technology, and business.

An unexpected but powerful source of ideas is Mary Shelley's small book, *Frankenstein*, which I've already mentioned. It is one of the greatest cautionary tales ever written about a quest for success. Her protagonist, the scientist Dr. Victor Frankenstein, was brilliant, passionate, resourceful, and determined in the pursuit of his goals. His vision was the ultimate creative endeavor. But he had failed to think through the consequences of his aims, and inadvertently launched into the world a monster he couldn't control. This is a powerful metaphor for so many of the leaders and high achievers of our time and their creative schemes that have gone awry. A close reading of Shelley's insightful story can shed light on the most pressing problems of the present day, as well as others that we may yet face in the future, as science and technology advance.

The most ancient epic we have, from around 2,700 BCE, is the story of *Gilgamesh*, a highly intelligent, strikingly handsome and talented individual who was simply a bad and oppressive leader, selfishly pursuing his own narrow interests at the expense of others, until some traumatic events woke him up to what life and leadership really are, and how they should be approached. In the end, this formerly narcissistic tyrant became a famous and celebrated king. What transformed him? What made the difference? There are some powerful lessons in his personal trajectory that can serve us all well. However technical your business might be, there's no reason you can't learn a lot from such an ancient tale.

I've also just mentioned the famous Anglo-Saxon epic of *Beowulf.* It presents us with a conquering warrior, unmatched in power and skill. He solved problems that no one else could touch, and seemed able to attain the unattainable. No human being could stand up to him. He was good, sharp, courageous, and loyal. But when he became a leader, he didn't see how some of his long-term habits of individual excellence on the front lines could ironically set him up, in his new position, for his own demise. He didn't understand the need for change in his habits and actions, or the importance of new forms of true partnership and collaboration with other talented and strong people. And, because of that, he went down in flames—literally in this case, because of a dragon, and he then became in his own right one of the great cautionary legends we have.

Machiavelli famously gave some of the best and worst advice for leaders ever assembled in one small book, *The Prince.* The inability to separate what's insightful in his thought from what's catastrophically bad has set leaders up ever since for unintentionally disastrous results. Some of the deepest ethical puzzles of business can be understood through a contemporary reading of this classic essay. And we live in a time when its lessons may be needed more than ever before.

Friends of Steve Jobs often spoke of a Good Steve and a Bad Steve, as the two sides of his personality. Sometimes, Jobs seemed to be, in many ways, a Machiavellian creation in two parts—with Good Steve acting as a charming, silver-tongued manipulator who could seduce anyone into following him, and Bad Steve raging as a fearful despot who could be immensely cruel when he thought this would be more effective. In either case, he appeared to be operating as an individual who often pursued his personal ends in a way that fell far outside the normal rules of moral behavior. And yet, he had great success. Could he have had even greater achievement without the cruelty and occasional deceit? I certainly think so. And most commentators agree. He surely could have had a less messy and chaotic personal life. He could have enjoyed more fulfillment and deep satisfaction in his experience and accomplishments. He could have felt a much greater measure of happiness along the way, rather than engaging in business as a constant battlefield experience. And this seems to have been born out in his more mature years, when he mellowed considerably and had arguably his best and greatest successes.

Perhaps, in his youth, he should have spent even more time in the humanities than he did, in alignment with his own philosophy and practice, and then he possibly could have understood earlier and more deeply the almost inevitable consequences of his less helpful habits and emotional dispositions. A treasure chest of insights awaits us in old books. We don't have to figure it all out from scratch. Wise people have lived before us, have faced great struggles, have made huge mistakes of their own, and have given us their hard won insights about how to endure and even to prevail. When we read the right things and read them well, we position ourselves to move forward with the wisdom to leverage our time and talents in the greatest ways.

3. Philosophize with Purpose.

A REPORTER WAS GOING TO WRITE A COVER STORY THAT WAS intended to be really nothing more than a puff piece on Steve and Apple for *Wired* magazine, a popular outlet for news in the technology world. Alan Deutschman recounts the meeting where Steve came in and looked uncomfortable about being interviewed at all on that day. The reporter initially asked some easy questions, including this:

"At forty-four, if you could go back and give advice to your twenty-five-year-old self, what would you say?"

Jobs answered, "Not to deal with stupid interviews." Then he said, "I have no time for this philosophical bullshit. I'm a very busy person." As his sister indicates in a novel about him, he might have been too busy generally to flush toilets, but he would often take the time to flush reporters he thought he didn't need to charm.

Some have taken that exchange to imply that Jobs had no time for philosophy, or for the activity of philosophizing that we're engaged in here. But that isn't true at all. He was distinctively philosophical in his intellectual leanings from a young age. Deutschman reports earlier in his book that the teenage Jobs would often take long walks with his friend Bob Fernandez and "talk about philosophy and life." His engagement with Zen in later years was primarily about the philosophy it propounds. He clearly didn't use it as a technique to become a calm and peaceful person. But it took him deeper in many other respects. The book we've discussed that he read every year of his life was in its own way a very philosophical tome. And Apple's great designer Jony Ive has said that he and Jobs would often have long and quiet philosophical conversations about design and meaning that the engineers around them would just tune out. It wasn't that Jobs didn't have time for philosophy. He had plenty. What he didn't have time for was what he considered "bullshit" in every form, and that included the philosophical variety. He didn't like any bureaucratic or design versions of the metaphorical bovine excrement, or its psychological forms. Philosophy itself wasn't at all the problem.

In the interview being referenced, Jobs purportedly couldn't see any benefit in imagining his then present self going back in time and giving his younger stage any sort of advice on the future—what was to him, in that present, already the past—either because he was entirely forward-looking in general, or because voicing such advice to a reporter would have meant baring himself a little too much, or even showing a vulnerability that he preferred to mask, since most of us would advise our younger selves, in such a thought experiment, to avoid things we had in fact done and that we had come to learn were unproductive or just wrong. Steve was not about to admit any such stuff to a reporter, or to anyone who was not a close friend, for what he apparently at that moment considered to be no good reason. At his best and most reflective, it seems he had a deep and extensive philosophy that, at his most impatient, he wasn't prepared to discuss.

During a memorial service held after his death, Steve's wife Laurene reflected a bit on his talents and thoughts and love of beauty. She said that living in California was important to him because of the quality of its natural beauty and the scale of it all, which, she said, was "the perfect setting for thinking big." She went on to add: "And he did think big. He was the most unfettered thinker I have ever known. It was a deep pleasure, and a lot of fun, to think alongside him." Some of the closest companions of Socrates were inclined to say the same thing.

Jobs seemed to embrace the humanities because of the resources he found there for moving forward and thinking big, and for understanding things that would make his work and his products stand out in a crowded marketplace that was, in his view, full of mediocrity, or worse—the "bullshit" he always wanted to avoid. He came to grasp quite deeply the fundamentals of aesthetics and the importance of beauty. He understood things about human nature that helped him get what he wanted from people. He may have personally misused some of that knowledge in his interpersonal interactions outside of work as well as within his professional endeavors, but his principle of immersion in the humanities as well as the sciences was a strong and astute perspective.

The humanities give us a deeper grasp of our basic human nature and our common condition, and the insights that result can then be used in very positive ways to build a business and a life. The sciences were, of course, unavoidable in the computer industry, and even in the very different business of digitally animated filmmaking that he pursued at Pixar. Everyone had to be comfortable with the scientific and technological side of things. But Jobs often stood apart by equally appreciating the humanities side as well—the importance of feeding your mind and spirit with resources that could be just as important, and at times even more vital to his aims of world-class innovation and the best customer experience.

Steve was indeed a busy man. He was too busy to philosophize without a purpose. But it was his philosophizing with purpose and creating a big vision philosophically that, along with his energy and charisma, set him apart in a distinctive way. And without the vision, the charisma could have gone nowhere. The energy would never alone have changed the world.

14

Stay Hungry, Stay Foolish

Did we not place hunger, thirst, and the like in the class of desires?
Socrates

As a young man, Steve had loved *The Whole Earth Catalogue*, the hippie-era compendium of all things needed for living independently and self sufficiently on the land. Their last print issue had featured on its back cover a picture of a country road and the valedictory injunction, "Stay Hungry, Stay Foolish." This advice appealed deeply to Jobs and it would become something like an inner mantra, a line that he used to great effect in his life, as well as in his famous Stanford University Commencement Address, which in its transcript form is perhaps one of the most widely read talks to graduates in modern history. This short directive became his advice for the young people gathered there, and as one of his own life imperatives is one of his central principles for any business leader who would seek to do great things.

Our philosophical guiding light, Socrates, was certainly a man hungry for wisdom, and he was known primarily as such. But true wisdom is often foolish in the eyes of the world. So the great thinker was likely to be seen as foolish by the majority of people who encountered him or heard of his mission. Dreamers, pioneers, and world changers throughout history have often been viewed in the same way. So, to those who would be world-class revolutionaries like Socrates or Steve Jobs, or any of the other greats who disrupted and innovated in their own times, this advice can resonate deeply. But exactly what does it mean?

A hungry person has some acutely felt needs and intense desires rooted in those needs. A truly hungry person is not comfortable or satisfied. He's highly motivated. A foolish person does not conform to the norms of those around him and does not bend to the accepted wisdom of the time. And, of course, Jobs isn't using these terms in their most literal senses, but in in a certain metaphorical and even ironic way—a favored approach to utterance often taken by the original Socrates. I suspect that Jobs thought of himself as always metaphorically hungry, and certainly as likewise foolish, at least in the eyes of the true fools of his time who could not fathom what he was doing or why he was doing it. Both of the adjectives in this famous piece of advice were certainly appropriated by Jobs to describe himself and then presented to others with more than a slight touch of self-referential irony. And both indicated something very important to him.

1. Passionate Nuts Own the Future.

Socrates sought to follow reason, but not in the way that his fellow Athenians did. To many of them, he seemed quite unreasonable in his dogged demands for truth and rationality. What then is it to be reasonable in this life? What is it to be unreasonable? George Bernard Shaw famously wrote these words:

> "The reasonable man adapts himself to the world. The unreasonable man persists in trying to adapt the world to himself. All progress, therefore, depends upon the unreasonable man."

Steve Jobs was clearly by this definition an unreasonable man. That's a big reason he was able to create such important parts of the future—now, our present—and certainly enable many more things that are still yet to come.

Most people who personally encountered Jobs in any context, or who worked closely with him, would later on, in reporting their experience of him, talk about his passionate intensity. He seemed to have an energy flowing in him and through him that was beyond normal human reach. The same was often said of Socrates, in his own time. There was an intense zeal that both men displayed and that tended to set them apart from the crowd.

In Steve's case, this often took the form of a magnetically attractive positive force that would dazzle people, charm them, lure them in, and bend them to his will. At other times, he could be "radiating hostility," in the words of one tirade victim, who later commented on the sheer force of the dark energy he experienced by saying of Jobs that, "He's got some heavy magic." This is clearly not a common sort of remark to make about anyone. Jobs somehow collected energy that he was then able to use, for good or ill.

In the realm of heavy magic, it's obviously better to be the great Dumbledore than to be the feared Voldemort. And Harry Potter, among others, knew that. Yet, for some of his adolescence, the young Harry felt the two possibilities warring within him. In the end, though, goodness prevailed. Steve seemed never to learn to tame this wild energy completely and use it for good alone. As long as he had it, he also had mixed success with handling it. The times he grew calmer and kinder, more subdued and humble and understanding, were often times when the energy had to an extent ebbed away, due to an inability to cope well with a business disaster—or later, because of the ravages of a serious disease. But whenever he had both health and success, he often appeared unable to manage the force in a way that was only honorable, with consistent kindness, and well. Yet, when his innate enthusiasm was positive and flowing and infectious, it did work like a good magic, and it launched the efforts for which we remember him.

It does seem that "nuts" own the future. Too often, bad nuts create massive havoc that we have to work hard to contain and control. They launch various disasters and calamities both within their own circumstances and around the globe. Their craziness creates its own gravitational field and deflects us from what we ought to be doing, instead of just responding to their chaos. But in the end, we all hope, the good nuts will in fact prevail—the hungry, foolish dreamers like Steve Jobs, and even old Socrates, who are able to step beyond the known and accepted ways of doing things and invent new possibilities for living and working in the world. And now we have an imperative principle from Steve that's reflective of this.

2. Never Be Satisfied with the Status Quo.

The point has often been made that Jobs was not an engineer or a technologist in any formal sense. He was a natural salesman. His problem was that, in his early years, he kept trying to sell the same thing over and over. He founded Apple Computer to make and sell computers. When he was forced out of the company in 1985 and then went through a period of debilitating depression, he came out of his funk and decided to start another company he called, simply, "NeXT." He saw it then as his new mission to make and sell more computers. His vision was that they would be better and more powerful than anything Apple had. And as a result, they would be more expensive. But he viewed his job as basically the same—making and selling computers.

When it soon became clear that the top team of people he had assembled at NeXT had built a remarkable and costly computer that few could afford or wanted to buy, but had also created new software that many companies both needed and wanted, he should have been able to shift gears quickly. But he found it hard to think of himself as doing anything else other than building and selling computers. Then, when he bought a small computer animation division from George Lukas, he thought at first that, in this other new venture, he would again *build and sell computers*—this time with some animation capabilities that were unique. But these computers were also far too expensive, and he couldn't find enough customers. With the blinders still on that came from what he had known in the past, he was lucky to have other people in his life, in these new contexts, who had sparks of insight that could point him in a different direction.

When John Lassiter started making short films to show what their animation computer could do, no one realized that the company, Pixar, would go on to be a major film production company, rather than an outfit that just made and sold specialty computers. Jobs certainly didn't see it that way—at least, not for a very long time. He was, during all that time of challenge and struggle, stuck on Hill A, and slow to change his vision for what he was doing—until he came back to Apple in 1997. Then he seemed, like never before, to be set on the sort of ongoing disruptive invention and change that had launched Apple in the first place. He had to learn never to be satisfied again with the *status quo*, and never to let anyone around him get complacent in that way. He finally understood that each adventure we're on prepares us for the next one that's to come, but often in ways we don't expect, and that our next adventures rarely should just replicate with minor changes the previous ones we've lived. The push is to do something radically, really, and freshly new.

The great irony is that those among us who are most satisfied with the *status quo* rarely end up being fully happy with the results of that satisfaction. When we keep doing the same things in the same ways, the world eventually passes us by. Yesterday's success too often becomes tomorrow's failure—at least, for those who fail to continue to pioneer. I think Steve Jobs finally came to understand at a fundamental level that life is change. Reality is dynamic. As the ancient philosopher Heraclitus said, "Everything is always changing." Our approaches to work should be as dynamic as the world in which we live. We need to be out front making change, and not just watching it, or even simply responding to it. We ourselves need to be masters of change. Ongoing innovation is certainly the only way to live and do business well in modern times. Only then can we continue to prosper.

In Steve's life, this dynamic philosophy really began to manifest itself during his famed second act at Apple. It became a time for thinking differently in major new ways. And his big departures from the ways things had long been done are what eventually set Apple apart and blazed the path to a new future. We're clearly most comfortable with what we know. But we're also most successful only when we move out into the unknown, bravely face the uncertain, and do genuinely new things.

The *status quo* is a subtly dangerous place to stay. Remember Hill A and Hill B. Hill A, representing your first big success, should always be your base camp for your next adventure, as you locate and ascend the next challenge, your Hill B. Part of being hungry is wanting more. Part of being foolish is leaving behind what you know; and in appearing to live dangerously, you may actually find the only path that's ultimately safe at all. Such paradox is often a sign of truth and even a pointer in the direction of greatness. And so we need a reminder.

3. Creativity Stays a Step Ahead of Normal

Jobs wanted his products, his people, and his companies to be extraordinary. I love the way the Oxford English Dictionary defines the word 'extraordinary.' It uses terms like 'exceptional,' 'surprising,' and 'unusually great.' By contrast, the word 'ordinary' gets this treatment:

> Regular, normal, customary, usual, not exceptional, not above the usual, commonplace...

There is, in principle, absolutely nothing wrong with what's ordinary—except when it's also poor-to-mediocre, or significantly less than our best. But that's exactly the problem, isn't it? That's just what ordinary most ordinarily is. The ordinary life is typically one defined by the past rather than by the possible, by other people's expectations rather than our own aspirations, or by what's easy rather than what's right, and by most often considering the safe path instead of the best one. Ordinary efforts seldom yield exceptional results.

Why should we settle for ordinary when so much more is available? Something extraordinary beckons to us all, whatever our circumstances, and simply awaits our response. And that's the perspective Steve Jobs was driven to bring to everything he did. He would not tolerate ordinariness. He was always in search of the magic that would take us beyond the mundane. He insisted that people rise higher and do more than they would ever have thought they were capable of accomplishing. And that's how he was able to fuel such innovation beyond the norm.

The people around Jobs often wished that he would be more normal in his emotions, actions, and general treatment of others. They wanted him to be calmer and kinder. When we study his life carefully, we quickly come to realize that there were deep and damaging forces mixed in with the positive impulses that drove him. We should never seek to replicate in our own lives those dark forces, or the actions to which they led. They were elements that often constrained and hampered him, rather than simply helping. They certainly pushed him along, but they also often tripped him up. Fortunately, they were connected in his life to other more positive elements and a persistent drive that aided him greatly. In most other contexts, the occasional, unfortunate behaviors that he was so infamous for would have been eventually self-destructive, to the extent that they would not have allowed for the sort of tremendous success he had. And we should never emulate that behavior in our own situations. But his desire to push beyond the normal in thoroughly positive ways, beyond the *status quo*, is something we can all aspire to in our work and lives.

The fourteen leadership principles first articulated by Walter Isaacson that we have examined here at length are clearly helpful guides to many of the things that animated Steve Jobs and assisted him to push through challenges and difficulties that would have defeated most people. They also offer insightful keys as to how he was able to do so many things spectacularly well. It's no surprise that a student of history and people who is as astute as Isaacson would be able to identify such core elements in the life of even so complex a figure as Jobs. And these principles have been quite productive to examine philosophically. I think we should get them all in view again for a moment, now that we've explored each in at least some detail.

The Fourteen Leadership Principles from Steve Jobs

1. Focus
2. Simplify
3. Take Responsibility End to End
4. When Behind, Leapfrog
5. Put Products Before Profit
6. Don't Be a Slave to Focus Groups
7. Bend Reality
8. Impute
9. Push for Perfection
10. Tolerate Only "A" Players
11. Engage Face to Face
12. Know Both the Big Picture and the Details
13. Combine the Humanities with the Sciences
14. Stay Hungry, Stay Foolish

These principles can help us to get our minds around the key lessons that are to be lifted from Jobs' own words, or that can be read off his customary practices. They distill the essence of a lot that he did well, and give us reminders that can be helpful in other, vastly different, business contexts, and various personal contexts, as well. They are a vital part of his personal philosophical operating system, the OS that lay behind his extraordinary success. But I think we can also go a step farther in our grasp of what made him great. There's still a measure of philosophical understanding yet to be achieved. And that's what comes next.

Part Two

The Seven Conditions

15

The Deep Operating System for Success

The builder won't make all his own tools—and he needs many.
The same is true, in like manner, of the weaver and shoemaker.
Socrates

Some people seem successful in nearly everything they do. Others struggle constantly, regardless of the situation. What makes the difference? Is there anything that all the most successful people have in common that helps lead to their accomplishments?

Here's another important question. In every period of human history, however tough and trying, there have been people who not only survived but flourished and thrived to the point that they experienced great success. Steve Jobs overcame heavy odds that were clearly stacked against him in so many ways, and he ultimately succeeded in his business endeavors to a rare and amazing degree. There are individuals who do so in nearly every period of time, across cultures and throughout the centuries. One question many people naturally ask, then, when contemplating figures like Steve Jobs is: How can I possibly be among such people in our own day? What tools do they use that are universal?

Throughout my unusual career as a public philosopher, I've had the great opportunity to speak with many extremely successful leaders across industries and various areas of human endeavor who have possessed an unusual talent, or knack, for doing all the right things throughout their own lives in order to achieve extraordinary degrees of success. But they have often confided to me that they've felt frustrated at the difficulty of articulating well enough to others, even within their own circle of direct reports, what exactly it is that they've intuitively done throughout their lives, and where likewise those lieutenants should focus their own attention, in order to keep the success going. It's a more common problem than you might imagine. It's one thing to be a top performer, another altogether to be a great coach or analyst and commentator on the particulars of such performance. Doing great things and teaching others how to do great things are very different endeavors.

Highly accomplished individuals can't always explain to other people what they have innately done. Sometimes, they simply can't find the words. And when I've had a chance to help them with that, they often come alive with relief and even a measure of genuine excitement. As a philosopher whose primary challenge is to unearth hidden concepts, analyze complex behaviors, and articulate deeper truths, I've often been able to help top leaders to become good teachers in this one crucial way. And when they can clearly explain what they've naturally done and want to see others do well to carry on their mutual enterprises, they can then take those endeavors to even higher levels.

In case after case of discovering what accomplished people have done in their lives to bring new things into the world, I've come to believe that there is something like a deep personal and organizational operating system for success. In an older analogy, it can be thought of metaphorically as a toolkit. It's a logically integrated cluster of ideas that I first came to identify more than a quarter century ago as I studied the wisdom of the most practical philosophers throughout the ages, and the lives of highly successful people across cultures. I see this operating system, or this toolkit, or cluster of practical ideas, in the best work and highest accomplishments of Steve Jobs. The kit contains tools that we don't have to create ourselves. They're already available for us. They emerge from a deep understanding of human nature and have been identified by the wisest diagnosticians of the human condition who have ever lived. They've been used in every major culture. And they've proved their worth, time and again. Some people seem to be born with the inclination and skill to use these tools instinctively, and without a high degree of self-conscious awareness that this is what they're doing. But an effective use of the tools can be taught to anyone capable of learning, setting goals, and achieving things in the world.

These are ideas that have stood the test of time. And even though some are connected in one way or another to Isaacson's Fourteen Principles, they contain much that his framework of ideas doesn't identify, and much, I think, that benefitted Steve Jobs throughout his career. Jobs wasn't, of course, always acting in perfect accord with these conditions for success throughout his life, but whenever his actions were harmonious with them, he flourished. And whenever they weren't, he had trouble. To the extent that he succeeded out of all proportion to any reasonable expectations, I think these universal conditions for success will explain to us a large part of why. And, like the fourteen principles, they can equip us also for our own best forms of success.

From Plato and Aristotle, Lao Tsu and Confucius, throughout the centuries across various cultures and up to the present day, I would suggest that the wisest people who have ever thought about life achievement have left us bits and pieces of powerful advice for attaining success in nearly anything we do. Over the past few decades, I've worked to put these great ideas together into a simple framework that's ultimately settled in to seven universal conditions for success.

These conditions are universal in at least three ways. First, they are recognized across cultures in the best practical thought, historically and globally. Second, they apply to every aspect of our lives, personal or professional. And third, they govern team collaborations and organizational efforts, as well as individual challenges. I would also contend that any other condition or principle for success that we might be offered is either less than universal, or else can be viewed as an application of one of these seven conditions within specific circumstances. If I'm right, then these seven tools will give us the most universal toolkit for achievement. As such, the framework is as powerful as it is simple. And it can be used in any industry or challenge.

Since I was first able to identify these seven conditions in the late nineteen-eighties, I've been able to bring them to the attention of leaders and top practitioners across industries and professions, both in the US and in various other parts of the world. I've personally tested them in the cauldron of contemporary challenges. I've also talked about them at length with some of the most celebrated and outstanding achievers of our day.

As I've worked with these tools, I've discovered that the most successful people who've had a chance to study these ideas tend to endorse them immediately, instinctively, and resoundingly as describing what they've done in their own careers to produce and enjoy great accomplishments. I'm also convinced that they map out a good part of what we need to understand about the Socrates of Silicon Valley who is our topic of focus, and the revolutionary success that he managed to attain during his life, despite all the many obstacles he faced, both inner and outer. As I did with Isaacson's fourteen principles, I'll just lay them out here, at first, in the simplest possible way, as a basic framework, and then we'll briefly look at what they mean. Let's consider at a quick glance the particular sweep of the ideas, and then we'll descend into a more detailed look, with an eye to Steve Jobs and his habits of mind.

The 7 Cs of Success

For the most deeply satisfying and sustainable forms of success, we need to bring into any challenge, opportunity, or relationship these inner traits, or facilitating conditions:

1. A clear **CONCEPTION** of what we want, a vivid vision, a goal clearly imagined.
2. A strong **CONFIDENCE** that we can attain that goal.
3. A focused **CONCENTRATION** on what it takes to reach the goal.
4. A stubborn **CONSISTENCY** in pursuing our vision.
5. An emotional **COMMITMENT** to the importance of what we're doing.
6. A good **CHARACTER** to guide us and keep us on a proper course.
7. A **CAPACITY TO ENJOY** the process along the way.

The 7 Cs of Success give us what may be the most universal, logical, integrated, and comprehensive framework of facilitating conditions to position ourselves for success in whatever we do. There are certainly many other concepts and techniques, habits and bits of advice often associated with success, but as I've mentioned, I'm thoroughly convinced that every one of the ideas not found in this list either falls short of the universality test, or else is just a partial version, or results from a particular use, of one or more of these seven ideas in specific situations. I have also come to believe that these seven concepts give us the most fundamental personal operating system underlying the astonishing success that Steve Jobs was able to attain by the use of the particular principles we've already examined. I'd like now to share a bit of explanation about each.

We need first in any challenge or enterprise:

1. A clear CONCEPTION of what we want, a vivid vision, a goal clearly imagined.

In any facet of our lives, we need to think through as clearly as possible what we want to accomplish, and what exactly we'd like to see happen. True success in challenging endeavors always starts with an inner vision, however incomplete it might be. The world as we find it is just raw material for what we can make it. We're meant to be artists with our energies and our lives. And the only way to do that well is to structure our actions around clear goals. Vague thoughts cannot motivate specific and productive behavior. We need clear and well-defined goals, as precise and detailed as we can make them. In times of change, this is more important than ever, however difficult it might seem. The fight for clarity in our vision for what we want to make happen is well worth the ongoing effort it takes.

Two great pieces of advice on goals come down to us from the ancient world. First, every exercise in goal setting should be an exercise in self-knowledge. Who am I as a person? What's right for me? What do I love? What do I not like so much? What are my resources and skills? What's my network of relationships? At an organizational level: Who are we as a business? What's our mission? What's our position in the market, or in our overall context? How can we make our best difference now? What's right for us? What sorts of partners might further empower us? Answering such questions is crucial, and for a simple reason. Goals give us structure. Proper goals give us the right structure. Goals that are rooted the most deeply in self-knowledge are the most powerful of all.

Second, we need an ongoing inner boldness for setting new goals, bigger and different targets as we move forward, realizing that this sort of exercise in structuring and guiding new behavior should never stop. Life is indeed supposed to be a series of adventures. Great goals produce great adventures. And then, in turn, great adventures produce more great goals. It's what philosophers call a virtuous cycle. Michael Moritz, who knew Steve Jobs for many years and was a sort of mentor for him, has said about him, "He was curious and adventurous and open to the sensations of life." That ongoing curiosity and adventurous openness to the new powered him forward and led him intuitively to the goals and challenges that could change industries.

One of the qualities that made Steve such a powerful and effective leader was his strength and clarity of vision. He wasn't always right, but he was almost always vivid in his conception of what was needed next. In the few cases where he was not able to clarity his vision for a product, as for example the Lisa computer, things went very badly. But there aren't many such instances to cite. He was typically gifted with great clarity. And he communicated his goals clearly, firmly, and even at times loudly, and always without compromise. It's never enough for a leader to have clear goals—everyone on his team and in the organization needs to understand and share those goals, and with the highest clarity that can be communicated to them.

Even when we set the wrong goals, the clearer and more vivid they are, the better we're able to act on them and the sooner we can then see that they need to be adjusted or replaced with alternate aims. Clarity never hinders. It always helps. Whenever we're mired in vagueness or inner conflict, we have to fight through the confusion to attain the clarity that's needed. In any creative endeavor, and with any attempt to make a new product or construct a new service, conception precedes creation, and then benefits from it. The clearer the conception is, the better the overall process can work. Next, we need:

(2) A strong CONFIDENCE that we can attain the goal.

INNER ATTITUDE IS A MAJOR KEY TO OUTER RESULTS. OVER a century ago, the prominent and groundbreaking Harvard philosopher and psychologist William James learned from a study of championship athletes that a proper confidence should be operative throughout our lives. In any new enterprise or challenge, we need, up front, a strong initial faith in what we're doing. And we need resilient confidence, a form of assurance that can take its lumps and keep on going. James called it *precursive faith*—a faith that "runs ahead of" the evidence, according to the etymology of the phrase he coined. Sometimes we have to work hard to generate this attitude. It's not often easy to run ahead of the evidence we have and stretch out into an uncertain future. But it's also well worth the work it takes, because it raises our objective prospects for success. With a strong enough belief in ourselves, we eliminate, or at least reduce, the inner psychic obstacles to our own performance, opening up the way to a full use of all our resources.

As a classic narcissist, Jobs didn't have a problem with showing confidence. Narcissism is just a strong defensive mindset that typically arises out of an emotional wound of some sort in early life. You could never please your demanding mother or dismissive father. You felt an early rejection or abandonment. And so now you have to win and please the world. This mindset then involves many shields developed to block or deflect any further painful messages from life. A narcissist easily becomes self-absorbed in grand tasks through which he plans to prove himself to be worthy and valuable. He often lacks empathy for the feelings of other people around him, and especially when that empathy might interfere with his own sense of progress. He almost always maintains and displays a high degree of positive self-confidence that comes, more often than not, from a deep need for a sense of mastery rather than from any particular degree of rational preparation. And yet, an intelligent narcissist will do the preparation to further enhance his chances of success. The confidence that he can do any needed preparatory work effectively even typically runs ahead of the evidence.

The interesting thing about Jobs, and something that he shared with most narcissists, is that an ongoing and overt display of strong self-confidence came quite naturally—he tended to believe he was right, even when he was pretty obviously wrong. Sometimes, this got him into trouble, but most often it was an important contributing cause of his success. He captivated and enthralled many other highly successful people with the strength of his confidence. They saw in him what they had presumably felt in their own hearts and too rarely witnessed in the lives of others around them. It was one of his qualities that the best people he was recruiting often responded to very favorably. It generally drew other highly accomplished individuals to him with a special magnetism. People wanted to be a part of whatever he was doing. And this attribute of self-assurance frequently propelled him through difficulties that would have stopped most people.

Associates sometimes talked of Jobs as demonstrating grit, determination, and incredible perseverance, or a stubborn persistence through daunting challenges. And despite being a man who was almost always in a hurry, he was often able to exercise tremendous patience in developing a product, or a company like Pixar, over time. These qualities are almost impossible to possess and exercise without a baseline of strong confidence underlying their demonstration. Confident people can work and wait for the best results. Confident people don't give up.

The best confidence, of course, naturally arises out of a strong competence, and then augments it. It's certainly no guarantee of success. But it is among the chief facilitators or contributors to it. In times of great change and economic uncertainty, personal confidence is one of the first things to diminish and disappear. If we're concerned with proper accomplishment in our own lives, we should follow the champions on this point and guard a proper boldness of confidence in our hearts.

If you find that you need help with your level of confidence, one ancient solution is to try to help someone else with his or her own confidence, and then you may be surprised by how it quickly rises within your spirit as well. We learn best when we teach. By giving, we receive. And we are always deeply helped when we ourselves offer help. This is a beautiful paradox of the spirit. Then, in our march toward success we next need:

(3) A focused CONCENTRATION on what it takes to reach the goal.

BIG DREAMS JUST LEAD TO BIG DISAPPOINTMENTS WHEN people don't learn how to chart their way forward, step-by-step. One of the greatest pieces of advice ever given about achieving any big dream is to "Divide then Conquer." Divide it up, break it down, and then take it on, focusing on what's needed, step-by-step. If I want to be at a certain point a year from now, where do I have to be six months from now? How about three months from now? What can I be doing today and then tomorrow? Daunting goals become manageable objectives as we divide and conquer. We need to learn to focus on what's first, and then on what's next. Real success at anything that's challenging comes from planning your path forward and then putting that plan into action.

The focused concentration we need has to be intellectual and practical, a focus of thought and energy leading to action. As Socrates once said, "Nothing that is really good and admirable is granted by the gods to men without effort and application." When we concentrate our thoughts, energies, and actions well, we can make progress.

Psychologists teach us that a new mental focus often generates what we can think of as having the impact of new perceptual abilities. Concentrating your thought and energy in a new direction, toward a clear goal, you begin to see things around you that you might have missed before—things that relate to the goal you've set and that can help you attain it. This new focused concentration can allow you then to set effective intermediate goals and also even more immediate ones to get your plan going, and then guide you in action and adaptation as you go. Even a flawed plan can start you off and help lead you to where you can more likely discover a better one. A continually focused concentration of thought and action throughout the process of your goal pursuit is key.

Steve Jobs clearly had intense focus and a formidable power of concentration. It was one of his most remarkable qualities and was often commented on by others. He wasn't an inventor of new technologies. But when he had a clear goal, he knew how to find the people and ideas already out in the world that he could use to move toward attaining the goal. In many ways, he was clearly masterful at developing a focused concentration on how to use other people's ideas better than they themselves would likely ever have been able to do so. When he famously visited a research division of the Xerox company and first saw a graphical user interface on a monitor, one that was roughly akin to the use of desktop icons that he would go on to make ubiquitous and necessary in personal technology, he focused his thought and actions on how it could all be put to use in his new computer. He was later to say that if Xerox had only done what he went on to do, they could have owned the computer business, and the history of technology would have been quite different.

It was an interesting thing about Jobs. He often put other people's ideas and inventions to better use than they could themselves. In an interview, he once said, "Who cares where the good ideas come from? If you're paying attention, you'll notice them." He was opportunistic in the best possible way. And sometimes, even great creativity is just the proper repurposing of what's already available. A focused concentration makes that possible.

Steve Jobs had a distinctive and characteristic ability to attain a strong focus, and became legendary, in part, because it was a main ingredient in his capacity to create legendary results. All great jobs require great focus, with a concentration of thought and energy working together. Next up, we need:

4. A stubborn CONSISTENCY in pursuing our vision.

The word 'consistency' comes from two Greek roots—a verb meaning "to stand" and a particle meaning "together." Consistency is all about standing together. Do my actions stand together with my words? Do my reactions and emotions stand together with my deepest beliefs and values? Do the people I work with stand together? Do the various departments and divisions of the business stand together? Even on a personal level we can ask: "Do the members of my family stand together, or are we pulling apart?" This is what consistency is all about. It's a matter of unifying our energy and efforts in a single direction, personally or collectively. It won't allow for contrary and self-defeating uses of time or energy. It keeps us on course.

Chinese philosophers often refer to this sort of consistency as harmony, and to illustrate the nature of a strongly consistent movement forward despite any presence of obstacles, they use the image of moving water, which can flow around any obstruction, or push an obstacle out of the way. They say, "Be like water." Flow forward to your goals, adapting to your circumstances and, at the same time, staying true to the essence of who and what you most deeply are—making sure that your actions are harmonious with what you fundamentally value and desire. Inconsistency defuses power. It scatters focus and energy. Consistency marshals power and moves us toward our goals.

Being consistent in our goal pursuit doesn't mean always doing things in the same way. That's just being stuck. It means doing things together in the most powerful ways. Steve Jobs was often to be seen trying to get everyone on a project to stand together and work hard in the same direction. He wasn't great about the emotional side of harmony—and too often, this problem hampered or even defused his efforts. It was an area that could have used a lot of work in his life. But in matters of project focus and product quality, he was usually to be found demanding the highest consistency and relentlessly urging it on others, despite the difficulty of it in other areas of his life. Design, function, packaging, sales—everything about the Apple experience had to be consistent, and consistently great. The fact that he was able to get so much accomplished and at such a high level of overall consistency is eloquent testimony to his ability to motivate the people around him to stand together on a project, working powerfully toward the desired and deeply harmonious results.

Consistency, at its best, isn't backward looking or blindly repetitious. It's forward thinking and doing. It's about acting in concert, and in harmony with both our highest goals and our deepest values. It's about maximizing our efforts and pushing through our difficulties with a clear aim in view. It can require frequent adjustment and adaptation along the way in support of our goals. It has thus a paradoxical relationship with change, both embracing it and yet always ordering it to the end in view. In changing times, one of the most common sources of failure is inconsistent behavior, action contrary to our own goals and values. We have to insist on consistent conduct in support of our goals, and do everything possible to encourage consistency within our teams and organizations. We need consistency. And with it, we also need:

5. An emotional COMMITMENT to the importance of what we're doing.

IT'S HARD TO BE CONSISTENT IF YOU'RE NOT COMMITTED. Passion is at the core of extraordinary success. It's a key to overcoming difficulties, seizing opportunities, and getting other people excited about your projects. Too much goal setting in the modern world of business has been an act of the mind without a full engagement of the heart. It's been all about ideas and the rational intellect, and reasons and numbers, and yet has ignored feelings and passions. We philosophers certainly are among the first to appreciate the role of rationality in human life. But we know that it's not just the head, but also the heart, that can guide us on to the tasks that are right for us, and keep us functioning at the peak of our abilities. To quote again the eminently quotable Pascal, "The heart has its reasons of which reason knows nothing." The mind alone is never enough for achievement through challenge. Reason and emotion should be put to work in tandem. Then, powerful things can happen.

I advise people to do what they're passionate about, or else to find a way to be passionate about what they do, and then to communicate that enthusiasm and commitment to their associates and clients, showing an equal commitment to them as collaborative partners for the goals that can best be pursued together. People are attracted to people who care. Anyone who demonstrates a properly committed care for any noble cause can, as a result, go far. And any good cause can be made noble by the right attitude.

A contemporary of Pascal, Nicolas Herman, who joined a monastic order and took on the name Lawrence of the Resurrection, but has become known most widely as Brother Lawrence, talked of doing everything for the love of God, whether he was working in the kitchen or caring for the sandals of all the other brothers. In Zen, it's said that the unenlightened man chops wood and carries water, while the enlightened man chops wood and carries water. It's not the activity, but the inner perspective that makes all the difference. When I was a professor, I'd notice two students in the big auditorium sitting side by side. One was bored. The other was enthralled. They were hearing the same words. A great lesson in life consists in realizing that it's up to use what we bring to our situations. When we bring commitment and passion, our activities light up with a new sense of value and importance, and even nobility. And that quickly can become contagious for the other people around us.

This may be the one positive thing in the life and personality of Steve Jobs that people who personally knew him talked about the most: his passion, his enthusiasm, and his seemingly endless emotional commitment and energy for what he was doing. He was extreme. He brought intensity to everything he did. He was crazy on fire with his vision for how he could change the world, and he didn't often know how to turn down the volume or reduce the heat a little for what he felt, in a way that might be more sensitive or appropriate to the situation or context he was in.

Henry Nicholas, the founder of Broadcom, once commented on his interactions with Jobs and put the point like this:

> I never knew when Steve was going to call. But I knew that when he did, it would probably be in the middle of the night. In 2001 my company was developing Ethernet chips for Mac computers. Steve was enormously excited about our product. He was enormously excited about everything. And restless and sometimes agitated—and frankly, he could be a bit of a pain. He was like a bulldog. He worked all the time, day and night, and he expected everyone around him to be that way, too.

In a widely watched video online, Jobs talks about the power and necessity of passion for attaining the persistence that worthy endeavors in life require. Most valuable things are much harder than we think they'll be to accomplish or secure, and we'd just give up if we didn't have a passionate commitment to what we're doing. In that video, Jobs even talks about genuine love as necessary for hanging in there when the results just aren't yet coming. It's all about a deep and ongoing emotional commitment, at every level.

My friend Tom Looney has shared with me a small trove of personal emails from Steve when they were working together at NeXT. I'll reproduce one below in its entirety just to demonstrate how his commitment and the passion that resulted could be demonstrated in a business email, in response to some good news.

Content-Type: application/x-nextmail
Mime-Version: 1.0 (NeXT Mail 3.3 v116.1
From: Steve Jobs <Steve_Jobs>
Date: Thu, 13 Oct 94 21:33:48 -0700
To: tlooney
Subject: Re: Note from Gerdelman

Yippie !!

The recipient of this email often spoke of Steve's passion, or "zeal"—a word that has often been used of Socrates and his own indefatigable energy. Steve's commitment, in both its depth and height, was responsible for his widely recognized charisma, but also in another way for his angry tirades and strange, occasional bouts of uncontrolled sobbing in business meetings when things were not going his way. It wasn't all just cold and calculated manipulation. That commitment of the heart was a wellspring of emotion for him, as well as of action. Steve couldn't stand to be resisted or thwarted, and he couldn't usually control his expressions of emotion as most of us seek to do in normal business and life settings. The passion did propel his success. But its more egregious manifestations often created problems, as well. And this just reflects a deep truth about life: Our greatest strengths are often related very closely with our greatest weaknesses. In the life of Steve Jobs, a strong emotional commitment was a crucial part of his operating system. A better, more modulated control of its expression could probably have allowed him to go farther, and even faster—as hard as that might be to imagine. But in addition to passion, we need:

6. A good CHARACTER to guide us and keep us on a proper course.

This condition was perhaps in a great many ways the biggest challenge and signature weakness for Jobs. It's important for us to understand it, both for grasping what he often did without, in the view of many around him—especially in his early years—and for seeing clearly the role of this strongly facilitating condition, generally, for achieving long-term, sustainable, satisfying success in any challenge. But first, I need to provide a quick clarification of the logical status for these conditions we're considering.

The components to be found in The 7 Cs of Success don't make up what philosophers call "logically necessary conditions" for the achievement of any particular goal or any specific level of accomplishment. They aren't individually necessary and jointly sufficient for any particular desired achievement. They're rather what can be considered facilitating or enabling conditions for success. They contribute to raising the probability, or objective likelihood, of success in any challenging endeavor, but can't promise or guarantee it. They merely position us in the best way for both sustainable and satisfying success in any challenge. And having a good character for inner guidance and support is one of these facilitating conditions. A low level of one condition, or a lack of it, is then not guaranteed to torpedo any given success, but will decrease the probability of its initial attainment, and its likelihood thereafter of lasting. Most successful people operate most of the time in accordance with at least five or six of these seven conditions. But it's ideal to act in harmony with all seven.

Let's start off our discussion of this condition in the life of Steve

Jobs with a classic understanding of moral character as that cluster of inner strengths and weaknesses we bring to any situation of dealing with the world and other people around us. So, in this sense, we'll initially understand good character in a broad stroke way as involving such qualities as honesty, integrity, courage, and kindness. We'll go into more detail shortly. But in this initial sense, there are some things we've understood since ancient times. Character inspires or erodes, or actually extinguishes trust. And trust is necessary for people to work together well. Good character is required for great collaboration. In a world in which innovative partnerships and collaborative strategies are increasingly important, a broadly moral foundation for working well together matters more than ever before. And good character does a bigger job than just provide for trust. It has an effect on each individual's own freedom and insight.

Bad character not only corrupts and diminishes, it also blinds. A person whose perspective has been deeply twisted by selfishness, or dishonesty, or cowardice, cannot understand the world in as perceptive a way as someone whose sensibilities are morally or ethically well formed. A bad character will inevitably distort our sensibilities and judgments, and limit our ability to grasp important features of the world around us. Good character, by contrast, through its enhancement of keen perspicacity, raises the likelihood of sustainable success in the company of others, and in the world.

Good character also makes you a more persuasive person when working with others. Aristotle believed that to be great at selling ideas or new possibilities, to be convincing with others, you need to be a master of thee things: Logos, Pathos, and Ethos—Logic and information; Passion and emotion; Character and integrity. This is the foundation for masterful persuasion and lasting success.

Steve Jobs did not have a spotless character record throughout his life. But then again, who does? And, yet, when he fell short, he fell big. There were, as a result, some sizable spots on his character. It's well known that he apparently deceived his good friend and business partner Steve Wozniak on at least one occasion in their very early years of working together. He secretly withheld money that Woz should have shared. For years, he tried to ignore the existence of his first child and the financial plight that she shared with her mother, his former girlfriend, who had to live on public assistance while he was busy amassing a fortune. He could be completely self-absorbed and apparently without feelings regarding the welfare of others, on at least some occasions. At other times, he could be kind and generous. But he often seemed willing to twist facts and dissemble mightily to suit his own interests.

One man who knew him well for many years has told me, on the general issue of character, that, "Steve didn't chase secretaries and run through quick marriages with four or five of them, like so many other business founders and leaders in Silicon Valley." And that was good. However, it's almost all that this personal confidant could say in a positive vein on the general issue of Steve's character. Sometimes, Jobs showed great affection and concern for others, and even real loyalty. But many business associates, friends, and employees who were the occasional recipients of this distinctively nice treatment, would reflect, years later, that it could all have been part of an overall effort at subtle and effective manipulation. Even when he seemed to be acting in a way that showed good ethical character in his business endeavors, the evidence we have is apparently compatible with his mindset having been anything but resoundingly virtuous.

Machiavelli argued in his famous little book *The Prince* that it's better for a leader to put forth the appearance of being good, rather than actually being good. The argument was that evil adversaries could easily take advantage of a truly good person; whereas, a shrewd individual merely using the appearances of goodness for his own ends was less likely to be tripped up by an enemy. Machiavelli, of course, seemed to ignore altogether what such manipulative behavior would do to the prince himself, and to his relationships with his closest allies and compatriots—the people on whom he would have to depend for getting things done. For the most part, smart people eventually recognize manipulation for what it is and come to resent it deeply. It simply alienates them. The manipulator in some way inadvertently reveals his true colors. And, because of this, he can't sustain many positive relationships, and will almost inevitably suffer their untimely end.

It might be helpful to have something like a checklist here on the notion of character. Let's look for a moment at Aristotle's classic conception of the virtues, or the individual human strengths that together form good character. From the wealth of what's been written and said about Jobs, from various candid reports by people who knew him, and from what he himself has said across various media, we can perhaps assess how he stood, as a leader and a businessperson, on each classic virtue. Our assessments will be quick here, but will give us a useful overview. We'll begin with what Aristotle thought of as the most important of all the virtues, one that would be needed for embodying any of the others in challenging circumstances.

Courage: a commitment to do what's right, despite the risk—Jobs scored well in many ways here, but not if "right" is meant in a narrowly ethical way. He was courageously committed to doing what was aesthetically right, and technologically best. But he sometimes lied and broke promises, and deprived people of what was rightfully theirs. It may even be that his worst personal failure, to accept and love his first child as his own, was due to a fear of not being able to balance a family with the work he felt he had to do. And this may have been his deepest and most regrettable lapse of courage.

Temperance: a moderation and proper self-restraint—Well, this was not a general strength for Steve, especially in his treatment of others. But in odd ways, he was a man of moderate appetites and needs, at least in things like clothing, home furnishings, and food choices. Yet, his obsessions were many. And his intemperate anger was legendary. So we have a clearly mixed report here.

Liberality: a freedom in giving to others what can help—Advice? Yes. Great work associates? Definitely. Good working conditions? Ok. At least, we can grant this if we discount the constant pressure, the often oppressive secrecy, and the many insane deadlines. But the buildings were nice. And yet, we have to ask: What about his tendencies for giving in other ways? Think: stock options. He could be churlish and even miserly with others, and withhold what they both needed and rightfully should receive. His approach to stock options at both Pixar and Apple resulted in fiercely fought battles, ill will, and long-term resentments, at least until someone else stepped in and insisted on the right thing. And not even that always worked. Was he liberal with encouragement, praise, and even human basic kindness? No. And yet, I know of some moving personal stories where Steve was surprising generous in attitude and in a sincere offer of help for an associate who was in the midst of adopting a child. He could go out of his way to be solicitous and helpful. Let me give an example. A trusted and highly valued colleague suddenly had to take a leave of absence right before what would be a crucial time of business transition. It was possible that the leave might end up being a more permanent departure. And this was a man expected to play a crucial rôle in the changes that were about ready to happen. The Steve we hear so much about could have gone ballistic. But his actual response, quickly sent by personal email was:

From: Steve_Jobs (Steve Jobs)
Date: Wed, 10 Feb 93 09:40:24 -0800
To: Tom Looney <Tom_Looney>
Subject: Re: Looney's Personal Decision about NeXT

> I am sad to lose you, but I understand. Thanks for doing this now, rather than a month from now. If you ever want to return, just call me. I think very highly of you.

The recipient of this kind response was my friend Tom Looney. As a matter of fact, he did return after his leave to have his best years at NeXT during the time that was also the best stretch for the company, building up the business that would eventually be bought by Apple and lead to the return of Jobs to the position from which he would go on to change the world. This one short private email has a tone that we haven't heard a lot about in Steve's conversations and correspondence with his closest associates, but it was just as much a part of the man as those aspects that repeatedly have been played up in the press and in various biographies. He could be kind and authentically generous. And yet, he could be frustratingly inconsistent in this Aristotelian liberality of giving graciously, and in his attitude toward it.

Magnificence: a capacity for acting on a grand scale—YES. Certainly, this was a talent. Jobs had a flair for the dramatic and the grand far beyond what most people ever display. He had an expansive capacity to act on the biggest stage imaginable. This, we can certainly grant him. No scale of difficulty would hold him back. In fact, he seemed to relish the biggest challenges and launching the most massive changes.

Pride: a true sense of honor and worthiness—The "true" part is, of course, the hang-up here. Jobs certainly displayed a firm grasp of his own self-worth and value, but his real inner self-esteem was something that, deep down, was likely a big problem for him. He was clearly proud of his many accomplishments, in the sense of the things he had created, and the way he was making his big dent in the universe, but I think this attribute was problematic for him in many ways. Proper pride never shades into arrogance or presumptuousness or any hint of braggadocio. It's not overweening or overwhelming or loudly insistent. It's rather calmly and firmly confident in itself and its prospects.

Good Temper: an inner calm displayed outwardly—Well, Ok, Apparently Not Often. Despite all his keen, ongoing interest in Zen and the meditative traditions of the east, he seemed a troubled soul throughout much of his working life, and was prone to emotional outbursts whenever his desires weren't being satisfied. He could hold a grudge and nurse a sense of grievance like no one else. There was an inner turbulence never fully resolved. But as he aged, the inner sea seemed to calm a bit, and he was less prone to shocking outbursts in his reactions of disappointment or frustration at the actions of other people.

Friendliness: the demeanor of treating others sociably—Not always, it seems, or at all consistently. He could certainly be nice to people when his inner storms weren't raging. He did have some relatively close friends, and perhaps a few lifetime buddies. But, again, even in the estimation of some who were close to him, much of his friendliness could have been a subtle form of manipulation. There are plenty of stories about egregious rudeness to waiters and others in service positions whose favor and esteem he obviously didn't feel he needed. And such behavior is always telling. Plus, one of his very talented associates, Bas Ording, finally stopped attending meetings with Steve because he was so often unkind and even aggressively "nasty" to people in the room for no reason. And this was long after Jobs supposedly matured and changed during his exile away from Apple. The same old Steve seemed to be lashing out regularly, years after his return to the company that would change the world. Ording later commented on his decision about not attending meetings with the boss by saying, simply: "No, Steve's an asshole."

Truthfulness: a strong disposition toward openness and honesty—Not a good track record here at all. Jobs certainly didn't like hearing difficult truths from others, and would often explode in anger when someone warned him about a problem with a pet project. He could also be very loose with the truth while talking to outsiders, or even with such a close partner, at one time, as Woz. Jobs often seemed to have said what he wanted others to believe, whether he was actually convinced of it or not. He sometimes claimed credit for ideas that weren't his or even technologies he didn't develop, and seemed so self-assured about it all that he himself may have come untethered from the truth. And yet, he was not a source of the sort of mendacious shenanigans often seen in the lives of corrupt CEOs who fabricate financials and abuse businesses for their own personal greed and gain. Steve was different from such more outrageous deceivers. And later in his life, he does seem to have become more consistent in both speaking and receiving difficult truths.

Wittiness: the ability to see and express humor appropriately—Not that often, it seems. But at times, he could crack a joke or point out the humor in a situation, just not a lot at work. He did this more in performance situations than in private with colleagues or at work, by all reports. His wife Laurene told one of the authors of Becoming Steve Jobs that he was often funny while goofing around with their kids. He certainly had the intellectual capacity for seeing and appreciating humor. But he didn't often seem to have the demeanor, or inner emotional life to encourage its expression. With a bit more robust a sense of humor, more regularly displayed in appropriate ways within professional contexts, he might have been able to get along better with his associates at Apple and create a robustly finer environment for their creative best work.

Justice: a basic commitment to treating others fairly—Not for much of the time, or by most people's definition. Jobs could be massively resentful, hold a grudge, let anger unhinge him, and treat people very unfairly. He sometimes seemed to have a storm of emotions deep in his soul swirling about and distorting how he saw the people around him. Justice never appeared to be a top primary consideration to him, at least, in dealings with many of his associates. He could sometimes do the right thing, but there are so many stories of the opposite. Again, he occasionally could be kind and generous and respectful, but was terribly inconsistent in such matters.

So, on the question of whether Steve Jobs lived up to Aristotle's account of what good character is, the available evidence seems fairly negative, at worst, or mixed and conflicted, at best. Actually, on this issue, I think most observers would judge that the overall score looks pretty bad. Steve Jobs, it seems, wasn't just an imperfect person trying his best in a flawed world. His personal psychological problems and emotional needs seem to have undermined several aspects of what's traditionally and normally meant by good character—at least in the early parts of his career, and perhaps even sporadically at much later times. And, in a real sense, this just makes his actual level of success all the more surprising. He was an outlier in more than one way. He was wounded and weakened on the most basic personal level and still managed to do what he did. It's actually astonishing, and yet not at all in this particular respect, admirable.

There are also, of course, broader conceptions of the virtues, and different understandings of character, in accordance with which Jobs would score a bit better. For example, in line with what some have thought of historically, following Homer and others, as warrior virtues, the quality of steely determination can be seen as a virtue and as a part of good character. Persistence can be viewed in the same way. An ability to stay true to your vision, despite contrary opinions all around you would also qualify—and on this count, Jobs would do well. In that sense, he did often display what Aristotle thought of as the crucial virtue of courage. He took chances. He believed in what he was doing. He wanted to make the world a better place, no matter what it might take. He was innovative to the maximal degree. He was opportunistic. He kept trying. He stood up to obstacles. He spoke his mind.

In classical Japanese Samurai culture, or in the modern stream of Bushido thought, the moral virtues are thought to be such things as frugality, loyalty, and honor, as well as involving a mastery of martial arts. Jobs certainly lived in many ways frugally, compared to his peers, and he had a fierce loyalty to his mission, and would have defined his own sense of honor, I think, in connection with that. He was a distinctive character who had a distinctive character, but not with the full integrity we normally think of in connection with this universal facilitating condition for success.

Jobs would often get high marks from acquaintances on avoiding the duplicity of fake friendliness, or hypocritical niceness, which is apparently the bane of certain circles in California, and is also to be found in a type of old culture in the southern United States. Marc Andreessen, the founder of Netscape and the cofounder of the venture capital firm, Andreessen Horowitz, once reminisced about this side of Jobs in an interview with Charlie Rose:

> "We use the phrase 'California casual,' or 'California fake-casual,' which is that a lot of people here want to go along and get along, and everybody's nice to each other, smiles to each other's faces. Then when somebody leaves the room, they're like, 'Oh, that guy's a real son of a whatever.' Steve's not like that. Steve was never like that. He was always somebody who told you exactly where you stood, exactly what he thought. The clarity of the communication you could have with him—there was no wasted time. There was no wasted effort. Everything was crystal clear and unbelievably effective. I think that quality permeates Apple's culture, and it's one of the reasons they're such an amazing company."

And surely these can be virtuous things, or qualities ingredient to good character that Andreessen is pointing to. But it would be hard to argue for a definition of character that only accommodated such matters and avoided Aristotle's other virtues altogether, a conceptualization that would give Jobs overall a better assessment here. There's no getting around it. In many ways, there were character issues. And they created problems.

This takes us back to our important point that the conditions of The 7 Cs of Success are not necessary and sufficient conditions, logically attached to sure results. Human achievement in a dynamic, complex, and messy world is not like that. The conditions we're considering are strongly facilitating factors, things that will help position a practitioner of them for the likelier attainment of success at a given challenge. It seems clear that Jobs struggled with issues of character at many points throughout his life. But it's also clear that some of the people who worked with him saw character traits in him that led them to trust him on the whole and remain loyal to him. One promise he never broke was clearly the most important promise he ever made, at least in the hearts and minds of those who stayed with him: He promised them that together they would change the world, put a dent in the universe, and do something insanely great. Our need for such a lofty purpose in our work can overshadow many other matters. And in the lives of those who remained loyal to Steve, I think this did.

No doubt, Jobs changed some over time, as reported in the excellent book *Becoming Steve Jobs*, as well as in the fine Ed Catmull book *Creativity, Inc.* on the rise of Pixar. Steve mellowed out some with age and experience. He became more humane and pragmatic. He learned how to love in new and deeper ways, and especially in connection with Laurene and his children. He grew a bit less mercurial. And he turned into a better leader. My judgment on this character condition of success, overall, is that, to the extent that Jobs did act in accordance with it, it helped him greatly, and to the extent that he did not, he hindered himself from what could have been an even broader and deeper form of personal achievement.

And then, in addition to these six conditions we've considered, we need one more trait to position us for the greatest forms of success:

7. A CAPACITY TO ENJOY ***the process along the way.***

Most of the best practical philosophers who have written about various forms of worldly success have pointed out the importance of enjoying the process along the way. We all want great results. But the results will necessarily arise out of a process. The more we enjoy the process itself, the better we'll typically do at making it the best effort it can be for producing precisely the best results. Throughout the sweep of human history, most highly accomplished people have had a love for what they were doing, a deep enjoyment that transcended any externals concerning money, power, fame, or status. That true enjoyment, or that love, gave them the intrinsic rewards that we're now coming to understand are so important for attaining and sustaining excellent results.

And this is deeply related to the other facilitating conditions for success. The more you can enjoy the process of what you're doing, the better your mastery of the other six conditions naturally tends to be. When you're really enjoying your work, many benefits accrue. It's easier to set creative goals. Confidence will come more naturally. Your concentration can seem effortless. Consistency will not be a battle. The ongoing emotional commitment will flow. And the various issues of character will not be as difficult to manage. Anyone taking great pleasure in his work is typically found to be in a better mood and consequently will treat others around him better than would someone else who is miserable in his efforts. A capacity to enjoy the process is entwined with every other facilitator of success in a great many ways. When you can relish the journey, you can be delightfully surprised by the results.

So, here's the final question: Did Steve Jobs enjoy his work? Did he love what he was doing? Did he relish his project of building a company and changing the world? Or was he simply obsessed with it, compelled to do it, and relentlessly driven by his emotional needs for success on a massive scale? Was he forced by a deep personality disorder, or two, or more, to work hard and achieve big, in a grim effort to prove that his birth parents should never have given him away, and that he was, after all, worthy and important?

There's evidence on both sides of the issue. On the one hand, obsessed and driven people are often on an emotional hair-trigger, given to immense frustration and outbursts of anger when disappointed by others or blocked by circumstances. And this certainly seemed true of Jobs. Plus, obsessed and compulsive, driven people don't typically smile and laugh a lot in a genuine spirit of good fun and delight. Unfortunately, Steve was not known for a generally pleasant or joyful disposition, offstage and in personal settings, to put it mildly, indeed. Rarely did people seem to see him laugh or crack a smile, except when he was on a stage, and even then just in order to attain his immediate goals.

There were a few exceptions, though. For example, Jim Allchin, former co-president of Microsoft's Platforms and Services Division, wrote after Jobs' death:

> "I never had a conversation with Steve I didn't enjoy. Whether sparring over technology, laughing over technical issues (dual booting a PC, etc.), or later talking about cancer. I remember once he and I were on an industry panel, at some conference or another, together with many other vendors in the early '90s. We both spent most of our time doing one-liners about the other's technology during the demos. It was as if the other vendors weren't even in the room. The audience had a great time laughing as we poked fun at each other. Then, when we got off the stage, Steve

> said a classic Steve line of something like 'Everyone else hasn't got a clue, but ... we've got to work together.'"

This was apparently not an everyday occurrence. Steve didn't go around cracking jokes and laughing at the absurdities and joys of life. But did he still enjoy himself? Did he love what he was doing? At a retreat for about fifty members of the Mac team in 1982, he spoke at the end of their days together on the beach in Monterey and said:

> "I know I might be a little hard to get along with, but this is the most fun thing I've ever done in my life." (143)

Love produces passion and commitment, and, as we've noted, Jobs seemed to have had those two qualities regarding his work, and in plentiful amounts. In fact, when I posed our question about enjoyment to my friend who worked closely with Jobs for years and knew him well, the short answer I got in a long and interesting email was this:

> "Complex guy. He enjoyed work more than life itself." (Tom Looney, email)

And that seems like an answer that resonates with all the facts available to us. So it's no surprise, in this regard, that his work succeeded in ways that his life, overall, did not.

The individual conditions within the framework of The 7 Cs of Success are not, again, simple guarantees of achievement. They don't give us anything like a science of accomplishment, but something more like an art, as I've explained at length in my book, *The Art of Achievement.* They are the most universal supportive and facilitating factors for attaining our goals, dealing with challenges, and making the most of opportunities. They position us as well as possible for success. Certainly, many other factors can be helpful in achievement, but only as applications or supports of these ideas. That's my assessment. So, in all, I view The 7 Cs as the only deep universal philosophical operating system for success that underlies anything else that's helpful for achievement. And I see these philosophical conditions as powerfully, though not perfectly, undergirding the work and accomplishments of Steve Jobs.

Crucially, for those of us who would like to attain even a small measure of the success that Jobs had with this operating system, we need to understand that these tools, and the overall framework of The 7 Cs, can be used in three distinct ways. We work better and attain more success throughout our adventures when we understand that the framework should be used in each of these three different capacities:

1. **As a test for any potential goal:** Ask whether you can attain a clear conception of that goal, a vivid vision for it, planted firmly in your imagination. Can you be confident in pursuing it? Can you focus your concentration on what it will take? Can you pursue it consistently with your other commitments and activities? And so on. If a potential goal can't pass the test, you need a different goal, or else other changes in your life that will make the goal appropriate.
2. **As a support for your pursuit of a chosen goal:** These seven conditions are meant to be tools for the accomplishment of our goals. They can be used and consulted on a regular basis. Am I maintaining a clear conception of what I'm doing? Am I acting consistently enough here? Am I fully committed? Am I enjoying the process? And so on.
3. **As a diagnostic template for assessing any difficulty:** If things aren't going as well as you would like, you can troubleshoot with The 7 Cs. Use the framework as a self-diagnostic grid, or as a systematic diagnostic test for your organization.

> How have you been performing on each of the conditions? How are you doing right now on them? The key to strength in any challenge is to realize that the ones you're doing right can help you to rectify those on which you're not doing well.

The greatest jobs ahead of us will call for all seven of these facilitating conditions of success. An occasional individual with the right cluster of talents, appearing at the right time, in the right industry, can do amazing things with only most of the operating system provided by The 7 Cs functioning well in his or her life. Steve Jobs was, I think, a prime example of that, since he struggled so much with the character condition. But for the deepest, most satisfying, broadest, and most sustainable success, it's my view that all seven factors are needed.

Steve had deep flaws and many obstacles to overcome throughout his life. What's so surprising is how his intense dedication to the principles and conditions of action that did animate him took him and his associates, and as a result, our contemporary popular culture, so far. If Socrates himself were to reawaken in Silicon Valley today and wander around the area in conversation and inquiry, I suspect that he would see much to admire and a lot to question. Some of his personal qualities might remind a few old-timers of certain things they had seen years ago in the life and work habits of the great Steve Jobs. But his personal commitment to truth and, especially, to goodness would perhaps offer a nice augmentation of how his more modern counterpart followed and cherished the other ideal of beauty in engineering and design. And it's of course a supreme irony that our modern alternative Socrates became a billionaire while his predecessor was put on public trial, convicted of false charges, and sentenced to death. And yet, after that death, those who knew him well called him the best and wisest of all men. And perhaps that, in the end, is the most important thing of all.

Those last few sentences would have been a great way to close our exploration together. But there's just one more thing. As Steve lay dying, surrounded by family, we're told that he gazed quietly and intently into the eyes of his loved ones for the longest time, as if he was holding them with that final gaze and did not want to let them go. Then, he looked up over them, as if toward the corner of the room, apparently seeing something that no one else there could see. And he said, simply, "Oh, Wow." Then he said it again. "Oh, Wow." And, finally, a third time: "Oh, Wow."

The man who so wowed the world during his life was apparently, in his last lucid moments and at the portal of death, himself suddenly wowed by something that only he could see—which is so great and appropriate and just like Steve Jobs. I like to hope that he and the original Socrates are having quite a time together now, in a realm and adventure that perhaps he then glimpsed. That indeed would be such a cosmic and philosophic Wow.

Appendix One

A Self-Diagnostic Check-Up on The 7 Cs

Know thyself!
Socrates

In the set of questions here, you can go through an exercise in self-knowledge relevant to The 7 Cs, something Socrates would approve and that Steve Jobs could have benefitted from in his lowest times. I recommend you do this periodically as a diagnostic test. Answer each question as honestly as you can. Write down the number that applies to you, "0" representing the lowest possible self-score, and "10" the highest.

(C1) CONCEPTION
I have a clear conception of what I am pursuing in my activities.

0 1 2 3 4 5 6 7 8 9 10

I have a vivid vision for what I'm doing that appeals to my imagination.

0 1 2 3 4 5 6 7 8 9 10

(C2) CONFIDENCE

I'm confident in my ability to attain my current goals successfully.

0 1 2 3 4 5 6 7 8 9 10

I display a confident attitude and help to enhance the confidence of people around me.

0 1 2 3 4 5 6 7 8 9 10

(C3) CONCENTRATION

I'm well focused on the next steps I need to take to reach my goals.

0 1 2 3 4 5 6 7 8 9 10

I regularly take action in small ways as well as larger ways to implement my plans.

0 1 2 3 4 5 6 7 8 9 10

(C4) CONSISTENCY

I monitor my daily behavior well for consistency with my goals and deepest values.

0 1 2 3 4 5 6 7 8 9 10

I seek to help everyone working toward goals with me to be as consistent as possible.

0 1 2 3 4 5 6 7 8 9 10

(C5) COMMITMENT
I'm emotionally committed to the importance of what I do.

0 1 2 3 4 5 6 7 8 9 10

I'm emotionally committed to the people I work with in pursuit of my goals.

0 1 2 3 4 5 6 7 8 9 10

(C6) CHARACTER
I'm sure that my actions in pursuit of my goals satisfy high standards of character.

0 1 2 3 4 5 6 7 8 9 10

I seek to surround myself with people of strong character.

0 1 2 3 4 5 6 7 8 9 10

(C7) CAPACITY TO ENJOY
I've been enjoying the pursuit of my goals lately.

0 1 2 3 4 5 6 7 8 9 10

I work toward my goals in such a way that I can enjoy my life more broadly.

0 1 2 3 4 5 6 7 8 9 10

Grading Yourself on the Checkup

Add up all your self-scores on this checklist and write down your current total. If it's over 120, then you're in pretty good shape in the recent stages of your journey of success. Keep up the good work and build on your accomplishments.

If your score is under 120, you should very seriously rethink the goals you are pursuing and how you are working toward them. If your total is over 120 but under 140, pay attention to what could use a little more work. You're just fine-tuning an already viable enterprise, for greater levels of satisfying accomplishment.

A Second Opinion

You might want another person's feedback in this process too. Imagine if Steve Jobs had done this and gotten feedback. Yeah. I know. But you can. Give a copy of the unmarked questions to a co-worker, spouse, friend, or child and ask them to mark the questions independently in the way that they think you should. Comparing their assessments with yours can be interesting on many levels, advancing your quest for self-understanding and providing new and useful information concerning the relationship the two of you have.

Life should involve an ongoing process of self-evaluation and self-correction, self-knowledge and self-mastery. Repeat this check up at regular intervals, act on the information you generate, and you will move progressively more in the direction of achieving all that you are here on this earth to do. Plus, of course, you can do a version of this self-diagnostic not focused on yourself personally, but on your department, division, or team. That makes for an interesting and sometimes revealing exercise. When all team members do it, it can often yield surprising results that are good for anyone in a leadership roll to have.

Appendix Two

A Short Formula

And shall I suggest that we talk a little
of the probabilities of these things?
Socrates

There are many reasons for the success of Steve Jobs. We've explored the philosophical side of those reasons in this short book. But if asked to give a 40,000 foot summary of what made it all work for Jobs, I might say something very simple. At the most general level possible, it all boils down to: Purpose, Passion, People, Process, and Products. These categories give us a different lens through which to view Job's success as an innovator and leader.

Purpose.

Steve had a purpose: to change the world, to revolutionize the way we live. And he never let people forget that purpose. It wasn't about the money. It wasn't about profits, or fame, or power. It was about making a ripple in the universe. And by having a purpose like this, he attracted and engaged the right people. Everyone wants to matter. We all want to make a difference. And we all have somewhere within us a deep need to feel that we're making a big difference. Hidden away in our hearts, we all want to be heroes at some level, and in some way. A big, audacious, and noble purpose gets the attention of the best people. And then by having great people around him, Steve Jobs was able to get them aligned around processes and values that could lead to the right products. The talented designers, engineers, and manufacturing people that he brought together were then able to create some extraordinarily great things.

Passion.

But, underneath it all, and just as important as purpose for attracting the right people, was Steve's passion. I think he had a deep and abiding passion for what he was doing that was always evident, and that was strongly contagious. People are indeed attracted to people who care. No one wants to sleep walk through the day. We need something we can believe in and deeply care about.

Philosophers, who in a way are our paradigms of reason, have long told us that more often than not, reason is the servant of emotion, or passion. When people see true passion for something good, they figure out a reasonable way to be a part of it and stoke the fire in their own hearts.

Many people say that Jobs was immensely charismatic, that he was the most enthusiastic and energetic person they had ever met—that he could walk into a room and the energy level would just change throughout the space. It was because he was so passionate. He brought heart to everything he did. If you take a great purpose and align it with real passion, then you're going to attract the people, and you're going to develop the products that maybe, in your own area, will make a dent in the universe. That's what Steve showed us.

People.

Hardly anything extraordinary, world changing, and creative on a massive scale is ever accomplished alone. Recent studies have shown that underneath some of the most innovative ideas and products ever have been teams of exceptional people working together for a shared purpose. In fact, in his book *The Politics*, this was basically Aristotle's formula for great good:

People in Partnership for a shared Purpose.

We've long been seduced by the myth of the lone genius who breaks away from the crowd and finds his own path. But when we look more closely into great works of genius, we often find teams of talented people who have made those things happen together.

Process.

Steve didn't just conjure up a grand purpose, get passionate about it, find great people and hope for the best. He designed what amounted to a process that emphasized such things as focus, simplicity, leapfrogging the competition, using our intuition, and always pursuing perfection. A great purpose needs to give rise to and guide a great process. Passion then energizes the process. The right people can help create it and adopt it, spread it, and implement it. And then, when a great process is given a chance to work over time, great things can happen as a result.

Products.

Often, a business is developed around a product idea. So, it may seem that products should come first in our list. But philosophers would draw a distinction between the order of discovery and the order of implementation. Even when a business is started around a clear new product idea, everyone involved in the initial stage of envisioning the product needs to make sure that a sense of purpose ignites passion, attracts people, and launches a process that can make the envisioned product all that it can be. This five-stage checklist will then allow for other product ideas to develop around the vision, or purpose. So, even when the product seems to come first, its refinement and even perfection will result best from the other things we've reviewed—purpose, passion, people, and process. When everything else is working well, we get spectacular products—perhaps even to the point that, as Brian Merchant says in his recent book *The One Device*, "The iPhone might actually be the pinnacle product of all of capitalism to this point." Steve Jobs seemed to understand this on a deep level, and when we let his example reinforce it in our own minds, we learn the best lessons he has to pass on to us.

Appendix Three

The NeXT and Last Horizon: On the Death of Steve Jobs

By Tom Looney, Op. Ed. October 6, 2011

Now the hour to part has come. I go to die, and you go to live. Which of us goes to the better lot is known to no one—except the god.
Socrates

For six years I had the unique opportunity to work closely with Steve Jobs at NeXT. He has called it one of the most creative periods of his life, so you can imagine what a special time it was for this mere mortal. Apple bought the firm, and our technology was at the heart of Apple's remarkable renaissance.

Life with Steve Jobs was exhausting, challenging, and exhilarating. His magic was his ability to convince average people like me to believe that WE could change the world, and he prodded us to "dare to be great" and produce "insanely great" results.

Enduring Steve's withering "you're doing it all wrong" criticism was a rite of passage on the way to peak performance, and I never worked with a more talented group of people than the gang at NeXT. Thank goodness great men like Steve dream of a world yet to come, because dreams of the future are not coming from our politicians, bankers, and industrialists.

For Steve, re-imagining the world and making it better was a responsibility, something owed to our children's children, a gift to a future begging for his type of rare vision and selflessness. In his epic Stanford University speech in 2005, he said, "Death is very likely the single best invention of life. It is life's change agent. It clears out the old to make way for the new." How cool is that? The immortal Steve Jobs at his best.

Rest in peace, Steve.

For Further Reading

A Few Books Mentioned, Consulted, or Recommended

Brennan. Chrisann. *The Bite in the Apple.*
Catmull. Ed. *Creativity, Inc.*
Cervantes. Miguel. *Don Quixote.*
Christakis. Nicholas. Fowler. James. *Connected.*
Csikszentmihalyi. Mihaly. Flow: *The Psychology of Optimal Experience.*
Deutschman. Alan. *The Second Coming of Steve Jobs.*
Friend. David. *More Reflections on the Meaning of Life.*
Friend. David. *The Meaning of Life.*
Grant, Adam. *Give and Take.*
Holt. Jim. *Why Does the World Exist?*
Isaacson, Walter. *Steve Jobs.*
Isaacson, Walter. *The Innovators.*
Johnson. Paul. *Socrates.*
Kahney, Leander. *Inside Steve's Brain.*
Kelly-Gangi. Carol. (ed) *The Wisdom of Steve Jobs.*
Laertius. Diogenes. *Lives of Eminent Philosophers.*
Lashinsky. Adam. *Inside Apple.*
Levy, Lawrence. *To Pixar and Beyond.*
Malone. Michael. *Infinite Loop.*

Merchant. Brian. *The One Device.*
Moritz. Michael. *Return to the Little Kingdom.*
Morris. Tom. *If Aristotle Ran General Motors.*
Morris. Tom. *If Harry Potter Ran General Electric.*
Morris. Tom. *The Art of Achievement.*
Morris. Tom. *True Success.*
Murdoch. Iris. *The Sovereignty of Good.*
Pink. Dan. *Drive.*
Plato. *Dialogues.*
Polanyi. Michael. *Personal Knowledge.*
Polanyi. Michael. *Tacit Knowing.*
Powers. William. *Hamlet's Blackberry.*
Rendall. David. *The Freak Factor.*
Schlender. Rick. And Tetzeli. Rick. *Becoming Steve Jobs.*
Sculley. John. *Odyssey: Pepsi to Apple.*
Segall. Ken. *Insanely Simple.*
Simpson. Mona. *A Regular Guy.*
Snow. C.P. *The Two Cultures.*
Yogananda. Paramahansa. *Autobiography of a Yogi.*
Xenophon. *Conversations of Socrates.*

Acknowledgments

I want to thank Michael Brannick, who as CEO of Prometric first asked me to reflect on Steve Jobs and speak on the philosophy underlying his extraordinary success. I thank also the other companies and associations who have shared the enthusiasm to learn more about this topic and how it could apply in their own work. Thanks also to Geoffrey Dorhmann, CEO, IREI for his early enthusiasm on this topic.

I'd also like to thank all those who knew Steve or who knew those who knew Steve well and have been willing to share their insights on his life and work. I thank especially the insightful and gracious Tom Looney for his thoughtful and analytical take on Jobs and for perspectives that I have found revolutionary in helping me to grasp some of Steve's rough edges that are so well known. I thank my friends Bruce May, for his editorial guidance, Ed Hearn for his never failing support, Don Sharp for leading me to stay healthy during it all, and Tom Ryder, for his help and generously shared connections. Many other friends have indulged my enthusiasms about Jobs and Socrates as we've talked about the insights I was having and working through in the preparation of this text. I've especially enjoyed talking about the book with Vinod

Rangra and have benefitted immensely from the encouragement and suggestions of Dr. George Manning.

I heartily thank as always my wife and family. And I want to express appreciation again to my daughter Sara Morris who provided the cover design, and to Abigail Chiaramonte for the interior and final design elements of the book. Everyone in the Wisdom/Works family provided great assistance in getting this to print. To GT, Ollie, Abbey, Wes, and Odie: Many thanks for the various roles you've played in keeping me semi-sane and productive.

About the Author

Tom Morris is one of the most active philosophers and public speakers in the world. A native of North Carolina, he's a graduate of The University of North Carolina (Chapel Hill), where he was a Morehead-Cain Scholar, and he holds a Ph.D. in both Philosophy and Religious Studies from Yale University. For fifteen years, he served as a Professor of Philosophy at the University of Notre Dame, where he was one of their most popular teachers. You can find him online now anytime at:

www.TomVMorris.com.

Tom has been honored with the University of North Carolina's Distinguished Young Alumnus Award, as well as with honorary doctorates in recognition of his work. He has been a George A. and Eliza Gardner Howard Foundation Fellow through Brown University, and has been a Fellow with the National Endowment for the Humanities. Tom is also the author of over twenty-three pioneering books. His twelfth book, True Success: A New Philosophy of Excellence, launched him into an ongoing adventure as a philosopher working and speaking throughout the world. His audiences have included a great many of the Fortune 500 companies and dozens of the largest national and international trade associations. His work has been mentioned, commented on, or covered by NBC, ABC, CNN, CNBC, NPR, and in most major newspapers and news magazines.

He's also the author of the highly acclaimed books *If Aristotle Ran General Motors, Philosophy for Dummies, The Art of Achievement, The Stoic Art of Living, Twisdom, Superheroes and Philosophy*, and *If Harry Potter Ran General Electric: Leadership Wisdom from the World of the Wizards*, as well as many others. His most recent books include the philosophical prologue to a pioneering fiction series, *The Oasis Within*, and the subsequent series novels, *The Golden Palace, The Stone of Giza, The Viper and The Storm* and *The King and Prince*. He just may be the world's happiest philosopher.

As The Socratic Philosophical Midwife
Of Modern Technology Famously Said:

*And most important, have the courage
to follow your heart and intuition.
They somehow already know what you truly want to become.
Everything else is secondary.*

Steve Jobs
Stanford Commencement
2005

www.ingramcontent.com/pod-product-compliance
Lightning Source LLC
Chambersburg PA
CBHW021824090426
42811CB00032B/2011/J
* 9 7 8 0 9 9 9 3 5 2 4 1 0 *